Change in tourism

Change in tourism

People, places, processes

Edited by
Richard Butler and Douglas Pearce

London and New York

First published 1995
by Routledge
11 New Fetter Lane, London EC4P 4EE

Simultaneously published in the USA and Canada
by Routledge
29 West 35th Street, New York, NY 10001

© 1995 Richard Butler and Douglas Pearce

Typeset in Times Ten by Florencetype Ltd, Stoodleigh, Devon

Printed and bound in Great Britain by
Biddles Ltd, Guildford and King's Lynn

British Library Cataloguing in Publication Data
A catalogue record for this book is available from the British Library.

Library of Congress Cataloging in Publication Data
A catalog record for this book has been requested.

ISBN 0-415-11486-1

Contents

Illustrations

PLATES

FIGURES

TABLES

Contributors

Richard Butler Department of Geography, University of Western Ontario, London, Ontario

Erik Cohen Department of Sociology and Anthropology, The Hebrew University of Jerusalem, Jerusalem

Graham Dann Department of Government and Sociology, University of the West Indies, Bridgetown, Barbados

William Eadington Department of Economics/Institute for the Study of Gambling and Commercial Gaming, University of Nevada, Reno, Nevada

Nelson Graburn Department of Anthropology, University of California, Berkeley, California

Baodi Mao Department of Geography, University of Western Ontario, London, Ontario

Josef Mazanec Institute for Tourism and Leisure Studies, Vienna University of Economics and Business Administration, Vienna

Dennison Nash Department of Anthropology and Sociology, University of Connecticut, Storrs, Connecticut

Douglas Pearce Department of Geography, University of Canterbury, Christchurch, New Zealand

John Pigram Department of Geography and Planning, University of New England, Armidale, New South Wales

Linda Richter Department of Political Science, Kansas State University, Manhattan, Kansas

Stephen Wanhill School of Consumer Studies, Tourism and Hospitality Management, University of Wales, Cardiff

Acknowledgements

The preparation of any publication inevitably involves a great many people who contribute significantly, either directly or indirectly, to the completion of the volume. This book is no exception, and we would like to express our appreciation to the following groups in particular.

First, to the Korean hosts of the meeting of the International Academy for the Study of Tourism (the Korea Transport Institute, the Korean National Tourism Corporation, Korean Air Lines, and the City of Seoul) for providing the Academy members with a stimulating and enjoyable setting for the meeting for which these papers were prepared, and to Dr Jong-Yung Ahn and Dr Young G. Kwon for their individual efforts to make the meeting a success.

Second, to the authors of the papers, who prepared them for the meeting in Korea, and then revised them, in a spirit of true collegiality, after the comments and suggestions from colleagues and editors.

Third, to Routledge, our publisher, and especially to Francesca Weaver and Laura Large, for their assistance, patience and encouragement.

Fourth, to the unsung secretaries and cartographers in the various universities who translated academic scrawl into readable computer input. In particular, the cartographic and secretarial staff of the Department of Geography at the University of Western Ontario, especially Pamela Brown, for assembling and combining the various drafts into the final manuscript, overcoming unreasonable demands on eyesight, and patience, in the process. Any errors and omissions are the editors' responsibility.

Finally, to our families, for accepting the periods of absence, both physical and mental, and the bouts of indigestion, frustration and confusion which occur whenever academics attempt to co-ordinate the work of eleven colleagues from different disciplines and continents, and still providing us with support and the comforts of home.

Richard Butler and Douglas Pearce
1994

Chapter 1

Introduction

Richard W. Butler

In his opening paragraph of the final chapter in the second publication of the International Academy for the Study of Tourism, Ritchie (1993: 201) noted:

> the period of the 1990s and beyond is showing itself to be radically different from the three previous decades. While technological change has been with us for some time, it continues to accelerate and its impacts increasingly reverberate throughout society. Added to this, the dramatic political changes that have occurred in recent years are only manifestations of more deep-seated social and cultural transformations which reflect changes in human priorities concerning the way the populations of the world wish to live. Tourism, as a phenomenon, is clearly affected as much and perhaps more by these changes as any other sector.

Similar comments have been made in many publications about tourism, emphasizing the dynamic nature of the phenomenon, and the fact that while it responds to changes in the world in which it exists, it is also capable itself of generating significant change (Hall 1991; Nelson *et al.* 1993; Poon 1993). While each generation probably thinks that its time is one of singular change, the current generation might be forgiven for feeling that it is more justified than most for feeling that way.

The response of tourism to change in society and the environment in which it exists has not been the explicit focus of a great deal of research. Indeed, it can be argued that on a global or macro-scale there has been relatively little change in tourism. Statistics on tourist arrivals and receipts for the period from 1960 to 1993 show virtually no change in the relative ranking of the major areas of the world in terms of numbers of tourist arrivals and receipts generated

(World Tourism Organization 1994: 9). Europe still dominates both tourist arrivals and tourist receipts, with America in second place and East Asia/the Pacific in third place. Such large-scale figures hide many significant and important changes which have taken place in tourism over the last three decades, however, such as the relative rates of growth of tourism in different parts of the world, and very different forms of tourism which have appeared in recent decades. They should serve to remind us that most change in tourism is evolutionary, and its effects take time to appear (Butler 1993). What has made the period from the mid-1980s of particular significance to tourism is the fact that much of the change which has taken place in society during this period can be regarded as more revolutionary than evolutionary.

This comment applies particularly to political events. The collapse of communism, bringing with it the fall of the Berlin Wall and the dissolution of the Soviet Union; the disintegration of Yugoslavia, and the emergence of new states amid civil strife; the possibility of permanent peace between Israel and its neighbours, with subsequent impacts throughout the Middle East; the Gulf War and at least temporary political realignments in that area; civil unrest and response in China, with possible economic repercussions; coups in Fiji and Haiti; and the end of apartheid in South Africa, were unexpected events to say the least. All of these have had, or will have, major effects on tourism. Considerable attention has already been paid to the effects of the rapid and major political changes which have occurred in eastern Europe (Alkjaer 1990; Hall 1991; Davidson 1993; Harrison 1993; Mazaraki and Voronova 1993; Smeral 1993), but it is clear that the full impacts of the political upheavals have not yet been felt, and that much more change is going to take place (Hall 1992). Very little of what has happened from 1987 to 1994 could have been predicted at the beginning of that period. The conclusions of the unanimous report by tourist experts on megatrends in Europe to the year 2000 reported by Lickorish (1987), while still valid, pale when placed alongside the new trends and likely developments which have already appeared only half-way through the period being considered.

In addition to the political events noted above, the last decade has seen a continuation of the unpleasant face of politics in the forms of terrorism and extreme nationalism and fundamentalism. The civil strife in the Balkans has ended much of the tourism industry of the former Yugoslavia. Fundamentalists have threatened the previously strong tourism industry in Egypt, by targeting tourists and tourist facilities, although few tourists had actually been harmed by early 1994, and a similar fate may occur in Algeria. Kurdish nationalists in Turkey have deliberately taken international tourists hostage to dramatize their struggle for independence, although they have so far kept their word and released unharmed all those taken. It is unlikely that this phenomenon will disappear in the near future, and its effects on tourism will remain an unpleasant reality (Ryan 1993). In the same vein, what are now old political problems still impact upon the patterns of tourism today, as can be seen for example in the cases of Cyprus (Andronikou 1993) and Gibraltar (Seekings 1993).

As well as major political change, the world has seen significant economic restructuring and general recession and downturns in traditionally strong economies. These changes have been marked by an increasing reluctance and/or inability of governments to invest in or support areas such as tourism and, for the first time since 1939, a decline in global tourist arrivals, an event which occurred between 1990 and 1991 (WTO 1994). The negative effects of the Gulf War were undoubtedly also significant in this one year dip in international tourist numbers, but the long-term effects of economic recession are widespread, even affecting the normally resilient element of business tourism (Davidson 1993). To some degree, however, it may be argued that tourism has benefited from the recession and economic restructuring which has taken place in many western industrial countries. The economic downturn and the loss of traditional employment opportunities, in many cases permanently, have forced governments, often for the first time, to look seriously at tourism and its potential for economic development and revitalization (Lowyck and Wanhill 1992). This is particularly true in areas never previously thought of as suitable for tourism, such as former urban industrial centres (Cooper *et al.* 1993).

One of the other effects of reductions in public sector expenditure has been the increasing substitution of the private for the public sector in often traditional sectors of society. In the context of tourism, transport is of particular significance. In some western countries reductions in subsidies to rail travel, for example, have seen both the disappearance of often traditional tourist routes and the replacement of public service by private companies. The privatization of part of the TransCanada railroute and the reappearance of the Orient Express in recent years are examples of this process. In early 1994 another private sector venture, the Channel Tunnel, will be opened, which is likely to significantly alter international tourist travel between Europe and the United Kingdom, and have considerable impact on both sides of the Channel (Gibb *et al.* 1990; Garnett 1993). In a similar vein, one might also note the problems caused by improvements in aircraft range and fuel consumption which have allowed carriers to over-fly destinations whose tourist trade relied heavily on their critical location as refuelling stops, such as Ireland and Fiji (Qere-qeretabua 1990).

In contrast to tourism in urban and central locations has been the increasing spread of tourism to remote and relatively untouched areas, following, and in some cases leading, the revital-ized environmental consciousness of the 1980s. The growth of a variety of forms of what has come to be called alternative tourism (Smith and Eadington 1992) is one of the distinguishing charac-teristics of tourism since 1980. The public's apparent increased interest in and concern for the environment has been more than matched by the ability of the tourism industry to provide 'green' or nature-related opportunities. The result has seen a dramatic growth in such specific elements of tourism as ecotourism, nature tourism, and special interest tourism (Hall and Weiler 1992), although this growth has attracted considerable criticism and scepticism about its effects and authenticity (Butler 1992; Wheeler 1993).

Shifts in societal values may take a long time to materialize and affect elements such as tourism. One major social change which has been affecting tourism and leisure for several years, and which is inevitably going to have greater effect in the next few decades, is that of the ageing of the western population. While the older generation may not immediately alter fashion and tastes in tourism, it may over time radically alter consumer requirements and prefer-ences. Such consumers are not tied by the traditional obligations of work or family, or even in some cases by financial limitations, but they may face other constraints of mobility, energy and discrimina-tion. Their numbers and purchasing power, however, are likely to ensure that ultimately their needs and desires are met, and their importance has been recognized by industry and government (Viant 1993). Other significant social changes which have resulted in changes in tourism include the rise in feminism and a reduction in discrimination on the basis of colour, race or other personal characteristics, as noted below.

Anticipating and predicting the future in tourism and leisure, even when some trends may seem clear, is not an easy task, although it has attracted considerable attention (Butler 1989; Poon 1993). The speed with which many of the changes noted above have come into being makes such prediction even more difficult. When the likely effects of the future generation of computers and electronics is taken into account the picture becomes even more uncertain. The introduction of new technology holds considerable potential for change in tourism (Poon 1993; Stipanuk 1993), and can not only increase the numbers of tourists, it can also significantly alter the nature and scope of the attractions which they can travel to see (Martin and Mason 1993).

The preceding discussion highlights only some of the significant changes which have occurred in the world in the last few years. Such changes have dramatic and severe impacts upon tourism, and present many challenges for researchers in tourism. Traditional ways of identifying and measuring tourists and elements of tourism may not be realistic or accurate in a rapidly changing world, where the distinctions between work, leisure and tourism are becoming increasingly blurred. Accepted models and concepts of relationships between tourism and economies have to be reassessed in the light of changing roles of the public and private sector, and different expectations and demands upon tourism. Procedures in the industry are coming under increasingly close scrutiny, both from social and environmental viewpoints, and the industry and tourists individually are being expected and required to shoulder more responsibility for the effects of travel and behaviour on host environments, both physical and human. Policies towards tourism and processes such as planning and development are being revised in the light of new political and economic developments.

All of these changes require research and attention. While the literature already cited shows that considerable interest has already been shown in these problems, the actual process of change in tourism itself as a phenomenon has been little studied. Rather attention has focused on topics such as how tourism itself causes change, how the market changes, and how technology changes, with subsequent innovations in transport and communications. It was the need to identify and address some of these broad issues from a systematic and conceptual viewpoint that provided the focus and theme for the third meeting of the International Academy for the Study of Tourism, held in Seoul, South Korea, in June 1993, which was 'Tourism Issues of the 90s: Current and Emerging Trends'.

The Academy was established in 1988 and has as its purpose 'to further the scholarly research and professional investigation of tourism, to encourage the application of findings, and to advance the international diffusion and exchange of tourism knowledge'. Its first bi-annual meeting was in Zakopane, Poland, with the theme of 'Alternative Tourism' (Smith and Eadington 1992). In 1991 the Academy met in Calgary, Canada, and addressed the theme of 'Methodological and Conceptual Issues in Tourism Research' (Pearce and Butler 1993).

The chapters in this volume represent revised versions of some of the papers presented at the Academy meeting in Seoul; in particular, those papers which focused on the theme of change in tourism. They represent an attempt explicitly to discuss the relationship between change in society and change in tourism, and provide a range of examples of how change in tourism can be examined in the context of problems of scale, data, methodology and philosophy.

They begin with papers which address some of the broad social aspects of change in tourism, tourism places and tourists. Cohen's chapter focuses on the apparent changes in attitude of tourists towards attractions and the relative importance of the authentic versus the contrived nature of tourist environments. He notes that this shift is likely to continue and to be emphasized by the effects of new technology and opportunities such as 'Virtual Reality', and suggests that the availability and popularity of new attractions will affect the need to protect natural and vulnerable attractions from overuse and misuse.

Some of these points are taken up by Nash, who, using an anthropological perspective, continues the discussion on the relative and changing relationship between tourism, work and leisure in society. He discusses the fact that traditionally leisure has only been possible when society has produced a surplus over what was needed, or else reduces its requirements. In a period of economic change and recession his comments have particular relevance. He notes the changing role of leisure in society and its dependence upon the basic structure of society, which itself is changing. Nash uses two examples to illustrate how changing social habits and images of people and places reflect the nature of tourism as super-stucture in society.

Graburn (Chapter Four) also focuses on change in society's tastes, and uses the rise in popularity of nostalgia in Japan as his example. He explores the way in which this phenomenon has been marketed and integrated into the changing yet conservative Japanese society, and how it relates to other elements of tourism and recreation. There are clear implications for other societies from the Japanese example, and similarities with the arguments made in Chapter Two by Cohen on the way in which people's tastes change and can be encouraged to change.

As noted above, two of the major social changes which have taken place in recent decades have related to the treatment of gender and race. Richter discusses these two variables in the context of tourism and the way they are bringing about major changes in the way tourism is organized, operated and sold, rather than as explanatory variables affecting tourist behaviour which has been the traditional approach to these topics. She makes it clear that compared to other industries and subjects of study, tourism lags behind in dealing with these important social and cultural variables, and that it is impossible to separate these factors from the political settings in which tourism occurs and operates.

The political setting for tourism is the focus of Chapter Six by Butler and Mao, which examines the problems created for tourism as a result of political change, and the establishment of new political units, some of which may take a considerable time to reach full statehood. The concept of the 'quasi-state' has particular relevance at this time, given the rapid dissolution of some states and the re-establishment of others in the recent past and the foreseeable future. The changes in the world's political realm in the last few years, and the probability of continued instability and change, suggest that the conceptual and applied problems raised in the discussion will continue for some time.

The shifts in tastes and preferences of tourists are discussed by Cohen, Nash and Graburn in the early chapters in the volume. In Chapter Seven Dann examines the shift in perceptions of tourists after they reach a tourist destination, and the changing manner in which they describe their images of the destination. His analysis of responses to images, visual and non-visual, builds on some of the issues raised in the discussions of Nash and Graburn, on the way in which attractions and destinations are portrayed and marketed, and the methods used to create and maintain images. Dann's arguments on the way in which perceptions and images appear to change with experience have interesting implications for the way tastes and preferences may also change with experience and travel.

The problem of improving ways to identify, segment and explain an apparently increasingly fragmented tourist market is the topic addressed by Mazanec (Chapter Eight). As both industry and government are forced to examine their expenditures more and more closely, it becomes essential that expenditure on marketing is based on an accurate understanding of the market which is being courted. Mazanec presents and describes a new approach to segmenting and analysing the tourist market, which allows for greater detail to be obtained, a prime consideration when niche marketing and the identification of increasingly specialized parts of the market have become much more important.

The relatively recent concern of many western governments with budgets and deficits is implicit in the chapters by Eadington and Wanhill. Eadington (Chapter Nine) reviews the major changes which have taken place with respect to commercial gambling and the effects which these have had upon tourism. Although gambling and tourism have a relatively long history together, in the last ten years there has been a concerted effort in several countries, particularly the USA, Canada, Australia and New Zealand, to stimulate both tourism and government revenues by legalizing and developing commercial gaming. Casino and other forms of gambling are discussed by Eadington, along with the implications of the diffusion of gambling into locations and societies in which it had previously been prohibited. He notes the adoption of gambling on Indian reserves in the United States, and the high but often unrealistic expectations of communities about to become involved in the activity.

Commercial gaming represents a somewhat unusual situation in tourism where the public sector is actively encouraging the private sector to develop a newly legalized activity in order to stimulate economic growth and employment. In his chapter, Wanhill looks at other public sector involvement in tourism, and presents a review of the availability of financial support from the public sector for tourism projects. He notes the increasing expectations of the public sector in terms of performance and return on investment in employment and revenue. He presents models which predict the likely result of investment in specific situations and uses a case study by way of illustration.

As well as being concerned with economic matters, increasingly government agencies and the tourism industry are being forced to consider environmental and planning issues. The final two chapters in the volume, by Pigram and Pearce, address aspects of these concerns. Pigram (Chapter Eleven) examines the specific environmental issue of water, which is assuming critical importance in many tourist destinations, and which may become the critical constraint on tourism developments in some locations. He demonstrates how little attention has been given to this issue in the past, and how it has often required an environmental crisis to provoke some response from agencies responsible. He illustrates what can be achieved by far sighted planning and management of scarce water resources, even in an arid location, to allow the development of a successful and major tourism industry.

The theme of planning is further addressed by Pearce in Chapter Twelve, in which he proposes an innovative approach to the planning of tourism destinations. Using a case study approach, he illustrates the application of the technique and its strengths compared to a more conventional approach. He incorporates elements of marketing and resource evaluation noted above, and relates these to the changes taking place in the demand sector, as well as alternative sources of supply or competition. Original and adaptive approaches to planning destination regions will assume greater importance given the rapid changes occurring in both the demand and supply elements of tourism at the international level.

The chapters in this volume do not cover all aspects of change in tourism. They do, however, identify significant elements of change in tourism, and in the cultural, economic, political and environmental sectors of society. By examining these elements of change, the way that they relate to each other and to society, they throw considerable light on the process of change, both in tourism and in the world at large.

REFERENCES

Alkjaer, E. (1990) 'East meets West – Europe's changing tourism', *Tourism Management* 11, 3: 174–175.

Andronikou, A. (1993) 'The hotel industry in Cyprus: problems and future prospects', *Tourism Management* 14, 1: 67–70.

Butler, R.W. (1989) 'The future', in G. Wall (ed.) *Outdoor Recreation in Canada*, Toronto: Wiley, 277–310.

—— (1992) 'Alternative tourism: The thin end of the wedge', in V. L. Smith and W. Eadington (eds) *Tourism Alternatives*, Philadelphia: University of Pennsylvania Press, 31–46.

—— (1993) 'Tourism – an evolutionary perspective', in J.G. Nelson, R.W. Butler and G. Wall (eds) *Tourism and Sustainable Development: Monitoring, Planning, Management*, Waterloo: University of Waterloo Press, 27–43.

Cooper, C., Fletcher, J., Gilbert, D. and Wanhill, S. (1993) *Tourism Principles and Practices*, London: Pitman.

Davidson, R. (1993) 'European business tourism – changes and prospects', *Tourism Management* 14, 3: 167–172.

Garnett, C. (1993) 'Impact of the Channel Tunnel on the tourism industry: a sea of change in cross-Channel travel', *Tourism Management* 14, 6: 411–418.

Gibb, R., Essex, S. and Charlton, C. (1990) 'The potential impact of the Channel Tunnel on Devon and Cornwall', *Applied Geography* 10: 43–61.

Hall, C.M. and Weiler, B. (1992) *Special-Interest Tourism*, London: Belhaven Press.

Hall, D. (1991) *Tourism and Economic Development in Eastern Europe and the Soviet Union*, London: Belhaven Press.

—— (1992) 'The changing face of tourism in Central and Eastern Europe', in C. P. Cooper and A. Lockwood (eds) *Progress in Tourism Recreation and Hospitality Management* Volume 4, London: Belhaven Press, 252–264.

Harrison, D. (1993) 'Bulgarian tourism: A state of uncertainty', *Annals of Tourism Research* 20, 3: 519–534.

Lickorish, L.J. (1987) 'Travel megatrends in Europe to the year 2000', *Annals of Tourism Research* 15, 2: 88–89.

Lowyck, E. and Wanhill, S. (1992) 'Regional development and tourism within the European Community', in C.P. Cooper and A. Lockwood (eds) *Progress in Tourism Recreation and Hospitality Management* Volume 4, London: Belhaven Press, 227–244.

Martin, B. and Mason, S. (1993) 'The future for attractions: meeting the needs of the new consumers', *Tourism Management* 14, 1: 34–40.

Mazaraki, A. and Voronova, E. (1993) 'Prospects for tourism in Ukraine', *Tourism Management* 14, 4: 316–317.

Nelson, J.G., Butler, R.W. and Wall, G. (1993) *Tourism and Sustainable Development: Monitoring, Planning, Management*, Waterloo: University of Waterloo Press.

Pearce, D.G. and Butler, R.W. (1993) *Tourism Research: Critiques and Challenges*, London: Routledge.

Poon, A. (1993) *Tourism, Technology and Competitive Strategies*, Harmondsworth: CAB International.

Qereqeretabua, R. (1990) 'Going global: an insight into the impacts on, and the concerns of, a small island nation of the globalization of the tourism industry, and reactions to it by the Fiji islands', Paper presented at Pacific Asia Travel Association Conference, Vancouver, Canada, April.

Ritchie, B. (1993) 'Tourism research: policy and managerial priorities for the 1990s and beyond', in D.G. Pearce and R.W. Butler (eds) *Tourism Research: Critiques and Challenges*, London: Routledge, 201–216.

Ryan, C. (1993) 'Crime, violence, terrorism and tourism', *Tourism Management* 14, 3: 173–183.

Seekings, J. (1993) 'Gibraltar: developing tourism in a political impasse', *Tourism Management* 14, 1: 61–67.

Smeral, E. (1993) 'Emerging eastern European tourism markets', *Tourism Management* 14, 6: 411–418.

Smith, V.L. and Eadington, W.R. (1992) *Tourism Alternatives*, Philadelphia: University of Pennsylvania Press.

Stipanuk, D.M. (1993) 'Tourism and technology: interactions and implications', *Tourism Management* 14, 4: 267–278.

Viant, A. (1993) 'Enticing the elderly to travel – an exercise in Euro-management', *Tourism Management* 14, 1: 52–60.

Wheeler, B. (1993) 'Sustaining the Ego', *Journal of Sustainable Tourism* 1, 2: 121–129.

World Tourism Organization (1994) *Tourism in 1993 Highlights*, Madrid: WTO.

Chapter 2

Contemporary tourism – trends and challenges
Sustainable authenticity or contrived post-modernity?

Erik Cohen

Tourism is essentially a modern western phenomenon. Although travel for religious, cultural, educational and medical purposes, and even for entertainment, can be found throughout human history, this author claims, in contrast, for example, to Nash (1981), that the motivations, roles and institutional structures of modern tourism differ significantly from those of pre-modern and non-western forms of travel, and are closely related to some other crucial characteristics of modernity (Cohen 1972: 165). These motivations and structures have changed and continue to change over time as tourism itself changes. This chapter examines, from a sociological perspective, the changing nature of tourist attractions and places, noting their shift from the natural and authentic to the artificial and contrived, and the implications of related changes in tastes and preferences of tourists in different societies. It cannot be denied, however, that modern tourist travel has spread in recent decades virtually throughout the world. Contemporary Japanese, Taiwanese, Koreans and members of many Third World societies are also tourists in the western sense of the term, even though their specific mode of travelling may incorporate elements from their own cultural traditions (Graburn 1983, Chapter Four; Ikkai 1988).

The early work in the sociology of tourism, therefore, focused on the modern western tourist. This work was concerned at first with the changes which occurred in the motivation and role of pre-modern travellers as they became modern tourists (Knebel 1960; Boorstin 1964: 77–117), and, later on, with the nature of the relationship between tourism and modernity (MacCannell 1973, 1976). Here, the principal question of concern became that of the 'authenticity' of the tourist experience (MacCannell 1973; Cohen 1988a): in effect, to what degree modern tourists are in quest of authenticity and, if they are, whether they are able to realize their aim. The destination, the site of their experience, was in this early work seen mainly as the medium for the realization of the tourists' motivations. To be sure, there existed from early on a wider concern with the 'impacts of tourism', the balance of desirable and undesirable consequences of tourism for destinations in the ecological, economic, social, political and cultural domains (Noronha 1977; Cohen 1984: 383–388). However, in the spirit of the focus on the tourist and the quality of his or her experience, much of this work, within the confines of the sociology of tourism, was concerned with the changes that tourism imparts to destinations, changes which may eventually have a negative feedback impact on their touristic attractiveness.

A major theme informing the sociological discourse on tourism impact was that of 'staged authenticity', a term coined by MacCannell (1973) to describe the artful presentation of contrived sites and sights as if they were authentic, when, in fact, they had already been transformed, partly by tourism itself. Such staging was seen to lead eventually to the emergence of a 'tourist space', which separates the sphere of tourism from the ordinary flow of local life, and thus prevents the tourist from experiencing its authenticity. The tourist was seen as caught in such a space, as if in a trap. Since the quest for authenticity was presented as a modern, secular substitute for the pre-modern religious quest, the denial of its fulfilment was at least implicitly seen as a negative consequence. It followed that tourism, by virtue of its very development, blocks the route to secular salvation, which it had initially promised (Dumont 1984: 140; Cohen 1988a: 372–373).

This trend of investigation at a later stage led to a growing concern with alternative tourism (Holden 1984; Cohen 1987; Vir Singh *et al.* 1989; Pleumarom 1990; Smith and Eadington 1992). That concept has several connotations, each of which shapes a different variety of this kind of tourism (Cazes 1989). This author called one of these varieties 'counter-cultural' alternative tourism (Cohen 1987), to indicate the opposition of its practitioners to the tourist establishment, and their desire to develop a style of travel studiously contrasting with that of routine mass tourists. This kind of tourism was supposed to re-open the path to salvation – enable the tourist, travelling alone or in small groups in the touristically unchartered territory beyond the limits of the 'tourist space', to have 'authentic' experiences. Such alternative tourism is often at least implicitly considered by its protagonists to be 'sustainable' – it is assumed that is does not significantly impinge upon the destination, and could therefore go on indefinitely. Alternative tourism, however, has a negligible impact only as long as its density is low – as long as few tourists visit remote locations at low frequencies. As the number of such tourists grows, they can engender considerable, though perhaps unsuspected, damage, precisely to sensitive outlying, as yet 'authentic', natural and cultural environments (Burns 1991; Butler 1992).

Under the impact of growing numbers of alternative tourists, their chosen destinations undergo a process of change. Tourism to such destinations, as Dearden and Harren (1994) have recently showed, then remains 'sustainable' only if the motivation of tourists to visit the destinations changes concomitantly. 'Sustainability', rather than indicating a static, unchanged state of affairs, thus becomes a dynamic concept: it comes to refer to the existence of some degree of congruence between two sets of changes, in the destination as well as in the motivations of tourists. The ultimate consequence of this process is frequently that ordinary tourists enter the area which has initially been opened by alternative tourists, while the latter penetrate ever deeper into as yet 'unspoilt' areas.

It turns out, then, that the idea of developing alternative tourism harbours a contradiction, and that this kind of tourism in fact often serves as the spearhead of ordinary touristic penetration. Indeed, it is this dynamic element of tourism expansion which raises a fundamental question of social policy: namely, should tourists, even alternative ones, be encouraged, or even allowed, to roam freely around and invade any new area, or should they be contained within set confines, even if this might preclude their having 'authentic experiences'?

This question reflects a gradual shift in public concern in many countries from tourism development to the protection of local nature and culture from tourism impacts. This concern is in turn reflected in a gradual refocusing of the principal interest of sociologists of tourism, from the tourists and their experiences to the destination: not just a preoccupation, common in any comprehensive touristic planning process, with the problem of how the more undesirable consequences of tourism development could be ameliorated, while developing a destination for tourism; rather, it is a more radical concern with how the local environment and people could be protected from the 'tourist gaze' (Urry 1990, 1992: 12) in all its various manifestations. This, however, should not be construed to mean that sociologists, or anyone else, suggest that tourism should be stopped altogether – an impossible and preposterous proposition; rather, it means that they seek to deflect tourism to different kinds of destinations – primarily to the manmade ones, created specifically for tourism. Ironically, these are the very 'contrived' attractions (Cohen 1972: 170) which, at an earlier stage, have been condemned as embodiments of inauthenticity. This term will be used in the following discussion, but in a neutral and not in a derogatory sense.

'NATURAL' AND 'CONTRIVED' ATTRACTIONS

Two polar types of attractions can be distinguished: the 'natural' and the 'contrived'. As an ideal type, 'natural' attractions are completely 'unmarked' – sites and sights which have not yet undergone any intervention – physical or symbolic – to make them more appealing, accessible, or even more easily noticed by tourists. The polar type of 'natural' attraction is exemplified by physical, cultural, ethnic or archaeological sites which have not been tampered with for touristic purposes. On the other hand, 'contrived' attractions, as a polar type, are exemplified by sites and sights which were specifically created for touristic purposes and are wholly artificial in character – that is, they do not contain any 'natural' elements.

The polar extremes define a continuum of different admixtures of natural and artificial elements: thus, many basically 'natural' attractions may have some 'contrived' traits. National parks, even if essentially 'natural' attractions, are symbolically marked and physically marked off. They are also regulated – for example, the populations of some animal species may have to be controlled artificially, since hunting by surrounding native human populations may have been prohibited. All these are 'contrived' traits. Similarly, archaeological sites are often marked, reconstructed and adapted for touristic visitation. Museums, though they may collect 'authentic', 'original' objects of ethnic, cultural or historical significance, often display them in artfully 'contrived' settings. Moreover, some contemporary museums do not display 'original' objects at all, but only copies or reconstructions of historical or natural environments. Here we approach the pole of completely 'contrived' attractions.

Certainly the best-known 'contrived' attraction, emblematic of the type, is Disneyland. This kind of attraction was looked down upon as a tourist destination by some researchers in the past. Indeed, when Khrushchev visited the United States in the 1960s, *Time Magazine* poked fun at his 'corny' tastes, since he asked to see how Americans grow corn, and to visit Disneyland. Since then the assessment of Disneyland has changed considerably. Precisely because of its emblematic status it is instructive to consider the reasons for that change, since it may throw some light on the changing status of other 'contrived' attractions.

There is, first, the patina of age. Although created for commercial touristic purposes, Disneyland over time became an American cultural landmark. Despite its 'contrived' origins, it acquired a measure of 'authenticity'. Second, the analysis of the structure and symbolism of Disneyland has disclosed its deep-structural meaning in American culture (Moore 1980; Johnson 1981; King 1981; Gottdiener 1982). The fact that it is a 'contrived' attraction no longer automatically implies that it is meaningless. Finally, and most relevant to present purposes, attitudes to 'contrived' attractions have changed with the emergence of a 'post-modern' touristic ethos: tourists, less concerned with authenticity and the hierarchy of attractions, seem to care less for the origins of an attraction as long as the visit is an enjoyable one.

It is this last point which is of particular interest for this discussion, since it indicates a trend away from the paradigmatic dominance of the quest for 'authenticity' as the principal culturally sanctioned motivation for modern tourists, and towards a 'nivellation' of all attractions, 'natural' and 'contrived', realistic or fantastic, historical or futuristic, original or recreated, characteristic of the post-modern ethos (Feifer 1985: 259–279; Urry 1990: 83–103). This nivellation finds expression, among other things, in touristic markers (MacCannell 1976: 110–111) in recently established 'contrived' attractions. It is strikingly illustrated by the manner in which the 'Many Worlds' (Sentosa: 1992), the various groups of sights on a recently established major tourist complex, the island of Sentosa in Singapore, are marked. The island features such sights as a secondary rain forest in the 'Nature Walk', a fantastic 'Dragon Walk' and fictional monuments of an ancient 'Ruined City' and a 'Lost Civilization'. The markers on both the realistic nature sights and the fantastic fictional ones are formulated in the same serious, matter-of-fact language which could easily convince any undiscerning visitor of the reality of the historical existence of dragons.

While it is not the purpose of this chapter to explore in depth this post-modern touristic ethos, it should be noted that it is congruent with the idea, broached at the end of the preceding section, that tourism should be deflected from intruding upon the environment and culture of people towards specifically created, 'contrived' attractions.

Modern criticism of mass tourism is generally inimical to 'contrived' attractions. The (covert) staging of attractions to which tourists are then surreptitiously directed, and in which they are presented with an allegedly authentic rendition of a people's life and culture, is generally condemned in the literature as an expression of crass commercialism, and of a double deception in which a falsified reality is made to confirm and satisfy the false expectations engendered by images of the destination in the promotional brochures and advertisements (Adams 1984: 472). Indeed, much of MacCannell's work was intended to show, on the one hand, how the tourist establishment succeeds in staging authenticity, and on the other, how tourists seek to break through the 'front' so established, to the 'back', the real life at the visited destination (MacCannell 1973).

However, there is another way to look at staged attractions. Buck (1977: 207, 1978), in his study of tourism in an Old Order Amish community, was the first anthropologist to use Mac-Cannell's concept from a different perspective. Instead of focusing upon the tourists' desire to break through the staged front presented by the Amish in order to experience their authentic life in the 'back', Buck drew attention to the role which staging plays 'in maintaining their way of life in spite of the seemingly pervasive presence of tourists' (1978: 225).

Staged representations may thus be seen to play an important, though perhaps often unintended role, that of keeping the authenticity-seeking tourists out, to prevent their 'gaze' from disturbing the life and culture of the community. This role of staged attractions is becoming increasingly important for precisely the most vulnerable and touristically exploited people: the 'Fourth World' ethnic minorities, tribal groups and remnants of hunter–gatherer bands whose 'real' life is threatened to become a show for organized touristic visits. Regulation of tourist visits to such sensitive sites, and the creation of contrived and staged representations of the toured group's life and culture, is, under these circumstances, an alternative policy to unbridled penetration, and may enable the toured group to derive some benefit from tourism, while protecting it from disruption by outsiders.

Staged attractions may thus play a beneficial role with regard to ethnic and tribal groups which still maintain a viable culture. One could develop a parallel argument regarding physical attractions, namely that valuable environments, harbouring rare flora and fauna, can be protected from detrimental touristic penetration by the creation of regulated, segregated areas in which the most attractive features of the environment are presented to visitors, while the rest is closed to visitors. To some degree this is the philosophy behind the concept of zoning in national parks and other protected areas. Not all 'contrived' attractions, however, are covertly staged. Indeed, one of the important trends in contemporary tourism development is the growing number of attractions which are admittedly and overtly staged.

There is a growing scarcity and diminishing attractiveness of 'natural' attractions. With the rapid penetration of western technology, industrial products and lifestyles into the remotest parts of the world, ever fewer ethnic and tribal groups are able to preserve unaltered their inherited culture and ways of life, and ever fewer natural environments remain pristine and untouched. A growing gap has opened between the image of native people or wild nature in the advertised destinations and the reality which exists there (Cohen 1992; Nash Chapter Three; Dann Chapter Seven).

While the transformations which the cultural world and the natural environment of the more remote parts of the world undergo are of consuming interest to researchers, they are of diminishing interest to tourists, even to those alternative tourists who are in quest of authenticity. Under these circumstances, the establishment of living museums, reconstructed ethnic or tribal villages, theme parks, wildlife and nature parks, and similar partly or wholly 'contrived' attractions become an increasingly acceptable substitute for 'natural' attractions. The establishment of such attractions is a matter of growing concern for developers and policy makers, not only in developed countries such as Japan and Singapore, but increasingly also in developing countries.

The tendency for reconstruction can be found not only in the domain of nature and ethnic or tribal culture, but also, and perhaps even more strongly, in the domain of history. MacCannell (1976:

148) argued that the alienated moderns seek authenticity not only in other, that is, non-modern, places but also in other times, that is, in the past. Indeed, archaeological sites and monuments of ancient civilizations have been leading touristic attractions from the very inception of modern tourism. However, the accelerated rate of change of the modern world destroys at a rapid rate the remnants of even the recent past, both material and cultural, even as it uproots the modern and produces a sense of irretrievable loss. This loss finds its cultural expression in the theme of 'nostalgia' (Frow 1991), which, as Graburn (Chapter Four) clearly illustrates, has significant implications for tourism. A powerful motive for the preservation and recreation of the past thus emerges, leading in part to the proliferation of local history museums, protected buildings and neighbourhoods, and the designation of various remnants of the past as 'heritage centres' (Urry 1990: 104–134). As this growing concern with the past becomes exploited by the tourism industry, the past itself is 'commoditized' (Evans-Pritchard 1993). As a result, a 'heritage industry' emerges (Hewison 1987; Urry 1990: 104–112).

Not only have growing numbers of archaeological and historical sites been adapted, and often also at least partly reconstructed, for touristic visitations, but a new type of 'contrived' attraction has emerged. This takes the form of historical reconstructions such as the 'historic theme parks' (Moscardo and Pearce 1986), and more recently, a pre-history, in which not only the material remnants of the past, but also the environment, culture, and way of life of bygone eras are conjured up by modern technological devices. These reconstructions of the past are thus a counterpart, in the historical realm, to 'living museums', staged ethnic villages and similar 'contrived' attractions in the ethnic and cultural realm. The most recent development in this area is the partly imaginary 'reconstruction' of prehistoric environments, such as the 'Jurassic Parks' which proliferated in the wake of the phenomenal success of Spielberg's film.

In what sense can 'contrived' historical reconstructions be considered 'authentic' (Moscardo and Pearce 1986)? The problem arises from their paradoxical nature: on the one hand they are obviously and admittedly staged attractions. On the other hand, however, their claim to legitimacy consists precisely in the allegation that, within the constraints of technical possibilities, they are 'correct' reproductions of the past, and in this sense may be considered 'authentic': they are 'authentic reproductions'. Research on local history museums and similar 'contrived' historical attractions, however, indicates that a kind of 'secondary staging' usually occurs. Rather than being neutral reproductions, such attractions often embody the cultural values, ideological perspectives (Katriel forthcoming), or commercial interests (Urry 1990: 132) of their creators. They are in themselves 'cultural productions' of our own time.

'Contrived' natural, ethnic and historical reconstructions have become increasingly popular with the travelling public. A variety of factors may have contributed to their growing popularity, but only two are directly relevant to the present discussion. On the one hand, such attractions, as was already pointed out, are a substitute for 'natural' attractions, which are becoming ever scarcer and ever more despoiled in the contemporary world. The 'authentic' reproductions of the past (even barely 'authentic' ones, as Graburn Chapter Four points out) also seem to satisfy the nostalgic cravings of contemporary tourists for the past, the remnants of which are being rapidly destroyed. In this sense, the 'contrived' reproductions may satisfy the modern 'quest for authenticity', in MacCannell's sense, though in fact they may be doubly staged.

On the other hand, however, such attractions are also a 'show'; they therefore bespeak the tourist's predisposition for playfulness, his or her readiness ludically (playfully) to accept 'contrived' attractions as if they were real. This predisposition becomes culturally sanctioned by the post-modern ethos. 'Contrived' reconstructions thus seem to entertain an interstitial location between 'natural' attractions and completely imaginary 'contrived' ones; they therefore appeal simultaneously to the culturally sanctioned modern as well as post-modern touristic motivations.

The proliferation and growing popularity of the last type of attraction which will be considered here, the imaginary 'contrived' attraction, appears to be particularly well suited to the latter kind of motivations. Such attractions are usually high-technology simulations of either futuristic environments, such as the 'Future Worlds' at the EPCOT Center in the Walt Disney World (EPCOT Center 1987), which enable the visitor to experience a projected or imagined future, or simulations of fantastic environments, such as the Magic Kingdom (Magic Kingdom 1987) in the Walt Disney World, which may be based either on myths of the past or even completely invented. The latter enable the visitor to undertake a completely imaginary journey without any, even imputed, reference to the real world. Entertainment centres such as the Disneylands, theme parks, such as Sentosa Island, and similar commercial entertainment facilities often feature several kinds of such attractions, sometimes in conjunction with ethnic or historical reconstructions.

There is, in itself, nothing new in such facilities. Newfangled devices and fantasy rides have been common offerings at popular fairs for many years, although the technology was more primitive, and the experience perhaps less realistic. But the point to note is that those rather modest devices were located in the realm of the local entertainment business, and not of the tourism industry. Their catchment areas were local or at most regional; they usually did not attract a national or international touristic audience. In contrast, the large contemporary entertainment centres, such as the Disneylands in the United States, Japan and France, are complexes of huge proportions, involving investments of the order of hundreds of millions of dollars and the most modern technology and management techniques. The very scale of such enterprises necessarily limits their number, while the existence and profitability of each is dependent on a wide, preferably world-wide, touristic appeal. Indeed, not only the Disneylands, but many other similar complexes of less renown and of a more limited scale in recent decades, have been incorporated into the tourist itineraries of many countries, especially the industrial ones.

A variety of specific factors, related to changes in lifestyles, income distribution and mobility, could be invoked to account for the contemporary proliferation of these large-scale imaginary 'contrived' attractions. But for present purposes it is important to note that this proliferation corresponds to an apparently pervasive shift in the dominant mode of experience desired by contemporary tourists, sightseers or vacationers. This mode, which is congruent with, and derives its legitimation from, the emerging 'post-modern ethos', is that of playfulness (Cohen 1985). If the culturally sanctioned mode of travel of the modern tourist has been that of the serious quest for authenticity, the mode of the post-modern tourist is that of playful search for enjoyment. In the former, there is a cognitive preoccupation with the penetration of staged fronts into real backs (MacCannell 1973), in the latter there is an aesthetic enjoyment of surfaces, whatever their cognitive status may be. The ludic attitude to attractions is becoming culturally sanctioned, and may well in the future overshadow that of the serious quest for authenticity. Post-modern tourists are engaging in an 'as if' game with the attraction (MacCannell 1989: 1). In order to enjoy the experience they are prepared to accept, although not wholly seriously, an even totally fantastic 'contrived' attraction as real. This concern with the enjoyability of the surface appearance of the attraction, rather than with its 'reality' or 'authenticity', makes it possible for the variety of imaginary 'contrived' attractions to flourish.

One can, in fact, advance this argument, somewhat speculatively, one step further. It appears that post-modern tourists, owing to the nivellating tendency of the post-modern ethos, and its stress on surfaces, evince a readiness to reduce or suspend the saliency of the boundaries between different 'provinces of meaning' (Schutz 1973: vol. I: 229 ff.), between fact and fiction, reality, reconstruction and fantasy. This readiness makes it possible for different kinds of 'contrived' attractions to co-exist within the same complex, as it were, on an equal standing. With the rapid contemporary development in simulation technology, those boundaries will become ever more reducible, and the suspension of their salience ever easier.

The most advanced of these developments are the various techniques of creating the impression of a 'virtual reality' (Ernsberger 1990), an artificial environment which is so completely simulated that it resembles, for the observer or participant in the situation, the 'paramount reality' (Schutz 1973: vol. I: 229 ff.). In principle, any environment, natural, historical or fantastic, could thus be almost perfectly realistically simulated in any location.

The combination between the lowered saliency of boundaries between provinces of meaning for post-modern tourists and the development of such advanced simulation technology poses an unexpected potential threat to contemporary tourism, namely, the progressive disappearance of 'placeness' (Relph 1976). If any experience could be virtually had in every location, no experience will be place-bound any more; then why should one travel? The boundary between tourism and leisure seems thereby to be put into question.

TOURISM AND LEISURE

The literature on tourism does not draw a clear distinction between tourism and leisure. Many students of tourism come from

the field of leisure studies, and indeed, one of the proposed definitions of a tourist is 'a person at leisure who also travels' (Nash
1981: 462). The sociology of leisure has provided one of the major
theoretical approaches to the study of tourism (Cohen 1984: 375).
Nevertheless, modern tourism is not merely a leisure activity, it
possesses some crucial characteristics which distinguish it from
other kinds of leisure. Indeed, not all tourism can be seen merely
as leisure, and some definitions of tourism include aspects such as
business travel. Consequently, tourism research emerged in recent
years as a fairly distinct field, separate from leisure studies (Fedler
1987; Butler 1989).

The crucial distinctive feature of tourism is that it involves
travel; it is an activity carried out at some distance from home. The
distance is of sociological as well as spatial significance, and it
implies exposure to the strangeness of an unaccustomed environment, along with the experiences of novelty and change for the
tourist. This distinguishing characteristic of tourism, which is not
found in ordinary leisure, can be employed as a point of departure
for a sociological approach to tourism (Cohen 1972). It is the basis
on which a distinct institutional nexus, the 'tourism industry',
has emerged. Tourism is based in part on the assumption that
the experience offered by the destination is not available in the
tourist's home environment. (Although others (Pearce 1987, 1989)
have argued that at least some of the motivation for tourism is
to escape the origin, and that it is the conditions there that are
important rather than the attractions at the destination (editors'
note).) The distinctiveness of the destination could be termed
'placeness'. One theory of intervening opportunities (Stouffer
1940) teaches us that, if the same experience were available at
home, tourists would not have to take the trouble to travel.

It is this very distinctiveness of tourism, the 'placeness' of the
destinations, which is threatened by the deflection of much of modern tourism to 'contrived' attractions and by the emergence of
simulated environments which provide experiences approximating
'reality'. Some kinds of 'contrived' attractions, especially entertainment complexes like the Disneylands or Sentosa Island, can
in principle be established anywhere; there is no intrinsic connection between them and the place in which they are located, as the
examples of Disneylands near Paris (Privat and Gleizes 1992) or
Tokyo demonstrate. However, these attractions do still have a
fixed location; and, as they become part of the tourist system, they

themselves may endow this location with an image and character which it had not earlier possessed; 'placeness' is an emergent quality.

In contrast, the more advanced simulation techniques, conjuring up a 'Virtual Reality', are in principle not at all place-bound; they can, or soon will, be enjoyable in the privacy of one's home. Hence, the distinction between the experience of an attraction in the real world and its simulation in one's home environment may be gradually disappearing. Under the assumptions of a post-modern ethos, which tends to reduce the salience of the authenticity or reality of the source of the experience, and is concerned, primarily, with its 'surface' quality, the two kinds of experiences will tend to become asymptotically indistinguishable. The boundary between tourism and leisure may then become virtually erased and tourism, as an activity, lose much of its distinctiveness.

Hereby is reached a perhaps unsuspected, but certainly fundamental, challenge which tourism, as a distinct type of activity, will have to face and come to grips with in the foreseeable future. Tourists are being gradually deflected, for reasons elaborated above, from 'natural' to 'contrived' attractions. Such attractions, however, are increasingly less place-bound, and hence lack the distinction of 'placeness' characteristic of 'natural' attractions. As modern simulation techniques gradually erase the distinction between 'real' and simulated experiences, and as the post-modern ethos endows this distinction with less and less saliency, experiences which could previously be attained only by travelling to attractions can now be increasingly approximated at home. This trend towards the 'de-placement' of experiences which in the past were distinctly touristic thus poses a threat to the attractiveness of tourism in the future.

How realistic is this threat? It would be easy, but facile, to extrapolate from it a prediction that it spells the end of tourism. We can learn from past experience that historical trends rarely, if ever, lead to their ultimate consequences. It is, rather, more reasonable to predict that tourism will be reconstituted and given new, but as yet not clearly foreseeable, meaning, form and direction. The trend away from 'natural' and towards 'contrived' and increasingly home-bound attractions reflects, as we have seen, a more general trend of change in contemporary society and culture, expressed in the post-modern ethos. Post-modernism, however, as the term itself implies, is a transitional phenomenon, rather than a novel, well-integrated and permanent cultural system. It is, of course, difficult to foresee the defining traits of the cultural ethos which will supplant it, but one reasonable prediction is that, as a reaction to the nivellating tendency of post-modernism, a new hierarchy of phenomenological 'realities' and corresponding experiences will emerge. In the process, some experiential short-comings of de-placed, 'contrived' attractions and simulated en-vironments will be discovered or rediscovered and gain increased salience – such as the loss of remoteness, of genuine placeness or of a sense of unprogrammed adventure. While, for reasons discussed above, there are few resources left on this globe which will satisfy those longings – the endless expanses of the universe still remain unexplored. While space-tourism in the foreseeable future will be the privilege of a small elite, it may well become the frontier of a reconstituted tourism of the coming centuries (Kaufmann 1983).

CONCLUSION

In order to put the preceding discussion in a wider perspective three observations are offered by way of conclusion. First, the post-modern touristic stance of nivellation of attractions, natural and contrived, of enjoyment of surfaces and simulations, and legit-imation of ludic attitudes is not a naive, unwitting or unconscious one. Rather, it is a reflective stance, which could, paraphrasing Eisenstadt (1982), be called 'post-axial'. This stance is a conse-quence of the process of radical secularization (Cohen 1988b) and of the breakthrough (or breakdown) of all absolute ('privileged') criteria of judgement and evaluation, on which the 'post-modern' ethos is grounded. It is a studied stance, close to the post-modern equalization of high and low elitist and popular art. Hence it is different from the allegedly undiscerning attitude of the mass-tourist as portrayed earlier, for example, by Boorstin (1964). Post-modern tourists are sophisticated individuals, who choose not to discern, though they are aware of the possibilities of distinction. The tourists' tendency not to discern is the consequence of rational penetration of all criteria as socially constructed, a kind of 'Aufhebung' of modern distinctions, which endows them with a newly won freedom (though perhaps of the Sartrian kind).

Second, in the contemporary world there are, in fact, two trends at work: one, emphasized in this chapter, leads away from 'natural' to 'contrived' attractions and towards a fusion of tourism and leisure. But there is a contrary trend at work, indicated in the first section of this chapter – towards a more radical *preservation* of historic (heritage) monuments, ethnic culture and pristine nature. This indicates the continuing cultural importance of authenticity. However, such preservation is not necessarily intended to *serve* tourism but may be intended as a *defence* of such sites *from* tourism. In that sense this is a relatively recent trend.

Lastly, two contrasting processes of transformation can be discerned on the contemporary tourist scene. On the one hand, the very effort of preserving attractions, and their defence from touristic impact, often makes them more 'contrived'. Preservation often involves the need to create contrivances which at least change the outward appearance of authentic physical, historical or cultural attractions. On the other hand, a contrary process is at work. 'Contrived' attractions, originally created for tourist purposes, increasingly become part of the physical, historical or cultural environment – they become 'naturalized'. These contrasting processes eventually blur the distinction between 'natural' and 'contrived' attractions, making it ever harder to distinguish between 'natural' attractions to which 'contrived' elements have been progressively added, and initially 'contrived' attractions which became progressively integrated into their natural surroundings. This process is likely to continue into the future.

ACKNOWLEDGEMENTS

Thanks are due to Zali Gurevitch and Boas Shamir for their useful comments on an earlier draft of this paper.

REFERENCES

Adams, K.M. (1984) 'Come to Tana Toraja, "Land of the Heavenly Kings"', *Annals of Tourism Research* 11, 3: 469–485.

Boorstin, D.J. (1964) *The Image: A Guide to Pseudo-Events in America*, New York: Harper & Row.

Buck, R.C. (1977) 'The ubiquitous tourist brochure', *Annals of Tourism Research* 4, 4: 195–207.

—— (1978) 'Boundary maintenance revisited: Tourist experience in an Old Order Amish community', *Rural Sociology* 43, 2: 221–234.

Burns, F.A. (1991) '"Ecotourists" aren't all good', *The Nation* (Bangkok), 26 August 1991, p. B 4.

Butler, R.W. (1989) 'Tourism and tourism research', in T.L. Burton and

E.L. Jackson (eds) *Understanding Leisure and Recreation: Mapping the Past, Charting the Future*, State College, Pa.: Venture Publishing, 567–595.

—— (1992) 'Alternative tourism: The thin end of the wedge', in V.L. Smith and W.R. Eadington (eds) *Tourism Alternatives*, Philadelphia: University of Pennsylvania Press, 31–46.

Cazes, G.H. (1989) 'Alternative tourism: Reflections on an ambiguous concept', in T. Vir Singh, H.L. Theuns and F.M. Go (eds) *Towards Appropriate Tourism*, Frankfurt a/M: Peter Lang, 117–126.

Cohen, E. (1972) 'Toward a sociology of international tourism', *Social Research* 39, 1: 164–182.

—— (1984) 'The sociology of tourism: Approaches, issues, and findings', *Annual Review of Sociology* 10: 373–392.

—— (1985) 'Tourism as play', *Religion* 15: 291–304.

—— (1987) 'Alternative tourism – A critique', *Tourism Recreation Research* 12, 2: 13–18.

——(1988a) 'Authenticity and commoditization in tourism', *Annals of Tourism Research* 15, 3: 371–386.

—— (1988b) 'Radical secularization and the destructuration of the universe of knowledge in late modernity', in S.N. Eisenstadt and I.F. Silber (eds) *Knowledge and Society: Studies in the Sociology of Culture Past and Present*, in H. Kuklick (series ed.) *Cultural Traditions and the World of Knowledge: Explorations in the Sociology of Knowledge*, Greenwich: JAI Press, 7, 202–223.

—— (1992) 'The growing gap: Hill tribe image and reality', *Pacific Viewpoint* 33, 2: 164–169.

Dearden, P. and Harren, S. (1994) 'Alternative tourism and adaptive change', *Annals of Tourism Research*, 21, 1: 81–102.

Dumont, J.-P. (1984) 'A matter of touristic "indifference"', *American Ethnologist* 11, 1: 139–151.

Eisenstadt, S.N. (1982) 'The axial age', *European Journal of Sociology* 23: 294–314.

EPCOT Center (1987) *EPCOT Center Guide Book*, Walt Disney World (Brochure).

Ernsberger, R. (1990) 'Through the Looking Glass', *Newsweek*, 7 May, 44–46.

Evans-Pritchard, D. (1993) 'Ancient art in a modern context: Tourist arts and the commoditization of the past', *Annals of Tourism Research* 20, 1: 9–31.

Fedler, A.J. (1987) 'Are leisure, recreation and tourism interrelated?', *Annals of Tourism Research* 14, 2: 311–313.

Feifer, N. (1985) *Going Places*, London: Macmillan.

Frow, J. (1991) 'Tourism and the semiotics of nostalgia', *October* 57: 123–151.

Gottdiener, M. (1982) 'Disneyland: A utopian urban space', *Urban Life* 11, 2: 139–162.

Graburn, N. (1983) 'To pray, pay and play: The cultural structure of Japanese domestic tourism', *Les Cahiers du Tourisme*, Ser. B, 26: 1–89.

Hewison, R. (1987) *The Heritage Industry: Britain in a Climate of Decline*, London: Methuen.

Holden, P. (ed.) (1984) *Alternative Tourism: With a Focus on Asia*, Bangkok: Ecumenical Coalition on Third World Tourism.

Ikkai, M. (1988) 'The *Senbetsu-Omiyage* relationship: Traditional reciprocity among Japanese tourists', *Kroeber Anthropological Society Papers* 67/68: 62–66.

Johnson, D.M. (1981) 'Disney World as structure and symbol: Recreation of the American experience', *Journal of Popular Culture* 15, 1: 157–166.

Katriel, T. (forthcoming) 'Re-making place: Cultural production in Israeli pioneer settlement museums', in E. Ben-Ari and Y. Bilu (eds) *Fabrication of Land*.

Kaufmann, W. J. (1983) 'Tourism in the twenty-first century', *Science Digest* 91, 4: 52–64.

King, M.J. (1981) 'Disneyland and Walt Disney World: Traditional values in futuristic form', *Journal of Popular Culture* 15, 1: 116–140.

Knebel, H.J. (1960) *Soziologische Strukturwandlungen im modernen Tourismus*, Stuttgart: Enke.

MacCannell, D. (1973) 'Staged authenticity: Arrangements of social space in tourist settings', *American Journal of Sociology* 79, 3: 589–603.

—— (1976) *The Tourist: A New Theory of the Leisure Class*, New York: Schocken.

—— (1989) 'Introduction', Special Issue, Semiotics of Tourism, *Annals of Tourism Research* 16, 1: 1–6.

Magic Kingdom (1987) *Magic Kingdom Guide Book*, Walt Disney World (Brochure).

Moore, A. (1980) 'Walt Disney World: Bounded ritual space and the playful pilgrimage center', *Anthropological Quarterly* 53, 4: 207–218.

Moscardo, G.P. and Pearce, P.L. (1986) 'Historic theme parks: An Australian experience in authenticity', *Annals of Tourism Research* 13, 3: 467–479.

Nash, D. (1981) 'Tourism as an anthropological subject', *Current Anthropology* 22, 5: 461–481.

Noronha, R. (1977) *Social and Cultural Dimensions of Tourism: A Review of the Literature in English*, Washington: World Bank (draft).

Pearce, D.G. (1987) *Tourism Today: A Geographical Analysis*, New York: Wiley.

—— (1989) *Tourist Development*, New York: Wiley.

Pleumarom, A. (1990) 'Alternative tourism: A viable solution?', *Contours* 4, 8: 12–15.

Privat, P. and Gleizes, F. (1992) 'Presto! Let the magic begin', *Newsweek* 119, 15: 14–15.

Relph, E. (1976) *Place and Placelessness*, London: Pion.

Schutz, A. (1973) *Collected Papers*, The Hague: M. Nijhoff (3 vols).

Sentosa (1992) *Discover the Many Worlds of Sentosa*, Singapore: Sentosa (Brochure).

Smith, V.L. and Eadington, W.R. (1992) *Tourism Alternatives*, Philadelphia: University of Pennsylvania Press.

Stouffer, S.A. (1940) 'Intervening opportunities: A theory relating mobility and distance', *American Sociological Review* 5, 6: 845–867.

Urry, J. (1990) *The Tourist Gaze*, London: Sage.

—— (1992) 'The tourist gaze and the environment', *Theory, Culture and Society* 9: 1–26.

Vir Singh, T., Theuns, H.L. and Go, F.M. (eds) (1989) *Towards Appropriate Tourism: The Case of Developing Countries*, Frankfurt a/M: Peter Lang.

Chapter 3

An exploration of tourism as superstructure

Dennison Nash

When confronted by scepticism about their choice of subject matter, some researchers in tourism may justify themselves by pointing out that their research has to do with a great world industry. Anthropologists, such as this author, may go further by referring to the Third or Developing World in which many have done fieldwork. There, tourism has become an increasingly important developmental tool and a major agent of change. These justifications are true enough, but even normally robust tourism figures are sometimes elastic, which can be revealed in times of recession and economic stringencies, when tourism patterns and expenditures may change, a fact which reveals a dependent nature. This chapter, by looking at tourism as a kind of superstructure in the societies of humankind, explores the nature of that dependency and vulnerability to change. In doing this, it follows up the suggestion of Hamilton-Smith (1987: 343) to consider the relationship between tourism behaviour and home behaviour. Likewise, Graburn (1983a: 19), in laying out a new course of anthropological inquiry on tourism, much of which has been concerned with destination areas, argues that we ought to seek to explain 'why specific touristic modes are attached to the particular social groups at the historical period when they are found'.

In line with an emerging comparative trend in tourism studies (Pearce D. 1993), this issue is viewed here from a perspective that includes all of the cultures of humankind, including those in our changing, increasingly internationalized world. The conception of tourism as a kind of superstructure is well suited for analysing the changing nature of tourism in this, as well as all other social worlds, and allows researchers to look at change over time as well as cross-culturally. This viewpoint is discussed in this chapter, beginning with a review of the relationship of tourism, leisure and labour in society in the context of base and superstructure, followed by a brief examination of two examples of research which are used to illustrate the points made, and which clearly illustrate the role of tourism in social and cultural change.

Looking at tourism from an anthropological point of view, it is difficult to avoid the conclusion that it is a widespread – even universal – phenomenon. By defining the tourist as a leisured traveller it is possible to make the cross-cultural comparisons that are one of the hallmarks of anthropological research. True, there are differences of opinion about the nature of leisure (see Neulinger 1981; Kelly 1983; Cooper 1989), but there is considerable agreement that, at a minimum, leisure involves *freedom from* social obligations that are necessary for the maintenance of a society and its reproduction – obligations that Dumazedier (1968) refers to as 'fundamental' or 'primary' (such as work, domestic tasks and personal care). Many authors take these obligations to centre around work, broadly or narrowly defined, which is supposed (because it is socially essential) to have a more socially compelling nature. People who are not engaged in work or work-related activities are thought to enter the sphere of leisure time and realize leisure in various culturally constituted ways. According to this view, leisure activities are those which are performed in the time available 'beyond existence and subsistence time' (Clawson 1964: 1). Thought of in this way, leisure would seem to exist in all societies, but the amount, form and nature of its allocation in a population appears to vary cross-culturally and intra-culturally.

Evidence to support these propositions comes from studies of time use by anthropologists (see Gross 1984 for a review). Although not speaking directly about leisure, Johnson (1978), for example, divides up the days of the Machchiguenga, horticulturalists of Peru, into production time, which includes all forms of work, consumption time, in which goods and services are used or consumed, and free time. Though Johnson's notion of free time is more restricted than that used here, that is, the time left over from production-related activities, it does give us some idea of the cross-cultural variability of leisure. Compared to a sample of urban, middle-class French adults, the Machchiguenga were found to spend less time in productive activity. Johnson also found that women in both cultures tended to work more than men. Why the similarity and differences? It is with questions such as this (specifically regarding tourism) that this chapter will be concerned.

Consider the apparent universality of leisure in the cultures of humankind. The *Outline of Cultural Materials* (Murdock *et al.* 1982) accepts it as such. Universals in human affairs are often explained by anthropologists in terms of some evolutionarily-given attribute (Brown 1991: 39–53). In leisure studies, the existence of leisure sometimes is accounted for by a human need, either for leisure itself (Sayers 1989: 42–43) or for the maintenance of some personal existential state (Iso-Ahola 1983; Hamilton-Smith 1987: 333–334). The existence of such needs is hard to prove. Why not simply assume that in every society there are some activities such as work that, because they are more essential, are more socially compelling? When people are not engaged in such activities they enter the sphere of free or leisure time. It also should be kept in mind that there always is division of labour in a society, which means that leisure time will not be equally allocated. Servants, for example, must work so that their employers can play; children and old people generally work less than adults; and men less than women.

We should also bear in mind that different aspects of a people's social life are more or less integrated so that one can affect the other. However, not all institutionalized activities have equal shaping power, and some, the less essential, are more dependent for their nature on those others which are more necessary for a society's functioning. Play, for example, which has often been tied to leisure activity, has been suggested by Suomi (1982: 169) to be one of the least essential of human activities; hence, it would be one of the most dependent.

Given the relationship between production-related activities and leisure just discussed, it seems fair to say that the ultimate cause of leisure is to be found in the broadly conceived work of the world seen in economic terms; leisure becomes, in Sahlins' view (1972: 65), a 'superstructural counterpart of a dynamic proper to the economy'. In an early paper on tourism (Nash 1979: 4), this writer argued that leisure is a social production that is dependent on the nature and extent of a society's work and the capacity of that work to generate the surplus necessary to maintain those not working. In the West, we have tended to think that the road to this surplus (and hence leisure) is taken by increasing productivity, so we produce much. But, as Sahlins has made clear, it is possible also to produce a surplus by diminishing wants. Both of these strategies have been employed by the peoples of the world to produce the surpluses needed to support leisure activities.

Contrary to popular notions, more complex, industrialized societies do not necessarily have more leisure time. Sahlins (1972) cites reports on wandering hunters and gatherers like the San of southern Africa or the Murngin of Australia that suggest diminished wants. As a result, these peoples had considerable leisure time. Both Sahlins (1972: 35) and Chick (1986: 162) have offered 'evolutionary' hypotheses about the relationship between leisure or free time and social complexity, but considering all the problems of time allocation studies (Bird-David 1992), generalizations like these should be taken with a grain of salt. Moreover, in speaking of free time in the global, per capita sense, they tend to paper over the issue of the allocation of leisure in a society. In more complex societies, the intra-societal differences in work and, as a consequence, in free time, tend to increase, which means that the elite have more free time than others. In a typical agriculturally-based state, peasants have to work long and hard in order to produce the surplus necessary to support their rulers' leisure; and owners of large industries may have more free time than the most leisurely of hunters and gatherers, although perhaps not always as much as their employees. Much more research needs to be done in order to make assured generalizations about these matters.

What forms do the leisure activities of a society take? One form is travel, which is comparatively expensive in terms of the energy and productivity involved. Tourism, as conceived here, results from the wedding of leisure and travel. People can hang around at home chatting and sleeping during their free time, as do the San, but when they expend the greater energy necessary to visit and socialize with relatives in another band, they begin to look like those French worker tourists, many of whom take their vacations with relatives or friends (Boyer 1972: 50).

The *Outline of Cultural Materials* (Murdock *et al.* 1982) considers travel as well as leisure as a cultural universal. So far as is known, there never has been a society that conforms to the Taoist utopia in which people are entirely content to stay at home. People everywhere go abroad, but the rate of travel and its nature also is cross-culturally, as well as intra-culturally, variable. To cite one intra-cultural difference, travelling often has been linked with social status. Societies, also, differ in their rates of individual mobility.

Many authors have pointed to an association between mobility and social complexity. Lerner (1958: 247), for example, saw in the Middle East a line of social development that had been taken in the western world, that is, a movement towards greater physical mobility that resulted in 'people becoming intimate with the idea of change through direct experience'. Though the causal nature of the relationship between social complexity and individual mobility has not been proven, and though some tinkering still may be necessary at the hunting and gathering end of the continuum, the notion of a positive association seems to have stood the test of time. Leisure mobility undoubtedly reflects this association.

To summarize and tie together the preceding discussion, tourism has been conceived here to involve both leisure and travel, both of which are socially constructed. The social production of leisure derives from a productive system in which people labour to produce the resources necessary to sustain themselves in their work and in their free or leisure time. Whatever leisure time is generated by the system of production is allocated in ways that are consistent with its division of labour. In general, an increase in the division of labour, and hence social complexity, is associated with greater differences in the allocation of leisure time. The people of a society make use of the leisure time available to them in ways that are consistent with their social position and its resources. One such way is travelling, which seems to be associated with social complexity. Whether people travel in their leisure time, and so become tourists, would seem to reflect the general propensity for travelling in a society.

All of the preceding only establishes the minimal conditions or opportunities for tourism. Whether these opportunities are real-ized, and in what form, would seem to be dependent on more specific factors which account for the variability of tourism within and between societies. In a survey of tourism in pre-industrial societies (Nash 1979: 22), this writer found that, generally, 'higher ranking people were more likely to engage in protracted, longer range, more luxurious forms of tourism'. Why is this so? In an influential paper, Cohen (1979) suggests that tourists seek five kinds of experience in their travelling (recreational, diversionary, experiential, experimental, existential). What are the social condi-tions that generate one or another of these types? To answer such questions, one searches for, in Hamilton-Smith's words (1987: 333), 'the opportunities and social constraints imposed on the individual from without'. Questions such as these may be entertained by considering tourism as a kind of superstructure.

THE CONCEPT OF SUPERSTRUCTURE

The habit of looking at the activities of a society in terms of base and superstructure is most closely linked with Marxist materialist analysis. Godelier (1980), taking a rather broad materialist point of view, sees the social base, which consists of a society's productive arrangements, exercising a determinative role 'in the last instance' on all other aspects of a society including superstructural elements such as religion. Harris (1992: 297), also taking a broad view, argues that all features of a society are 'necessary components of social life', but they do not 'play a symmetrical role in influencing the retention or extinction of sociocultural innovations'. It is the productive base that has the greatest influence in this regard.

One does not have to be a Marxist to argue that not all sectors of a society are equally determinative in its maintenance and reproduction. Durkheim, a key figure in functionalist studies, takes a similar view in his analysis of religion (Lukes 1972: 462–477). For him, social structure acts as the determinative force, and collective representations, including religion, though capable of influencing social action, are ultimately responsive to it. Here, religion is a superstructural element, but not exactly in the Marxist sense.

Although tourism may, in the last instance, be dependent on the productive system of a society, the kind of questions usually asked about it, that is, about its variability, require more proximate, and therefore more varied, statements of causation. Here, tourism can be seen as dependent–responsive to a variety of social bases. We should not forget, however, that like all aspects of sociocultural systems, it also acquires a life of its own and is capable of influencing other elements in a social system. Further, one must insist on the agency of individual human beings. As Hardy (1990: 542–543) argues, patterns of tourism are not some mechanistic outcome of infrastructural arrangements such as social class. Rather, the (tourist) users 'contribute to a greater extent than is commonly acknowledged, to the formation of distinctive patterns of use and opportunity'.

What is the connection between base and superstructure where tourism is concerned? In leisure studies, two kinds of causal connection are generally acknowledged (Neulinger 1974: 12). One is the 'spillover effect' in which leisure phenomena are a simple carryover of infrastructural or base activities. So, alienated workers continue to be alienated in their leisure. In tourism studies, a well-known proponent of this point of view is Boorstin (1964), who sees the superficialities of modern life spilling over into touristic experience. The other effect which has been proposed is compensatory. So, instead of continuing on the same track during leisure time, the alienated worker seeks a less alienated, more authentic existence. In tourism studies, this point of view has become well known through the work of MacCannell (1976) who sees the modern middle class scouring the world for the authentic experience which has been lacking in their daily, alienated lives, although Cohen (Chapter Two) suggests this pattern is changing. Graburn (1989), who also subscribes to this point of view, goes so far as to suggest that tourism satisfies a need for alternation or inversion of existential state in all human beings.

Whether tourism is a spillover from, or a compensation for the home routine, both, or something else, is not the main issue here. What is more important is the recognition that the connection between tourism as superstructure and its social base usually is stated in a way that conforms to some notion of how human beings operate. Which principle obtains in a given case is determined, as Kando and Summers (1971) have suggested, by the nature of the activities involved. For example, people in more alienated social positions may show a greater tendency to seek diversionary touristic compensation, as in the case of English 'hooligan' outings to football matches on the continent.

The connection between base and superstructure cannot violate relevant principles of individual motivation, which, according to Pearce P. (1993: 116), 'is the global integrating network of biological and cultural forces which gives value and direction to travel choices'. What of the direction of the motive driving the tourist? Can it be conceived as a push, a pull, or both? Dann (1981: 190–191) argues that the general disposition to tour involves a push, while more specific dispositions such as destination choice involve a pulling component. Iso-Ahola (1982) speaks of avoidance and approach in his analysis of tourist motivation. Typically, according to Dann (1981: 190–191), the logical and temporal sequence begins with certain desires 'to which the (home) environment inadequately responds'. Travel of one sort or another is next thought to be the answer to these desires. Then, there is a casting about for destinations that might satisfy. This process, according to Crompton (1992), involves a progressive narrowing down of 'pulling' alternatives, which ought to vary by culture and subculture.

BEGINNING STEPS

Cross-culturally oriented research that can be linked with the concept of tourism as superstructure is still in its infancy. Calls by anthropologists to study the tourist-generating situation have been issued for some time now (for example, Nash 1981; Graburn 1983a; Crick 1989), but the number of research projects in this area are few, and generally of a preliminary and speculative character. Nevertheless, we do have something to go on. Using the notion of tourism as superstructure, and by reference to some of these investigations, the following discussion will demonstrate the viability of this approach in different situations, including those in our changing, increasingly internationalized world.

The social organization of Japanese tourism

Since the resurgence of their country following World War II, Japanese tourists have become a familiar sight around the world. Tourism has become an important aspect of Japanese life, and despite lapses here and there, for example during oil crises or the Gulf War, all relevant measures from the Japan National Tourist Organization (JNTO 1992: 1–10) indicate a continuing robust, upward trend. What is the typical nature of Japanese touring as compared with, say, that of Americans? Graburn (1983b, Chapter Four) inquires into the nature of the relationship 'between the two "spheres of life" – work and home vs leisure and travel'. Though Graburn considers a number of aspects of Japanese (especially domestic) tourism, including its target sites (for example, those in natural, cultural and religious settings), its timing (according to the yearly cycle of holidays or festivals) and style, as well as its historical basis in pilgrimage, only one aspect – its social organization – will be considered here. It is this aspect that provides perhaps the most obvious contrast with the tourism generated in contemporary Europe and North America. In the course of discussing the relationship between leisure and tourist activities and the more 'serious' side of Japanese life, Graburn (1983b: 36–37) argues that the (superstructural) fact that Japanese tourists tend to travel more in larger groups than in smaller groups or as individuals reflects the group-oriented structure (that is, the base) of Japanese society.

The collective orientation of the Japanese is well known, and it is perhaps because of this that Graburn (1983b) does not spend much time demonstrating its existence. However, he does give us some idea of the various group involvements of individual Japanese. Kinship groupings, school groups, work groups and friendship groups structure much of their daily life and, in an interesting illustration of the spillover effect mentioned earlier, carry over into the realm of tourism. For example, Graburn speaks of family trips to the seaside or amusement parks, educational school tours, recreational outings of friends and tours sponsored by employers such as companies or agricultural cooperatives, and notes the 'team spirit' that is supposed to prevail in such groups. He refers only in passing to the tours arranged by Japanese travel agencies or airlines, but such overseas travel was limited in 1983.

A further indication of the importance of the group to the Japanese tourist is to be found in the relationship between the traveller and the kinship group at home, which is 'cemented' with a variety of gifts. At a farewell party prior to departure, the traveller is given money, travel paraphernalia or good luck charms (*senbetsu*), the value of which must be carefully attended to. During the trip, the tourist is supposed to buy appropriate return gifts (*omiyage*) worth approximately half the value of each *senbetsu*, which are delivered at a welcome home party. He or she also brings back souvenirs, including photographs, of the various destinations on the tour to confirm the visits to the people at home. In addition, the home group may practise certain observances that aim to keep the traveller in mind. As Graburn (1983b: 46) points out, 'the traveller is "sent" as a representative of the enduring group, most of whom are left behind, and indeed travels "for them" and buys things that they would have bought if they could have gone too'.

At the time of Graburn's first study (1983b), there were Japanese tourists – most of them younger, more individualistic and adventurous types – who were beginning to go abroad. Moeran (1983) thought that this was the leading edge of a more individualistic form of touring among the Japanese. Graburn (personal communication) agrees that there has, indeed, been an increasing tendency to tour in small groups such as the family. Official figures show that this has been the case on the domestic front. In 1991, for example, 55 per cent of domestic touring took place with the family (JNTO 1992: 7). The individualizing trend undoubtedly has been facilitated by a Ministry of Transport policy to aid non-group overseas air passengers with lower air fares and to respond to 'individual needs and tastes' (JNTO 1992: 20), as well as the increasing use of the private motor car and improvement of roads for domestic travel (Graburn Chapter Four). In 1990, four times as many passengers travelled by private car as in 1975.

On the other hand, travel in larger collectivities is far from over. Japanese airlines have significant charter businesses which carry not only sightseers, who, according to Moeran (1983: 95) dominated in the 1960s and 1970s, but also large groups of Japanese men on sex tours, especially to southeast Asia (Mackie 1988). School trips, analysed by Graburn, continue to flourish. In 1990 more than 90 per cent of Japanese junior and senior high schools had excursions, some of which have now been extended abroad (JNTO 1992:7). Graburn (personal communication) argues that the tendency is towards a mix of individualized and collectivized tourism, with the former presently concentrated among younger adults. Assuming he is correct about how large groupings of Japanese travellers serve to bolster a certain timidity when away from Japan, then there is reason to believe that the collectivized component will remain significant in Japanese tourism, at least in the near future, despite the other changes which are taking place.

Moeran (1983) has also speculated that Japanese tourism was becoming increasingly capitalized and hence 'individualized' in the western pattern, and that the spearhead of this trend was in the overseas realm. For him (1983: 95), 'the era of the flag-bearing guide leading a party of bewildered Japanese tourists . . . was coming to a close'. In terms of the form of analysis used here, his argument is that this evolution of Japanese tourism reflects the advance of an increasingly individualized western capitalistic consumerism. Japanese development, therefore, will follow the western form. This view is contradicted by others, including Graburn (1983b: 66) who states that 'at no point in history will the range of tourist structures or motivations coincide between Japan and the West'. From the 'tourism as superstructure' point of view, this is because the basal structure of Japanese society will not permit it. As Nozumu (1988: 281) says, 'Japanese modernization presents problems in which communal relations of various kinds have survived without being completely dissolved'. Further research on the evolving individual-collective mix of Japanese tourism, as well as the basal structure of Japanese society, should help us to know who is right.

Picture postcards of American Indians

In a series of studies involving picture postcard representations of American Indians, Albers and James (1983, 1988) have argued that the romantic, stereotyped images of Indians on early-twentieth-century postcards and other touristic literature constituted an ideology that responded to the interests of white American society. Though they do not pursue the notion to the end, their work can be used to illustrate the utility of the conception of tourism as superstructure, and this section will continue and complete their analysis in the theoretical direction that is latent in their work.

Picture postcards of American Indians in the early twentieth century were initially for local touristic consumption. According to Albers and James (1983: 131), they 'showed a great deal about the ordinary and indigenous aspects of life', but as tourism became more important, this image changed in a way that would attract a wider range of visitors. In the American southwest, this change was especially apparent in the media productions of the Fred Harvey Company and the Santa Fe Railroad. The reality of contemporary Indian life, which had become pretty grim under white domination, increasingly was replaced in the postcards by idyllic, exotic scenes designed to meet the expectations of white American tourists. Albers and James do not address the issue of how such expectations were generated, which is to say they do not explore the connections between what have been referred to here as base and superstructure, but such connections can be suggested.

The call of the wild (to American whites), in which the American Indian played an important part, was heard from the early days of the American Republic. At first threatening, it became increasingly benign until, with the disappearance of the frontier and pacification of Indians towards the end of the nineteenth century, it represented a significant romantic vision, especially for city-dwellers. Then, according to Nash (1967: 231), 'enough doubts had arisen about the beneficence of civilization's achievements to make possible a widespread popular enthusiasm for the uncivilized'. To give one example, the *Handbook of the Boy Scouts of America* (Seton 1910: 1–2), an organization that was to become the largest youth group in the country, proposed the value of living 'the simple life of primitive times'. Theodore Roosevelt, who was a sort of grown up Boy Scout all his life (Miller 1992), put the power of the presidency behind such views. Thus, the images of the American Indian on the postcards seem to reflect an increasing popular enthusiasm for the primitive.

What was the function of this romantic ideology? It has been argued that images of a beneficent state of nature worked to compensate for the human problems generated by an increasingly urbanized, industrial, capitalist society by offering the opportunity for social rejuvenation. Heiman (1989), for example, emphasizes contradictions in the American capitalist base in looking at conceptions of the Hudson River Valley in this way. The postcard images of the Indian free of the trappings and problems of civilization may be seen, then, as one 'rejuvenating' response to the increasingly oppressive commercial or industrial side of American life. One may pursue the analysis still further by thinking that this romantic ideology was variously interpreted by potential tourists, each having their own set of motivations (for example, ego enhancement or relaxation). Such motivations, according to Dann (1981, Chapter Seven), would constitute 'push' factors that, in this case, responded to the 'pull' of pacified Indian territory that, according to Albers and James (1988: 151–152), was given a 'picturesque, exotic, and enchanted character' in the touristic media productions of the Fred Harvey Company.

Thus, in this brief overview, possible connections have been suggested between base, a touristic superstructure of American society, and individual touristic inclinations. Further, one might suggest the influence of all this on the dependent host region, as Weigl (1989) has done for the American southwest, which she thinks has become a kind of giant Disneyworld that has been developed to meet the interests of various touristic agencies (and the desires of tourists (Cohen Chapter Two)).

All of this rather wide-ranging discussion is derived from the suggestion by Albers and James (1988) that postcard images of the American southwest were an ideology created by (or for) white, American society. That suggestion appears to fit nicely into the conception of tourism as superstructure which has been developed in this chapter. Cohen's (1993) comprehensive scheme for analysing images of host peoples, their social production and their use is a further step in this line of research. His discussion raises the question of whether, for example, the images on postcards sold to mostly white tourists would be different if produced by Indians themselves, thus introducing the fact of acculturated 'Indianness' into their production. Such a scheme would seem to be absolutely essential for analysing the complex conditions of postcard image production in the American southwest today.

Since the days when the Fred Harvey Company had a virtual monopoly, there has been a dramatic proliferation of companies producing pictorial representations of the region, including images of its Indian inhabitants. The variety of postcard images of Indians has also increased, but there is significant continuity with the past (often, simply a reproduction of earlier images). Albers (personal communication) agrees about the considerable variety of images, but chooses to stress the commonalities in ways in which Indians are depicted. She (Albers 1992: 9) says that 'the essence of the written and photographic language which accompanies the region's tourism has remained remarkably stable and highly romanticized'. These commonalities in linguistic and photographic discourse are viewed by her as responses to demands that the novel or exotic be presented in a synthetic, sanitized way that appeals to a broad tourist clientele.

The variety of postcard images, however, continues to intrigue, and one is hard put not to see it, like the commonalities, as a super-structural response to basal forces in contemporary consumer society. As Baudrillard (1970) notes, such a society draws its members into an awareness of marked (through various signs) social differences. Individuals and social groups mark themselves off from others by the signs they manipulate and consume. From this point of view the images of the American southwest on picture postcards continue to emphasize the romantic vision established earlier, but now they constitute a more differentiated medley that would appear to respond to an increasingly individu-ated and play-oriented market concentrated in what Bourdieu (1984) refers to as the new middle class. From the point of view taken here, they are superstructural manifestations of develop-ments in the social base, which in this case is an evolving consumer society.

CONCLUSION

This chapter has explored the utility of the notion of tourism as superstructure for the comparative and change-oriented study of tourism. Unlike much of the anthropological study of tourism, which has been concerned with destination areas and the consequences of tourism for host peoples, the focus here has been on the social production of tourism in the tourist-generating situation. Here, touristic activities have been conceived as ultimately responsive to more socially necessary activities, the most essential of which, as far as tourism is concerned, involve production and travel. The response of tourism to changes in the base elements, and the ways in which tourism itself can promote change in societies and cultures, were noted. The suggested research agenda would attend to, first, relevant aspects of production and travel which establish the minimal conditions or opportunities for tourism, and second, various other social conditions that are linked to more specific forms of tourism that vary over space and time. Clearly, as these fundamental elements undergo change, as has happened on a large scale in western societies in the last decade or so, leisure and tourism will also be subject to change, both in scale and nature.

To show the cross-cultural applicability of this agenda in today's increasingly international and changing world, two examples of relevant research have been summarized and critically evaluated. The comparatively simple examples chosen, the social organization of Japanese tourism and the picture postcard representations of American Indians, have been taken to be superstructural manifestations of more basal elements of tourist-producing societies. A broad, exploratory analysis of these cases has been carried down to the present day. It is hoped that other more methodologically sophisticated comparative studies, using the same general perspective, will follow, allowing us to understand more about the process of change in tourism and tourism-related phenomena.

REFERENCES

Albers, P. (1992) 'Postcards, travel and ethnicity: A comparative look at Mexico and the southwestern United States', Paper presented at the meetings of the American Anthropological Association, San Francisco, Ca.

Albers, P. and James, W. (1983) 'Tourism and the changing photographic image of the Great Lakes Indians', *Annals of Tourism Research* 10, 1: 123–148.

—— (1988) 'Travel photography: A methodological approach', *Annals of Tourism Research* 15, 1: 134–158.

Baudrillard, J. (1970) *La société de consommation*, Paris: Editions Denoel.

Bird-David, N. (1992) 'Beyond the original affluent society: A culturalist reformulation', *Current Anthropology* 13, 1: 25–48.

Boorstin, D. (1964) *The Image: A Guide to Pseudo-Events in America*, New York: Harper & Row.

Bourdieu, P. (1984) *Distinction*, London: Routledge & Kegan Paul.

Boyer, M. (1972) *Le Tourisme*, Paris: Editions du Seuil.

Brown, D. (1991) *Human Universals*, Philadelphia: Temple University Press.

Chick, G. (1986) 'Leisure, labor, and the complexity of culture: An anthropological perspective', *Journal of Leisure Research* 18, 3: 154–168.

Clawson, M. (1964) 'How much leisure now and in the future?', in J. Charlesworth (ed.) *Leisure in America: Blessing or Curse?*, Philadelphia: American Academy of Political Science, 1–20.

Cohen, E. (1979) 'A phenomenology of tourist experiences', *Sociology* 13: 179–202.

—— (1993) 'Mitigating the stereotype of a stereotype', in D. Pearce and R. Butler (eds) *Tourism Research: Critiques and Challenges*, London: Routledge, 36–69.

Cooper, W. (1989) 'Some philosophical aspects of leisure theory', in E. Jackson and T. Burton (eds) *Understanding Leisure and Recreation: Mapping the Past, Charting the Future*, State College, Pa.: Venture Publishing, 49–68.

Crick, M. (1989) 'Representations of international tourism in the social sciences: Sun, sex, sights', *Annual Review of Anthropology* 18: 307–344.

Crompton, J. (1992) 'Structure of vacation destination choice sets', *Annals of Tourism Research* 19, 3: 420–434.

Dann, G. (1981) 'Tourist motivation: An appraisal', *Annals of Tourism Research* 8, 2: 187–219.

Dumazedier, J. (1968) 'Leisure', *Encyclopedia of the Social Sciences* 9: 248–253.

Godelier, M. (1980) 'The emergence of Marxism in anthropology in France', in E. Gellner (ed.) *Soviet and Western Anthropology*, New York: Columbia University Press, 3–18.

Graburn, N. (1983a) 'The anthropology of tourism', *Annals of Tourism Research* 10, 1: 9–34.

—— (1983b) *To Pray, Pay and Play: The Cultural Structure of Japanese Domestic Tourism*, Aix-en-Provence: Centre des Hautes Études Touristiques.

—— (1989) 'Tourism: The sacred journey', in V. Smith (ed.) *Hosts and Guests: The Anthropology of Tourism*, Philadelphia: University of Pennsylvania Press, 21–36.

Gross, D. (1984) 'Time allocation: As tool for studying cultural behavior', *Annual Review of Anthropology* 13: 519–558.

Hamilton-Smith, E. (1987) 'Four kinds of tourism?', *Annals of Tourism Research* 14, 3: 332–344.

Hardy, D. (1990) 'Sociocultural dimensions of tourism history', *Annals of Tourism Research* 17, 4: 541–555.

Harris, M. (1992) 'Distinguished lecture: Anthropology and the theoretical and paradigmatic significance of the collapse of Soviet and East European Communism', *American Anthropologist* 94, 2: 295–305.

Heiman, M. (1989) 'Production confronts consumption: Landscape perception and social conflict in the Hudson River Valley', *Society and Space* 7: 165–178.

Iso-Ahola, S. (1982) 'Towards a social psychological theory of tourist motivation', *Annals of Tourism Research* 9, 3: 256–261.

—— (1983) 'Towards a social psychology of recreational travel', *Leisure Studies* 2: 45–56.

Japan National Tourist Organization (JNTO) (1992) *Tourism in Japan: 1992*, Tokyo: Ministry of Transport.

Johnson, A. (1978) 'In search of the affluent society', *Human Nature* 9, 1: 51–59.

Kando, T. and Summers, W. (1971) 'The impact of work on leisure: Towards a paradigm and research strategy', in T. Johannis Jr and C. N. Bull (eds) *Sociology of Leisure*, Beverly Hills, Ca./London: Sage, 75–92.

Kelly, J. (1983) *Leisure Identities and Interactions*, London: Allen & Unwin.

Lerner, D. (1958) *The Passing of Traditional Society*, New York: The Free Press.

Lukes, S. (1972) *Emile Durkheim: His Life and Work*, New York: Harper & Row.

MacCannell, D. (1976) *The Tourist: A New Theory of the Leisure Class*, New York: Schocken.

Mackie, V. (1988) 'Division of labor: Multinational sex in Asia', in G. McCormack and Y. Sugimoto (eds) *The Japanese Trajectory: Modernization and Beyond*, Cambridge: Cambridge University Press, 218–232.

Miller, N. (1992) *Theodore Roosevelt: A Life*, New York: Morrow.

Moeran, B. (1983) 'The language of Japanese tourism', *Annals of Tourism Research* 10, 1: 93–108.

Murdock, G., Ford, C., Hudson, A., Kennedy, R., Simmons, L. and Whiting, J. (1982) *Outline of Cultural Materials* (5th rev. edn), New Haven: Human Relations Area Files.

Nash, D. (1979) *Tourism in Pre-Industrial Societies*, Aix-en-Provence: Centre des Hautes Études Touristiques.

—— (1981) 'Tourism as an anthropological subject', *Current Anthropology* 22, 5: 461–481.

Nash, R. (1967) *Wilderness and the American Mind*, New Haven: Yale University Press.

Neulinger, R. (1974) *The Psychology of Leisure*, Springfield, Ill.: Thomas.

—— (1981) *To Leisure: An Introduction*. Boston: Allyn & Bacon.

Nozumo, K. (1988) 'The concept of modernization re-examined from the Japanese experience', in G. McCormack and Y. Sugimoto (eds) *The*

Japanese Trajectory: Modernization and Beyond, Cambridge: Cambridge University Press, 264–283.

Pearce, D.G. (1993) 'Comparative studies in tourism research', in D. Pearce and R. Butler (eds) *Tourism Research: Critiques and Challenges*, London and New York: Routledge, 20–35.

Pearce, P. (1993) 'Fundamentals of tourist motivation', in D. Pearce and R. Butler (eds) *Tourism Research: Critiques and Challenges*, London and New York: Routledge, 113–134.

Sahlins, M. (1972) *Stone Age Economics*, Chicago: Aldine.

Sayers, S. (1989) 'Work, leisure, and human needs', in T. Winnifrith and C. Barrett (eds) *The Philosophy of Leisure*, New York: St Martin's Press, 34–53.

Seton, E. (1910) *Boy Scouts of America: A Handbook of Woodcraft, Scouting, and Lifecraft*, New York: Boy Scouts of America.

Suomi, S. (1982) 'Why does play matter?', *The Behavioral and Brain Sciences* 5: 169–170.

Weigl, M. (1989) 'From desert to Disneyworld: the Santa Fe Railway and the Fred Harvey Company display the Indian southwest', *Journal of Anthropological Research* 45: 115–137.

Chapter 4

The past in the present in Japan
Nostalgia and neo-traditionalism in contemporary Japanese domestic tourism

Nelson H.H. Graburn

One remarkable feature of dynamic capitalist societies is their constant production of new attractions (MacCannell 1976, 1992; Cohen Chapter Two). Nostalgia is one of the most important tropes imbuing such attractions with power (Davis 1979; Lowenthal 1985; Dann 1992). This is manifested in the paradox that the majority of 'new' tourist attractions are old, exemplified by the growth of 'heritage tourism' all over the world (Urry 1991; Dann 1993). The transformative power of the passage of time is strongly evoked in Marshall McLuhan's phrase 'All obsolete technology becomes art', an idea that has great relevance to the study of historically or cross-culturally based tourism.

This chapter examines some psychological and socio-cultural ideas accounting for the generation and power of nostalgia, and in the context of one geographical area analyses the cultural construction of attractions imbued with such power. In doing so, it may be better understood how some contemporary phenomena are in the process of being converted into nostalgic tourist attractions (Eadington Chapter Nine).

The present analysis here focuses on the modern, or some would say post-modern, nation of Japan (Miyoshi and Harootunian 1989). Though Japan may symbolize the exotic as a tourist attraction for westerners – either the exotic past, the exotic Other, or even the exotic future – an attempt is made here to understand developments in Japanese domestic tourism from the point of view of their needs.

Westerners imagine that Japanese overseas tourists are common in the West but, though increasing in numbers every year, in fact they only numbered twelve million in 1993, a much smaller proportion than for most other industrialized nations (Morris 1990; Graburn 1993). It is just that to westerners' eyes they are so much more 'visible' as wealthy people of colour, and they may be travelling in groups. In reality, 90 per cent of Japanese tourism is domestic tourism.

Japanese overseas mass tourism only started in 1964, but their domestic mass tourism has a much longer history than any other country (Ishimori 1989), and involves over three hundred million overnight trips a year. In relation to the social context which generates it, Japanese tourism has certain characteristics which differentiate it from the tourism of the contemporary West (Graburn 1983a). These range from physical and logistical factors to cultural attitudes:

1 The Japanese national landscape, though penetrable (by tunnels or winding roads), consists of steep and often volcanic mountains in over three-quarters of its area. The many narrow valleys, and the few densely populated fertile plains, contain both agricultural and urban areas.

2 Contemporary Japan has superb but expensive urban and interurban public transportation systems. However, outside of the urban areas the roads are relatively inadequate.

3 Japan now has very crowded living conditions in the overwhelming urban settings to which a large proportion of the population has migrated since World War II.

4 Most Japanese have very short vacation periods, fairly evenly scattered through the year, many of which workers do not take. In addition the timing of adult and children's vacations often do not coincide.

5 Nearly all Japanese children have undergone a kind of 'training system' for peer group outings (*entotsu*) and tourism which starts as early as kindergarten (*yochien*).

6 Compared to most Europeans and North Americans, the Japanese have a low sense of cultural self-confidence (Graburn 1983b; Ohnuki-Tierney 1990), and they usually only travel in groups or at least visit well-known 'culturally approved' attractions.

A DECADE OF CHANGE

One can summarize the major changes in the social context of Japanese domestic tourism since the time of earlier research in the mid- and late 1970s, published as *To Pray, Pay, and Play* (Graburn

1983a). These factors might be grouped, in order, as socio-economic and ideological:

1 There has been a rapid increase in the affluence and ageing of the population (Morris 1990). There has also been some increase in leisure time available to residents in urban and suburban areas – spurred by the government's effort to reduce the work week (to five and a half days) and to increase the length of vacation time *actually taken* (still only ten days a year).

2 There has been a great increase in personal car ownership (Japan has now surpassed Great Britain on a per capita basis). It now exceeds one car per family in some prefectures (*Japan Statistical Yearbook* 1992: 50, 305).

3 At the same time, the government has instigated an extensive national road-building effort, both for expensive inter-city toll roads (and bridges) and into previously isolated hinterland areas. The central government has also developed plans for recreational zones in these non-metropolitan areas.

4 These plans are linked and cater to the growing urban-based nostalgia for *furusato* 'old home/village' culture and disappearing

Plate 1   The image of an ideal mountain *furusato* village, Yunomine in Wakayama prefecture. This is an *onsen*, 'hot spring' resort, the building on the left is a *ryokan*, a hot spring inn.

'traditional' Japan (Takeshita 1987; Robertson 1991). This feeling has been aided by and is reflected in a national and regional – economic and ideological – *mura okoshi* 'village revitalization' movement that meshes with interests in ecology.

5 There has been a parallel rise in interest in things rural as representing 'tradition', such as traditional (natural) food and drink. These cultural trends have coincided with the development of rural tourism activities, for example, visits to the numerous *onsen* resorts, historical and archaeological sites and areas, museums and 'folk' theme parks, rural recreation, skiing and golf. A 1989 survey found that 'Tourism travel within Japan (summer, winter, hot springs, etc.)' was the second highest ranked leisure activity of the Japanese (Morris 1990: 13).

One might summarize this as an ideological shift from an idea of rich city–poor village to poor city–rich village. Consequently, the small towns and villages which have suffered from urban out-migration now compete to attract back the affluent and alienated urban population. To do this, they have been involved wholeheartedly in the 'invention of tradition' (Hobsbawm and Ranger 1983), with symbolic manipulation of their histories and geographies in intimate collusion with the media (Cohen Chapter Two).

TRADITIONAL TOURISM AND TRADITION

The nature of these emerging attractions and destinations is considered here in relation to traditional tourism and the nature of 'tradition' itself, to nature and to innovations based consciously on western models. However, rarely does any tourist institution or excursion encompass only one type of societally valued attraction (Graburn 1983c).

Traditional Japanese domestic tourism *kanko* (which literally means sightseeing) encompasses famous historical creations including shrines, temples, castles, gardens and festivals (*matsuri*). Their present appeal lies in their 'traditional' aesthetics and their atmosphere of *bonhomie* in an ever faster changing urban world of high pressure jobs (including child-rearing), tiny, barren apartments, huge high-rise buildings, homeless and drunken bums, crowded trains and fast foods. Most historical sites are in cities or

Plate 2 Traditional domestic tourism: visitors take their shoes off to enter the Phoenix Hall of the Byodoin Temple at Uji, near Kyoto.

in famous outlying towns with good mass transportation. Others, often those founded long ago by exceptional monks, priests or exiled nobility, are found in remote areas which require consider-able time and effort – in the form of organized pilgrimages – to visit. The most famous, such as Ise or Izumi shrines, have attracted millions of visitors a year for hundreds of years, either on foot or, after the Meiji era of railroad building, by train.

Yet the recent abundance of cars and the national highway construction programme have opened up greater access to some of the less famous sights where visitor numbers may have more than doubled in the past decade. There is a symbiosis between these venerable institutions and the newer more secular attractions which form the focus of this chapter, by which tourists may con-tinue to 'pray, pay and play', even in the relatively remote areas. For instance in mountainous central Wakayama prefecture near Osaka, the famous Kumano Hongu-taisha (great Shinto shrine) shares its visitors with more recently popularized attractions such as the nearby hot spring villages, as well as boat-trips, hiking and swimming.

Plate 3 Brochure combining religious and secular attractions: Hongu Kumano grand shrine on the left; Kawayu *onsen* – a whole river heated by volcanic hot water – in the centre; Wataze *onsen* with

HOT SPRING RESORTS

The past twenty years have seen an *onsen buumu* (hot spring boom), a rush to often rural or small town hot spring resorts, most of which used to be the province of local rural people or a few upper-class visitors (Hotta and Ishiguro 1986). Some of these, such as Beppu, Shirahama or Arima, had already become very large-scale, commercialized, urban vacation spots during the 'railway' era. Thousands of others in remoter rural areas have 'cleaned up their act' and become popular tourist destinations, very often with the help of national and prefectural *mura okoshi* – development grants. Prime Minister Takeshita created a 'Furusato Foundation' to give 100,000,000 yen (approximately £700,000) to each village. *Onsen* development has been complementary to related attractions such as natural and historical sites, skiing, golf, fishing, etc.

The epitome of these attractions are rural *onsen ryokan* which preserve a 'traditional' atmosphere of dress, decor, architecture, food and style of service, while at the same time upgrading their physical structures to provide every comfort for the now thoroughly modern urban clientele. This involves providing clean – and heated and cooled – 'modern traditional' rooms, that is with *tatami* (woven straw) floors, rooms with telephones and television, and *wafu* (Japanese clothing), such as *yukata* (dressing gown) and *zori* (slippers) or *geta* (wooden clogs).

Key attractions of the 'authentic' *onsen* are the baths and the meals. The baths are filled with constantly flowing naturally heated volcanic spring waters in which one soaks after a thorough washing or shower in facilities provided at the sides of the room. These natural waters are often said to have curative or at least recuperative powers (Yanagita 1982 (1940)), and *onsen* resorts and traveller's guides usually recommend specific diseases or conditions to be cured or even present detailed chemical analyses of the waters. Such is the joy that Japanese feel in anticipation and partaking of these *onsen* baths that some call Japan an '*onsen* civilization'.

The baths themselves may be enamel, tile or wood but are most chic when constructed from local rock so as to resemble a natural pool. Similarly the bathrooms may be functional tile with showers and faucets, but ideally are constructed of rocks with plants and flowing streams or rivulets of spring water.

Plate 4   Men's room with bath *ofuro* in the Yunosato *ryokan*, Totsukawa *onsen* in southern Nara prefecture.

These facilities are usually separated into men's and women's bath areas or rooms, and until recently the men's was always the larger and better appointed. However, with the increasing afflu- ence of women, especially young unmarried 'OLs' (office ladies), many inns regularly switch the gender signs so that the women have a daily allotted time in the 'better' bath area.

The highlight of the most attractive *onsens* is the *rotenburo*, the outside bath/pool 'in nature' with superb natural or constructed views. These well-advertised attractions are often gender neutral and may be occupied by single-sex peer groups as well as by families in the daytime, and by couples – unmarried and otherwise – in the evening.

Ryokan food, partaken at the early evening meal and at break- fast, is almost mandatorily served in one's room. The cuisine should be *kaiseki*, that is a tastefully presented, large array of small traditional dishes, using the freshest and most attractive of seasonal ingredients. This cuisine stemmed originally from the elegant small accompaniments to the Zen-inspired tea ceremony; the historic and refined ambience of this food is supposed to

Plate 5 Men's outside bath, *rotenburo*, in the Yunosato *ryokan*, Totsukawa *onsen* in southern Nara prefecture. Compare with brochure photograph in *Plate 9*, which shows no division between men's and women's bath areas.

connote upper or noble class fare. (Compare the menus of *ryokan* meals served to the Imperial Family (Statler 1961) which do not differ too much from average meals in good *ryokans* today.)

Thus in a promotional brochure the appeal is echoed in the invitation 'to eat' by the use of the elegant and slightly old-fashioned term *shokusu* as opposed to the more ordinary term *taberu*. *Kaiseki* cuisine is also available in expensive city restaurants. It shares with restaurants in touristic rural areas an emphasis on fresh, locally available foods such as *sansai* (mountain vegetables), for example, locally gathered fiddleheads and other wild plants.

Thus, both the *ryokan* (the traditional inn without hot spring baths) and the *onsen* (with hot spring baths) appeal to populations mourning an ever-decreasing experience of 'Japaneseness' as valued in both nature and culture. Their spacious and leisurely facilities are particularly attractive to harried white-collar workers who live in cramped conditions in city apartments (Kelly 1986). They serve an additional function for affluent grandparents who take their thoroughly modern grandchildren (and the intermediate generation) to these nostalgic repositories of 'pure' Japaneseness –

Plate 6   Brochure advertising the high-class food at an *onsen ryokan* in Kameoka.

an experience they fear that their adult children will not or may not be able to provide for the grandchildren.

It should also be pointed out that space and tradition are expensive. The multicourse cuisine and the personal service, as well as the size of the baths, are far beyond what ordinary people could enjoy at home. A typical good rural *onsen ryokan* might cost more than *ichimanen* (Y10,000 or about $US100) per person, though this is not nearly as expensive as the fancier *onsen* hotels in the famous urban hot spring resorts which might be double or triple the price. Both kinds of facilities are in turn much cheaper than similar accommodation in urban areas. In addition, the cost of transportation to and from the resort might be very expensive by foreigners' standards, especially for a large family group. Thus in terms of both living style and discretionary expenditure a trip to an *onsen ryokan* might be called 'Samurai for a Day' (see Gottlieb 1982). Indeed there are now vacation inns outside of Tokyo where one can go and 'play Samurai'.

Young unmarried adults maintain the group-activity orientation of Japanese recreation (Nash Chapter Three) during the two- or three-day vacation periods common to most adult Japanese. In the countryside, they may choose skiing or other more strenuous activities during their short vacations. This gives them a chance to experience 'nature', though wrapped in high-tech ski equipment on crowded slopes. It can often be combined with a sojourn at *onsen* resorts – a natural hot spring bath and good food and drink after a day on the slopes – or in clean and semi-traditional *ryokan*, or at their lower price homologues *minshuku*. The latter are family-run bed and breakfast accommodations, often based on farm houses but expanded to accommodate 20–60 young people (Moon 1989). Their emphasis is more on conviviality, for example, eating in a dining room rather than one's own room, and less on tradition when it comes to food and clothing.

Increasingly, some young people stay with their peer groups at a new type of accommodation, *pensions*, which have beds and cafés and have been superficially built on 'Alpine' rather than domestic traditions. Of course, where tourism has become truly mass, large-scale, urban-based chain hotels move in and provide a high standard of both modern and traditional accommodation for the more affluent and less adventurous traveller.

RECREATING THE COUNTRYSIDE

Since World War II Japan has recreated itself out of almost all recognition. The burgeoning, affluent but ugly and polluted cities are surrounded by vast belts of crowded suburbs. Here the uprooted newcomers are encouraged to recreate 'community' through a *matsuri buumu* of government-directed secular rituals (Robertson 1991: 33). Conversely, the Japanese countryside has suffered a disastrous *kasogensho*, rural outmigration. It is the policy of the national and regional governments as well as business to hold the line on population loss by replacing the declining industries – forestry, farming and fishing – with rural tourism. The task of attracting tourists to new rural attractions is very competitive. Given the previously mentioned proclivity of the Japanese not to explore, that is, only to visit generally approved places, every

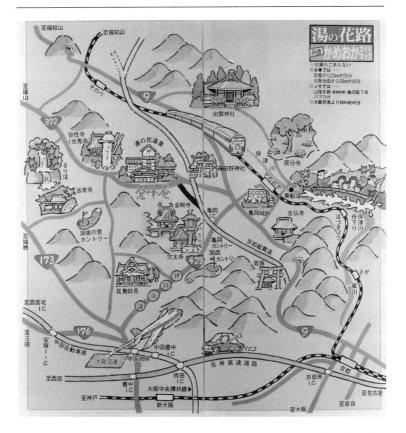

Plate 7   Brochure map of *onsen* and other natural and cultural tourist attractions in the Kameoka area.

destination has to 'invent its own approval' by getting itself literally and figuratively 'on the map'. Plate 7 shows a typical map filled with icons of the cooperating, and competing, tourist institutions of the Kameoka area near Kyoto and Osaka.

Each destination must have one or more socially approved *meibutsu* (famous thing) for it to be worth visiting. These *meibutsu* may be either local produce, for example the fruit grown in the piedmont area around Nagano City, local products, such as folk pottery (*mingei*) in Mashiko, or natural and cultural fixtures of the landscape, such as Sakurajima volcano in Kagoshima or the above-mentioned Great Shrine at Kumano Hongu.

These *meibutsu* become the icons which are represented on

Plate 8   Omiyage gift stand on the 'Apple Line', in Nagano prefecture, famous for its *meibustu* of apples and grapes.

maps, signs and brochures. They are also the basis of the enormous *omiyage* (gift) trade which is perhaps the most profitable component of the domestic tourist system (Graburn 1987). The things that are sold may be the actual *meibutsu* themselves (for example, fruit, vegetables, shells, rocks and wood, or metonyms of the famous attraction, such as volcanic sulphur standing for the nearby volcano of Mt Aso), or commercial representations of *meibutsu* that cannot themselves be sold (for example, buildings, trees, land and seascapes), in forms such as photographs, cartoons, models and postcards. The very crowds that gather at these places are another sign to the visitors that they must be at the right place.

Thus, off-site markers and signs (MacCannell 1976) are the key arena of competition, and the symbols (and icons) of *meibutsu* are the weapons. Off-site markers include above all placement on icon-filled tourist maps, a feature known in Japan for at least 350 years (Shiraishi 1987). Close behind are advertisements and brochures (Moeran 1983), available at travel agents or passed on by friends.

Third, and growing in importance, are television programmes (and like them newspaper and magazine articles) which are regularly packed with 'info-tainment' showing desirable attractions and convenient short tourist circuits. Television is most important, both for creating familiarity – and hence 'approval' – and it is, of course,

Plate 9   Brochure showing young women in the outside bath *rotenburo* in the Yunosato *ryokan*, Totsukawa *onsen* in southern Nara prefecture. Compare with Plate 5, which shows the bamboo 'divider'. Note also the functionless waterwheel.

tied in with selling the packaged place and the products for which it is famous. Typical are regional evening TV programmes which show young people (mostly attractive young women) touring rural regions, stopping nightly at clean and cute *ryokan* and *onsen* where they self-consciously bathe with tiny towels – or without them – in baths which appear to be frequented by both genders. These enticing images may be false representations, as in reality the baths may be gender-segregated; baths photographed at the opening (or after the refurbishing) of an establishment may later be divided by bamboo walls or other opaque structures.

On-site markers include photographs and ubiquitous brochures, as well as signs, façades and the architecture of the inns themselves (Ehrentraut 1993). Though the sought-after clientele ranges from old to young, families and singles, and men and women, all are subject to a broad range of appeal based on their shared urban, modern, affluent life-styles. The key emphasis is on 'tradition' which includes 'history' carefully cleaned up and 'nature' in select and tasteful doses. One text reads in part: 'Getting away from noisy busy life . . . surrounded by the quietness (*seijaku*) of the heartwarming mistiness of the mountains'.

An analysis of the markers for these rural institutions at first suggests the elimination of modern/western phenomena – a kind of ideological ethnic cleansing – and conversely the nostalgic highlighting of condensed symbols of 'Japaneseness' (see Moeran 1983). All written communications 'announce' the traditional nature of the experience: cosy-sounding rural names like 'The Summerhouse', 'The Old Village' or 'The Back of the Island', using phrases such as 'heart-warming and reliable service'. These are written with old-fashioned brush strokes and sketches, and use appealing words such as *natsukashii* (nostalgic), *furusato* (old home/village).

Both in the physical settings themselves and in their representations the visual and material emphasis is on history and 'obsolete technology' which, as Marshall McLuhan has suggested, invariably becomes aestheticized. Not only are traditional buildings shown – shrines, temples, public baths, farm houses – but reincorporated structures such as waterwheels, thatched roofs and wooden farm implements are displayed as non-utilitarian features of the environment. These are all anchored by signs pointing to historical (as well as mythological and archaeological) locales and events, often resurrected in local festivals, sets of stone markers and museums. By careful interweaving of historical tales and markers tourists are encouraged to feel that they are participating in traditional practices, such as pilgrimages, ablutions and worship.

One brochure shows the recently renovated mountain trail formerly used by retired emperors of the medieval period; about ten kilometres have been restored, signposted and cleaned up to encourage young people to 'trek' through the forested mountains to the pilgrimage (and tourist) sites of Hongu Grand Shrine and the associated Yunomine *onsen* village resort. The wording invites the visitor along the 'Path of History . . . to visit the Kumano Old

Plate 10 Yamaguchi *onsen* on the slopes of Mount Aso volcano in Kyushu. This *ryokan* shows a typical re-creation of rural nostalgia; note the thatched roof bathhouse in the lower centre.

Road . . . in Kiishu'. The latter word is the medieval name for the peninsula now known as Wakayama prefecture, rather like referring to part of England as Wessex.

Though Japan has long paid obeisance to *shizen* (nature), and natural things (food ingredients, flowers and plants, scenic vistas) have been highly valued, especially in refined culture, in reality Japanese life in the main shuns nature by Western standards. Not only are the farmers (24 per cent of the population) still 'fighting' nature with high-technology machinery and agricultural chemicals, but nature to most Japanese is boring to contemplate, dangerous to enter, and far removed from everyday life. It is only appreciated when it is strictly controlled (for example, only near sacred shrines are large trees allowed to grow to full size), and when it is 'naturally' represented and miniaturized (e.g. in *bonsai* and gardens), and socially approved for perusal (and photography) at the right seasons (Berque 1986).

Though there are national parks following the western model (Senge 1974) and famous natural sites have long been made sacred by religious shrines and markers, communing with nature, as in hiking, climbing, canoeing or bicycling, is almost invariably a *group*

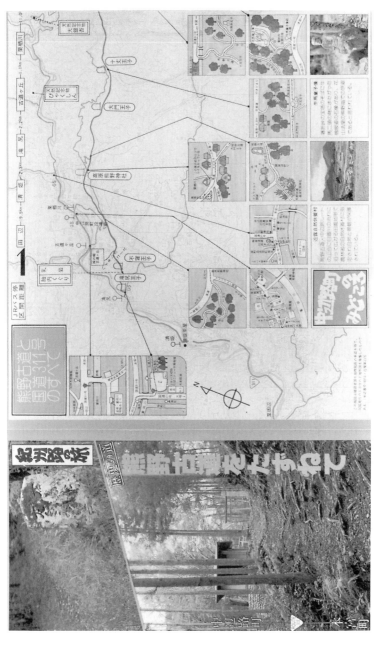

Plate 11 Brochure showing the reconstructed Old Kumano Road to Yunomine and Kumano Hongu in the mountains of Wakayama.

activity. Here, enjoyment stems more from sociality than from 'getting away from it all'. Rarely does anyone go anywhere alone, and loneliness, especially 'in nature', is to be feared above almost anything else in life. This in turn is expressed in the historical theme of admiration for hermits and ascetics, usually Buddhist, who avoid society and commune with nature.

Managed nature is represented not only for its own sake but because it, too, represents tradition. Sacred obeisance and awe of scenery such as volcanoes, mountains, rivers, caves, islands, rocks, trees and, especially, waterfalls, are timeless, shared features of Japanese culture – and most are imbued with *kami* (gods, spirits) whose presence is marked and elaborated by signs and buildings. It is in this form that nature is presented in touristic images and incorporated into the environment of touristic institutions. The seasonally appropriate viewing of nature – cherry blossom, wild azalea, autumn maples – is appropriately incorporated. Wild animals, always stuffed, reinforce the presentation of 'nature as it used to be'. For instance, *kitsune* (the fox), traditionally a powerful animistic messenger symbol, is culturalized in a pose of Buddhist blessing, while on the left in Plate 12 the *tanuki* (Japanese racoon dog), a powerful symbol of prosperity, is anthropomorphized as a golfer.

All this tradition must be carefully framed to avoid the common fear of the remote (*hikyo*), the rural uncouth (*inaka*) and the dirty (*kitanai*). Thus, signs of sociality, cleanliness and accessibility counteract these anxieties. One key multi-vocalic symbol is nubile young women, surrounded by clean and comfortable traditional settings, an ensemble which may be called *kawaii*, that is, 'cute'. On the surface this appeals directly to the increasing and affluent 'OL' clientele. Of course, it also appeals to the essential ingredients of sociality (fun, sex) for both younger and older men. For instance, a brochure advertising a large number of *onsen* resorts uses an old *waka* (historic nature poem) to suggest 'love nature, touch heart . . . with the one you like. . . . You might be able to find something . . . something might be born.' At a second level these symbolic presentations signal that these destinations are modern and clean enough to attract the most 'delicate' sector of the urban population.

Speculation may be made on a deeper symbolic level about the seeming paradox of the appearance of these fresh young women in places dedicated to nostalgic tradition and nature (Tanaka 1990). Perhaps these young women are supposed to represent *both* tradi-

Plate 12   Stuffed wild animals – a fox and a *tanuki* (racoon dog) – in cultural poses, in the coffee shop of the Rurikei Rural Recreational Area of Hyogo prefecture.

tion and nature: women are considered more 'natural' *vis-à-vis* the men who control the 'outside world' of work, technology, government, etc. For instance, *kirei*, which means both clean and pretty, is only applied to women, children and nature. At the same time, women are thought to be the 'bearers of tradition', the common defence in the home against these modern forces of the outside world. Thus, in the manipulative and sexist dominant gender ideology of commercial and political institutions of Japan, women – like nature – are aestheticized, preserved, displayed and seemingly granted the important role of providing continuity to the past. In addition, youth itself – *seinen*, literally the green years – is considered more natural than the constricted later years of adulthood. Representations of youth appeal nostalgically to middle-aged couples who may wish to visit these resorts to revive their youth and romance. As the brochures say: 'You can have energy from nature which, through the hot water, penetrates to your heart ... the warmth, the softness of nature.'

Though it is almost tautologically true that tourist motivations stem from the desire to experience a change (Smith 1989: 1), and that what the tourist desires is a direct reflection of the lacks or alienation in everyday life (Graburn 1983b, 1989), one must be careful of overgeneralization. For instance, one common explanation for the present nostalgia/heritage boom is that it is a reaction to a general 'crisis of confidence' in our war/ethnic strife/overpopulation/AIDS/nuclear age. But this is a weak and partial explanation, for Japanese history is no stranger to the longings of nostalgia; one might aver that for its production one only needs a sense of history and a feeling of anxiety. Indeed, the young but redoubtable Prince Genji waxed nostalgic in the late tenth century about the days of yore when the world and mankind were better (Murasaki 1970). Again during the isolationist Tokugawa period, Japan was said to have been nativistic and nostalgic in its attempt to indigenize foreign philosophies just as *nihonjinron* does today (Nosco 1990). Yet, as Koschmann points out (1991: 390): 'How does this "nostalgia" retain an essential identity throughout the centuries?'

CONCLUSION

This chapter has shown how rural tourism as epitomized through the images and reality, *onsen ryokan*, projects an ideal of continued tradition which caters, by inversion, to the needs of the urban middle classes. The on-site and off-site markers also demonstrate the construction of Japanese tradition by using multiple channels of communication employing all the senses. They include the visual: graphic, photographic and calligraphic, as well as architectural, decorative and sartorial; the aural, with reference to etiquette, and the sounds and silence of the rural milieu; taste is emphasized in the cuisine; the tactile is explicit in references to the water and the wind and suggestive in reference to human relations; and the olfactory with many references to the *kaori*, the fragrance or smell/taste of nature, as well as the nostalgic odour of the spring waters.

This analysis has emphasized the importance of the role of aestheticization; the careful manipulation of the essential channels to produce an image, more correctly, an atmosphere, which appeals to the needs of the urban-based tourist (as Nash Chapter Three has noted in other areas). As Bloch has shown for religious ritual

(1974), aestheticized phatic statements are far less challengeable than discursive truth claims. The use of aesthetics in the service of commerce is nothing new, but perhaps it has been stronger in Japan than in many other industrialized nations. In the case of *onsen ryokan*, there is a careful selection and highly aestheticized presentation of the nostalgic symbols to appeal to and to construct tradition using all the powers of modern media and technology (Cohen Chapter Two).

This preliminary research emphasizes merely one aspect of contemporary Japanese tourism, the other two being Japanese urban domestic tourism (Graburn 1983a), including all the new attractions such as Tokyo Disneyland (Cohen Chapter Two), and of course the ever-expanding Japanese overseas tourism (Morris 1990; Beer 1993). This research has not probed deeply the economic and cultural divisions which impel the Japanese to participate in these different forms of tourism. Thus it gives a perhaps unwarranted impression of a homogeneity of attractions and clientele, contributing to Japan's most important internal cultural debate, that of *Nihonjinron*, the theory of Japaneseness. Yet it can be seen from the case studies in this chapter that the widespread construction of and enthusiastic participation in these neo-traditional resorts are very much part of Japan's modern struggle to express and define its uniqueness which many feel is threatened on every side.

While Japan's expressive struggle resembles the 'heritage booms' of many Western countries, antidotes to a growing global homogeneity, the identity search is a tradition as old as Japan itself (Ohnuki-Tierney 1990). This backward looking search, like the pervasive nostalgia which is its twin, is found as far back as Japan's millennia-old origin myths. Japan, as a peripheral island nation, has had constantly to redefine its identity *vis-à-vis* China, Korea and the outside world, or to cut itself off from outside influence as it did during the 300 years of the Tokugawa shogunate. The rural *onsen ryokan* are like little islands of time, trying to temporarily recreate a peaceful and isolated world of yore, enabling the clients to forget the outside conflicts.

On a comparative level, the direction which Japan appears to be taking does parallel some of the trends of the Western world. For many social scientists, the main question is whether the trends in Japan – in tourism as much as in industry, education or family relations – represent a grand convergence of civilizations. For a while, it appeared that Japan was still 'catching up', and in the leisure arena the evolution from package tours to charter flights and individual travel arrangements lags behind the West. However, in creative neo-traditionalism they perhaps lead the world, and their customs of deep *ofuro* baths, *onsen* resorts, *tatami* sleeping arrangements and very fresh and seasonal local foods are being emulated by many in the West. Some Japanese, too, seem to be aware of their growing cultural 'leadership': their image of the United States now is of its heyday in the 1950s, as exemplified by a large billboard seen near Tokyo in 1991 advertising: 'Come to the California Café: See How It Used To Be!'

ACKNOWLEDGEMENTS

I express my deep gratitude to Dr John P. Knight (London School of Economics) and Dr John Nelson (Puget Sound University, Tacoma) for their introduction to – and many discussions of – the natural and cultural attractions of the Oku Kumano area of the hinterlands of Wakayama prefecture. My thanks are also extended to Jenny Beer, Dr Molly Lee, Dr Alice Horner and Dr Eiko Tai (University of California, Berkeley), Prof. Manar Hammad (Groupe de Recherches Semio-linguistiques, Paris), Prof. Jennifer Robertson (University of Michigan), Prof. Tomoko Hamada (College of William and Mary), to my family and to Barbara and Tak Tanizaki for many fruitful discussions about the content of this chapter. I am particularly grateful to Prof. Graham Dann for allowing me to see two of his manuscript papers on tourism and nostalgia. I also wish to acknowledge the extraordinary support extended to me during my visits to Japan in 1978–9, 1989–90, 1991 and 1993 by the National Museum of Ethnology, Osaka, particularly by Dr Tadao Umesao, director, and Prof. Shuzo Ishimori.

REFERENCES

Beer, Jennifer E. (1993) Packaging experiences: Japanese tourism in Southeast Asia, Berkeley: unpublished doctoral dissertation in anthropology.

Berque, Augustin (1986) *Le Sauvage et l'Artifice: Les Japonais devant la nature*, Paris: Gallimard.

Bloch, Maurice (1974) 'Symbols, song, dance and features of articulation: Or, is religion the highest form of traditional authority?', *European Journal of Sociology* 15: 55–81.

Dann, Graham (1992) 'Tourism and nostalgia: Looking forward to going back', Paper presented to the Working Group on Tourism of the International Sociological Association, on 'Le Tourisme International entre Tradition et Modernité', Nice.

—— (1993) 'Tourism: The nostalgia industry of the future', in W. Theobald (ed.) *Tourism in the 21st Century: Global Issues, Trends and Opportunities*, London: Butterworth-Heinemann, 179–198.

Davis, F. (1979) *Yearning for Yesterday: A Sociology of Nostalgia*, New York: Free Press.

Ehrentraut, A. (1993) 'Heritage authenticity and domestic tourism in Japan', *Annals of Tourism Research* 20, 2: 262–278.

Gottlieb, A. (1982) 'Americans' vacations', *Annals of Tourism Research* 9, 1: 165–188.

Graburn, N.H.H. (1983a) *To Pray, Pay and Play: The Cultural Structure of Japanese Domestic Tourism*, Aix-en-Provence: Centre des Hautes Études Touristiques.

—— (1983b) 'The anthropology of tourism', Special Issue of *Annals of Tourism Research* 10, 1: 9–34.

—— (1983c) 'Americans' vacations: Further comments on class and lifestyle', *Annals of Tourism Research* 10, 2: 270–273.

—— (1987) 'Material symbols in Japanese domestic tourism', in D. Ingersoll and G. Bronitsky (eds) *Mirror and Metaphor: Material and Social Constructions of Reality*, Lanham, Md: University Press of America, 15–27.

—— (1989) 'Tourism: The sacred journey', in Valene Smith (ed.) *Hosts and Guests: The Anthropology of Tourism*, Philadelphia: University of Pennsylvania Press, 21–37.

—— (1993) 'Review of Steven Morris 1990', *Annals of Tourism Research* 20, 2: 393–396.

Hobsbawm, Eric and Ranger, Terence (eds) (1983) *The Invention of Tradition*, Cambridge: Cambridge University Press.

Hotta, Anne and Ishiguro, Yoko (1986) *A Guide to Japanese Hot Springs*, Tokyo: Kodansha International.

Ishimori, Shuzo (1989) 'Popularization and commercialization of tourism in early modern Japan', in Tadao Umesao *et al.* (eds) *Japanese Civilization in the Modern World IV: Economic Institutions*, Senri Ethnological Series no. 26, 161–178.

Japan Statistical Yearbook (1992) Tokyo: Statistics Bureau, Management and Coordination Agency.

Kelly, William W. (1986) 'Rationalization and nostalgia: Cultural dynamics of new middle-class Japan', *American Anthropologist* 13: 603–618.

Koschmann, J. V. (1991) 'Review of Nosco 1990', *Journal of Japanese Studies* 17, 2: 386–390.

Lowenthal, David (1985) *The Past is a Foreign Country*, Cambridge: Cambridge University Press.

MacCannell, Dean (1976) *The Tourist: A New Theory of the Leisure Class*, New York: Schocken.

—— (1992) *Empty Meetings Grounds: The Tourist Papers*, London: Routledge.

Miyoshi, Masao and Harootunian, H.D. (eds) (1989) *Postmodernism and Japan*, Durham, NC: Duke University Press.

Moeran, Brian (1983) 'The language of Japanese tourism', *Annals of Tourism Research* 10, 1: 93–108.

Moon, Okpyo (1989) *From Paddy Field to Ski Slope: The Revitalization of Tradition in Japanese Village Life*, Manchester: Manchester University Press.

Morris, Stephen (1990) *The Japanese Overseas Travel Market in the 1990s*, London: *The Economist* Intelligence Unit, Special Report no. 2073.

Murasaki, Skikibu (1970) *The Tale of Genji* (trans. Edward Seidensticker), New York: Knopf.

Nosco, Peter (1990) *Remembering Paradise: Nativism and Nostalgia in Eighteenth Century Japan*, Cambridge, Mass.: Harvard University Press, Council for Asian Studies.

Ohnuki-Tierney, Emiko (1990) 'The ambivalent self of the contemporary Japanese', *Cultural Anthropology* 5: 197–216.

Robertson, Jennifer (1991) *Native and Newcomer: Making and Remaking a Japanese City*, Berkeley: University of California Press.

Senge, Tatsumaru (1974) 'Park facilities for the future', in Sir Hugh Elliot (ed.) *Second World Conference on National Parks*, Morges, Switzerland: International Union for the Conservation of Nature, 125–137.

Shiraishi, Toru (ed.) (1987) *Genroku Kyoto Rakuchu Rakugai oezu; Keio Gijuku Daigaku Toshokan* (Maps of Genroku éperiodè Kyoto inside and outside; held in the library of Keio Gijuku University), Tokyo: Benseisha.

Smith, Valene (ed.) (1989) *Hosts and Guests: The Anthropology of Tourism*, Philadelphia: University of Pennsylvania Press.

Statler, Oliver (1961) *Japanese Inn*, New York: Random House.

Takeshita, Noboru (1987) *Subarashii kuni Nihon: watakushi no 'furusato soseiron'* (Japan the wonderful country: My idea for the revival of *furusato*), Tokyo: Kondansha, Showa 62.

Tanaka, Keiko (1990) '"Intelligent elegance": Women and Japanese advertising', in Eyal Ben-Ari, Brian Moeran and James Valentine (eds) *Unwrapping Japan*, Manchester: Manchester University Press, 78–96.

Urry, John (1991) *The Tourist Gaze: Leisure and Travel in Contemporary Societies*, London: Sage.

Yanagita, Kunio (1982 (1940)) 'Fugo no Kigen' (The origin of *furo*), in vol. 14 of *Teihon Yanagita Kunioshu* (Collected Works of Yanagita Kunio), Tokyo: Tsukuman Shobo, 404–408.

Chapter 5

Gender and race
Neglected variables in tourism research

Linda K. Richter

Tourism research has accelerated dramatically in the last decade but, considering the size and scope of the tourism industry, the social science study of tourism is still in its infancy. As a consequence, the 1990s are an exciting period in which to examine the changing focus of tourism analysis. While issues of gender and race have been studied with increasing sophistication for more than two generations in the context of most social science disciplines, systematic attention to these two critical variables is largely absent from the critiques or analysis of tourism. Race and gender, arguably more central to most people than nation or class, are only recently being applied to the understanding of tourism. This is particularly surprising since tourism is a field of study itself profoundly influenced by perceptions of image and identity (Nash Chapter Three; Graburn Chapter Four; Dann Chapter Seven).

Studies of gender and race appear in many respects to have followed parallel intellectual and political histories. Preoccupation with biological differences gave way to the study of assigned social roles and the role socialization played in their development, and to a more holistic study of gendered society or society organized around issues of race (de Beauvoir 1953; Friedan 1964 and 1985; Wilson 1973; Hill and Jones 1993; Norris and Wall forthcoming). This general sequence of research approaches and policy emphases has been found in virtually all the social sciences. In the 1990s, one is seeing the study of gender and race, once considered such clear-cut variables, examined as cultural constructs rather than ordinal and timeless categories. Increasingly, one also finds analyses that study the *combined* and *interrelated* impact of these two variables (Hooks 1981; Rothenberg 1988; Collins 1990).

These research approaches have scarcely begun with respect to tourism, but they are under way and will surely reorder fundamentally our insights about tourism as they have so many other policy sectors. As a political scientist this writer finds striking opportunities to apply gender and race to a panoply of tourism issues focused on the distribution of power, privilege and political socialization. In 1991 this author began to look explicitly at gender as an element in dissecting tourism by examining tourism's impact as an independent variable on American women (Richter 1991). In 1992 parts of that analysis were recast into a global context and the basic patterns of gendered experience still held (Richter 1994). In this study, additional data on gender are included and the study is enriched by including the comparative element of race for analysis. Gender is itself a complex enough variable to examine, but there are some heuristic reasons why juxtaposing another neglected element, race, may in fact help to illustrate the *variations* in experiences and in responses to the dominant power structure.

Race is more complicated to discuss than gender and has, depending on conceptualization, a tendency to blur with ethnicity in many contexts (Van den Berghe 1992: 234–249). For most of this chapter race is examined by comparing dominant white or East Asian populations with a non-white and usually black population. This has been done, first, in order to delimit a vast and little understood topic. Second, most of the information has been drawn from the United States which has better data and more elaborate interest group organization for African-Americans than for other non-white racial groups.

Gender and race must be taken seriously both as independent variables impacting on tourism and as dependent variables affected *by* tourism. Specifically, this chapter seeks to explore first, tourism behaviour, followed by employment patterns, and then the gendered and racial patterns in advertising and in the attractions visited by the tourists. The final section of the chapter examines the economic and political control of the industry. The time is long overdue for such an analysis. Tourism is the largest industry in the world and yet it is perhaps the least critically assessed. Scholars still know relatively little about this phenomenon but it is clear tourism is not necessarily benign, frivolous, or self-evident in its impacts. The growing participation of women and racial minorities not only as tourists, but also as workers, politicians and consumers challenges scholars of tourism to acknowledge both their roles and the many constraints and opportunities they face as a consequence of the gender and racial patterns within and among the world's communities. All of the signs indicate that this involvement will continue to grow and will inevitably change the nature as well as the scale of tourism in many areas in the future.

TOURISM BEHAVIOUR

Tourism has long roots (Fiefer 1986) and many of the behaviours we bemoan today – graffiti, litter, uncouth travellers and ethnocentric behaviour – have been complaints that go back at least to Ancient Rome and Greece. Travel always has been differentially accessible (Nash Chapter Three). It has been said that, until the twentieth century, respectable women did not travel unless they were queens or pilgrims, missionary wives or colonizers (Enloe 1990; Robinson 1990), though at least one study of American women found a fair degree of travel freedom after independence until the 1840s (Cohen 1987). In Europe, as this writer has described elsewhere (Richter 1994), travel, while a capstone to a young male's education, was seen as compromising the reputation of young women – at least until Thomas Cook began to organize trips exclusively for well-bred ladies. While publishers are continually discovering and reissuing the diaries, journals and books of a few intrepid women adventurers, most women have had neither money, time nor the social indifference to risk such travels. Even leisure at home has been much more scarce for women than for men as virtually all labour studies demonstrate (Pruette 1924; Deem 1982; Colley 1984; Bella 1989). The very concept of 'the weekend' was one that for most of its existence has applied only to the public leisure of men (Rybezynski 1991: 107).

Today women comprise 40 per cent of US business travellers and have even been found to handle the stresses of business travel with more aplomb than their male counterparts. Of course, researchers speculate that this may be because they are able to get away from their 'second shift' at home when they are on the road, whereas men are forgoing a more relaxing and comforting environment when on the road (Del Rosso 1992). It has been argued that women are also the primary decision makers in terms of American family holidays (Smith 1979; Maruff 1993: 20), although other research suggests this may not be the case in other countries (Pearce 1989: 142). As a consequence, the industry has belatedly sought to accommodate their tastes, though this primarily has been focused on hotel security and amenities and much less in terms of creating destinations and attractions targeted to them (Kelley 1993; Militante 1993).

In Asia and Africa the business traveller is almost always male. Even when family travel is included, about two-thirds of all Asian travellers are male. However, important changes are occurring. Of the more than ten million Japanese international travellers in 1992, 3.7 million were female ('Japanese tourists abroad top 10 million', 1993: 23; Militante 1993: 17). Most of those were young women on modestly priced tour packages as befit their disadvantaged status in the labour market but as reflected in their enthusiasm for travel (Nash Chapter Three). Women constitute 40 per cent of the Japanese workforce but only 6 per cent of its managerial class (Militante 1993: 17). Another female market segment that is increasing is the *ajumah* market in Korea. These are married women who form small investment clubs and pool their savings for trips (Maruff 1993: 20).

For African and Asian men, travel has historically been either involuntary as during slavery or sharply curtailed to that which was absolutely necessary. In much of the world, tourism is something that non-whites participate in only as employees, if at all. Even in the United States until the 1964 Civil Rights Act declared racial discrimination in public accommodation illegal, most African-Americans found travel facilities scarce, segregated and of poor quality. That has changed. Non-white travellers are an increasing part of the international tourism market. It is difficult to remember that Americans in the 1950s were encouraged to travel to Japan to help the Japanese economy! The Japanese tourist is well known (Graburn Chapter Four), but even in very poor nations, where only a small percentage of the population has the means to travel for pleasure, large numbers travel for religious pilgrimage (Butler and Mao Chapter Six). Moreover, in countries with huge populations like India, even the tiny percentage that can easily indulge in luxury travel represents up to twenty-seven million people. Marketing assumptions often ignore how much travel goes on in developing nations.

Similarly, in the USA, media attention is so often focused on the plight of inner-city blacks that the growing affluence and size of the black middle class has been greatly underestimated. African-Americans constitute the fastest growing segment of the US travel market. Even as early as 1977 this market was estimated at over seven billion dollars (Hayes 1983: 6). By 1991 that figure had grown to twenty-five billion dollars ('Travelling the globe' 1990–91: 53, 56). Special interest tourism within the black community is still small but growing. As just one example, the popularity of Alex Haley's book and television mini-series *Roots* launched a number of black heritage tours to The Gambia and other historical centres of the slave trade (PBS 1978). Even the African-American *convention* market is huge. The National Coalition of Black Meeting Planners controlled over 2.6 billion dollars as of 1988 (Mills 1993: 50).

However, what is still not known about gender and race with respect to tourism behaviour is substantial. Rarely is the black or female travel market desegregated from general travel statistics. The same is also true for the Hispanic and native American travel market in the USA. Certain markets within the USA, such as those in Florida and California, have been identified as key destinations for Hispanics from Latin America, but Hispanic-Americans are all but invisible in the tourism statistics.

It is also important to deconstruct 'race'. Some nations keep statistics by race. These are becoming increasingly more problematic as racial groups intermarry. Moreover, for many kinds of uses the broad racial categories obscure as much as they reveal. African-Americans from the Caribbean, from Africa and those native-born in the USA may be treated as 'black' by the tourist industry and other economic sectors, but they may not identify with each other – let alone respond to the same historical markers, symbols, sports or other leisure activities (West 1993). Their income levels, religious affiliations and family structures may be markedly different when desegregated. Thus the tourist industry and the tourist and host communities increasingly need to recognize variations *within* as well as *among* racial groups.

EMPLOYMENT PATTERNS IN TOURISM

It is ironic that gender and race are usually obscured from an analysis of tourism except when it comes to employment. Ironic, because while employment in the tourism industry is disproportionately important to women and minorities, it is not necessarily a pattern that reassures (Ireland 1993). The industry is quick to note that one in every fifteen people in the world is employed in tourism (Edgell 1990). Over half of those so employed are women.

Within the United States, women constitute 52 per cent of the travel industry positions compared with 44 per cent of their share in all industries (US Travel Data Center in Smith 1989: 45; Edgell 1993: 18). Such employment data hide as much as they reveal. Certainly nowhere near half of the salaried income or half the work hours from tourism go to women or minorities. Rather, they constitute the base of a very steep pyramid, peopled at the bottom with low-paid, part-time and seasonal workers. There are few benefits and little security or mobility associated with such positions. The tourism employment pyramid is steep for everyone, but female and minority professionals are especially rare. Even those who make it to professional positions are paid poorly in comparative terms. That employment base is still very important, however, as in the USA, for example, the industry provides 4.6 million jobs for women, 970,000 for African-Americans and 765,000 jobs for Hispanics. In each case the travel industry has hired a larger percentage of women and minorities than most sectors of the economy (Edgell 1993: 18). However, for the most part the industry provides entry-level opportunities, and developing career ladders has been more problematic. Interestingly enough, when critics of tourism cite the low-level jobs associated with the industry, they often do so in gendered terms. There is far more concern that tourism is creating nations of 'bellboys' than concern about women becoming maids and prostitutes. Perhaps it is because the traditional *unpaid* labour of women in society in general is similar to their work in the industry that their condition seems to deserve no comment. The dignity of women seems to become relevant only if it reflects on the male's ability to protect his 'women' (Enloe 1990).

There *could* be more respectable roles for women in the industry if discrimination were not so pervasive. Even in a traditional nation like Pakistan in the 1970s, Prime Minister Zulfiqar ali Bhutto saw in tourism a way to create a new sector without the sex discrimination inherent in older sectors. He thought women would dominate the fledgeling industry. That was not his only political error in judgment. His execution by the coup leaders who deposed him in 1977 not only ended his life but signalled the retreat of women from the public sector in general and tourism in particular (Richter 1984), although his daughter has since continued his efforts from her position of leadership. In other Muslim countries there has been an effort to isolate tourism and reserve employment in this industry to men. The Maldives is a good example of a location where the effort to keep tourism away from women means that men working in the industry are physically removed from their families and kept on the islands especially designated for tourism (Richter 1989a: 163–168). Both sexes are disadvantaged as a consequence.

In general, however, tourism employment has been for many women in developing nations the only prospect for employment. As such it has been an important factor in the independence of some women (Swain 1993), in the integration of women into a monetized culture and in the creation of more modern values – all of which can be viewed as destructive or progressive depending on context. For example, Elmendorf (1981) talks of the many positive spillover effects that occurred after a road was constructed near a small Latin American village. Some of the young Mayan women left the village on a bus for the city to work in the hotels. They became bilingual; they became more self-sufficient. They brought money back to their families in the village. They postponed marriage a few years; they had fewer children, spaced further apart. They and their families were healthier and more prosperous (Elmendorf 1981: 149–162). Something similar happened in the North Aegean islands of Lesvos and Hios. Agricultural Tourist Cooperatives were established by Greece's Council for Equality of the Sexes. These cooperatives were designed to expand the economic opportunities of women. Women were encouraged to make use of traditional cooking, sewing, and farming skills and develop a homestay programme for tourists. Early results appeared promising both in terms of creating a viable economic base for the women and also in expanding opportunities for others on the islands (Van Houts 1983: 28–30; Melis 1986).

For every such success story, there are others of family stresses when gender power roles in the family are suddenly changed. Ireland's case study of an English parish offers an excellent longitudinal study of evolving gender roles as tourism develops and traditional occupations decline (Ireland 1993: 666–684). It is also important to recognize that tourism development may *displace* women from their homes and livelihoods. While employment may be created, the beneficiaries may not be homeowners, local farmers or fishermen, for whom access to lands and the sea may be denied. In developing as well as developed nations tourism's negative impacts are often the result of poor planning, hasty developments and inadequate provision for the very residents tourism was supposed to help ('Boholano women resist tourism project' 1992: 40). There is also a burgeoning literature on sex tours, paedophilia groups and gangster-controlled prostitution linked to tourism (Cottingham 1981; Thanh-Dam 1983; Richter 1989a; Moreau 1992: 50–51).

Even without dwelling on the more sordid forms of tourism employment, there is considerable disenchantment in some places with the impact of tourism on people's lives, especially women. One of the more systematic investigations is *Behind the Glitter* (Smith 1989), which details the impact of tourism on women in the American Southeast. This study, focused on Sevier County, Tennessee, illustrates the negative impact of tourism on women even when tourism is a 'success' story in terms of conventional economic measures. However, this critique of tourism needs to be considered in the context of options available to the women in the area. Historically, this area had been a very poor, traditional mountain culture. One should not romanticize life in such poor remote areas *pre*-tourism. It is not evident to this writer that life for women on balance in that area has deteriorated since tourism came on the scene, nor that the stresses associated with tourism are not in many respects synonymous with modern life – something that the mountain county sought to embrace. On the other hand it seems fair to acknowledge that a more gradual pace of tourism development and direct attention to the plight of women might have resulted in a wiser development process than that which has occurred.

Sexual harassment

As in virtually all employment sectors, sexual harassment is widespread in the travel industry (Belluccio 1983: 66–86). In fact some have claimed it may be twice as severe a problem as in most other occupations (Eller 1989; Nozar 1990; Brownwell 1993). There are, however, some features of the industry that make the problem especially severe. First, the industry operates in a 'sexualized environment' (Gutek *et al.* 1990). First is the nature of the promise implicit in tourism – escape, adventure and romance. Just as it weakens inhibitions to prostitution, it also weakens constraints on employee–client relationships. Women are routinely propositioned and harassed in the context of their waitress, chambermaid and other tourist occupations. In some cases this problem has been exacerbated by the outfits the women have been required to wear by their employers – clothing that invites leers and innuendo. In the United States in the last decade some women have been winning court cases against such uniforms, but the victories are time-consuming and costly – luxuries many women cannot afford (McConnell 1985: 78–82).

Second, most tourism businesses are sharply segregated both vertically and horizontally by gender. Men are typically in control, either over a mostly female workforce comprising such occupations as maids and waitresses, or above a largely female stratum in the same office, for example, clerical workers, travel agents or ticket sellers. Both situations are typical settings for sexual harassment. Finally, men rarely work as equals with women at the top of the tourism employment pyramid. There are few if any female chief executive officers (CEOs) of airlines, attractions and hotels. Women are also scarce in public sector tourism as major players (author's interviews 1993). Few women academics or travel writers breach the nearly exclusively male domain. Thus, it is small wonder that sexual harassment is rife in the industry and it appears behind other sectors in recognizing its vulnerability to legal action in this area (Belluccio 1983).

Neo-colonial hiring practices

In developing nations, employment typically follows a pattern of both assigning the poorest jobs to women and inferior jobs in general to minorities (Richter 1982, 1989a). This is reflective of a generally neo-colonial pattern in the industry. Even in Asian and Pacific countries, whatever ethnic or racial group is considered subordinate will be found assuming the least desirable positions. This was a major source of political strife in Fiji in 1987 (author's interviews 1987). In many societies multinational corporations will have largely expatriate male management assuming most of the choice positions. While some nations like the Philippines, Thailand and Pakistan have sought to assure that training programmes will move their citizens into leadership in the industry, progress has been slow and irregular. Multinational corporations have also been reluctant to lessen their reliance on a central purchasing source and to do more supplying of the industry from local resources. Major opportunities to create employment and diversification in the host societies are thereby lost, not to mention the loss or leakage of badly needed foreign exchange (Richter 1982, 1989a).

In some nations the country itself has projected a subservient image of its workers that works against the status of employment in the industry. In Jamaica, for example, efforts were made under former Prime Minister Michael Manley to encourage more respect for Jamaicans among the visiting tourists. Jamaica's tourism slogan during that period was 'Jamaica's more than a beach, it's a country' (Richter 1989a). Successor governments have been less nationalistic. The slogan after Manley was 'Jamaica's Jamaica again'.

The previous examples focus primarily on the negatives associated with tourism employment, but there are some pluses as well. Women own over half the travel agencies in the United States (Richter 1991: 161), they make up 81 per cent of agency managers and 84 per cent of agency sales agents (Kelley 1993: 17). They work in careers that often do accommodate child-rearing and an opportunity to learn on the job. The 'glass ceiling' is real and thick, but the opportunities to get started and own one's own business are perhaps greater for women in this industry than in almost any other.

Not so fortunate are minorities in most societies. The United States is a good example of just how limited the opportunities for African-American men and women have been above the employment base of the pyramid. Wylie Whisonant Jr was Deputy Under-Secretary of Commerce for Travel and Tourism from 1990 to 1992 – the first high ranking African-American in the US Travel and Tourism Administration (USTTA), but he was quick to recognize how limited minority participation in tourism has been above the most menial jobs (Hayes and Lawson-Burke 1990: 62–64). Only two African-American full service advertising agencies had travel accounts. There are fewer than 300 black travel agents in the nation out of a total of more than 37,000. There are only two black airline officers in the country, only thirty-five black general managers among 40,700 hotel properties, only one chief pilot for a major airline ('Travelling the globe' 1990–91: 52–57).

Employment in tourism is indeed structured by gender and race in ways that do great harm to notions of equality and individualism. Despite the small numbers, most black professionals have entered the tourism industry only since 1980. African-American interest in such careers is soaring today and the profile of the industry is expected to change dramatically by the year 2000 (Hayes 1993: 48).

WHAT DO WE SELL? WHAT DO WE REMEMBER?

For many years this writer has been struck by the way places and experiences are portrayed. It is important to understand this process in terms of how it socializes visitors and residents alike to a political impression of themselves *vis-à-vis* what they are seeing or remembering. Such impressions are not neutral. They imply gradations of power and influence, of value and dispensability, of what can be bought and what is not for sale (Dann Chapter Seven). School children on field trips may absorb such notions like popcorn. Adults may reinforce stereotypes or qualify them.

One of the first to examine the way in which tourism structures history and shapes a culture was Horne. His book, *The Great Museum* (1984), examines the very different way people and events are interpreted through the museums of Europe. He notes how antiseptic and quaint cataclysmic events such as the Industrial Revolution can become if only immortalized in villagers' homes or weaving shops. The Russian and French Revolutions are no more susceptible to balanced discourse, as he demonstrates with examples of the selective memories of various museums. As this writer learned, the Australian War Museum also furnished an example of the political subjectivity of exhibits. No curator by 1987 had been able to settle upon a representation of Australia's participation in the Vietnam War that met with universal favour. Was it a noble effort to defeat communism or a bloody blunder? The dedication, in September 1992, of the Australian National Memorial to those who died in the Vietnamese conflict has since gone some way to resolve this issue, but how we choose to remember and commemorate events is a very political act.

Advertising

Tourist advertising in Europe and North America assumes a white, indeed Anglo, tourist. This writer surveyed a wide array of travel advertising in both brochures and advertisements from most of the North American suppliers and found only a couple that included any picture, anywhere in their material, of a non-white, Hispanic, or semitic tourist (Dann Chapter Seven). An exception was Norwegian Cruise Lines which acknowledged in several pictures tourists with a variety of ethnic and racial backgrounds. So the industry starts with a myopic and inaccurate but still influential image of their clientele. That, in turn, shapes their notions of what their clients want to see. It also leads all tourists to assume that most of their travelling companions and fellow tourists will be white. Moreover, non-whites are shown disproportionate to their numbers in menial service roles catering to the tourist. One of the worst such examples was a full-page advertisement for a Caribbean vacation that had a smiling non-white staff of four – cook, concierge, maid and waiter – all waist deep in the ocean with trays of flowers and fruit proffered to a white couple sunning themselves on a rubber raft. Consider the racism implicit in this quotation from a brochure of the Jamaican government :

> You can rent a lovely life in Jamaica by the week. It starts with a country house or a beach cottage hilltop hideaway that comes equipped with gentle people named Ivy or Maude or Malcom who will cook, tend, mend, diaper and launder for you . . . giggle at your jokes and weep when you leave.
>
> (Erisman in Richter 1989a: 200)

Developing nations are not the only offenders. Air New Zealand used to advertise its friendly hospitality by showing a Polynesian woman lying in a wet sarong at the ocean's edge.

The USTTA, using American tax dollars, assists in the international marketing of the US Virgin Islands. But it was doing the islanders no favours with its large buttons with 'Try a Virgin' on them and only followed by 'island' in the tiniest of print (Richter 1989b: 4). In an age of AIDS, of complaints about sex tours, of supposedly heightened sensitivity to racism and sexism, one would think American tourism officials would recognize that such a use of government funds was inappropriate. Instead, it was left to the Caribbean Council of Churches and the Ecumenical Coalition on Third World Tourism to protest.

Attractions

Similar issues and problems arise with respect to tourist attractions, particularly in areas in which minority populations are becoming involved and incorporated into the tourism industry.

Much depends on whether the minority, often aboriginal populations, are used as attractions or involved in offering attractions based on their culture and history. Both New Zealand and Australia have struggled to use their minority populations to attract tourism while accommodating minority culture. Maori culture and aboriginal culture have in fact garnered more prestige with the dominant population in about the same proportion as they have attracted world-wide interest but aboriginal culture continues to be marginalized and caricatured (author's interviews 1987). The Public Broadcasting Service (PBS) 'Travels' presented the dilemma in its documentary on Australia (1993). In several scenes an aborigine was shown hopping like a kangaroo for the amusement of tourists who attempted to hit him with a boomerang. The tour promoter insisted tourists were much too inexperienced to actually hit the man but that they gained a respect for the aboriginal skill in hunting this way. The guide also claimed that the aborigine earned a good living from his role-playing. Both may be correct statements, but at what a price to the man's dignity and to the respect tourists might be expected to have of aborigines? Control and use of lands belonging to indigenous peoples are other major issues in many parts of the world. Altman (1989) explored the complexity of such relationships between governments, developers and indigenous peoples, and their implications for the aborigines.

Tourist attractions and their accompanying brochures have an especial modern power to educate that needs to be examined. Just as textbooks, stories and advertising have been scrutinized for latent sexism and racism, it is worth considering how cultural attractions, statues, amusement parks and ethnic displays expand or contract our perceptions of our fellow human beings (Cohen Chapter Two). There is some evidence that advertising, marketing and more racially and gender diverse tourism is already with us. Spurred on both by the rising economic clout of women and minorities and simply by a desire for new products and approaches, tourism is getting more historically grounded in reality, and old clichés are getting revised. (Although as Graburn Chapter Four illustrates, the newly romanticized past in the form of nostalgia is still a powerful selling point (Editors' note).) Slave life is the subject of many historic sites from the southern US to West Africa. The infamous concentration camps of Nazi Germany, Anne Frank's hideaway in Amsterdam, the Holocaust Museum in

Washington, DC, and the Museum of Tolerance in Los Angeles offer grim insights into a racist past. Some argue that bringing up reminders of cruelty and injustice only angers and increases hostility in those who see such museums and memorials. Others feel that events central to a nation's history – proud or shameful – need to be remembered and the moral lessons drawn.

Some of the most rapid growth in the establishment of new tourism attractions appears to be occurring through recognizing black culture world-wide as new sites are identified and in some cases the very race of familiar talents identified. For example, Alexander Dumas is well known as the author of *The Three Musketeers*, but much less well known is the fact that he was black. The château which he built in France is now open to the public (Hayes and Lawson-Evans 1988; Hayes 1989: 34). A major stimulus for attraction diversification is the economic power of international visitors and the growing affluence of American minorities (Hayes 1991: 52–56). Hayes explored the African heritage in tourism attractions and has chronicled for more than ten years the growing awareness of tourism within black communities. In 1988, Hayes with David Edgell Sr highlighted the *international* black marketing initiatives and entrepreneurial activity in places like Harlem, New Orleans and the US Virgin Islands (Edgell and Hayes 1988: 8–9). Similar marketing efforts are aimed at encouraging black travel in Africa, and The Gambia, for example, has hosted 'Roots' tours.

Women too have been, belatedly, the subject of the latest tourist attractions in many cities, though they have been more likely black women than white. Harriet Tubman's heroic efforts to bring southern slaves to freedom in the American North is just one example featured in tours of the American South. Sojourner Truth's powerful advocacy of women's rights at Seneca Falls, NY in 1848 is also memorialized in the museum there. This suggests that black heritage advocates have been more successful in showcasing talented blacks than the dominant culture has been at discovering the accomplishments of its women (Hayes and Lawson-Evans 1988: 38). Two major and recent attractions commemorating women's contributions deserve specific comment. The first is the National Museum for Women in the Arts in Washington, DC – the only museum in the world devoted exclusively to the art of women. The other attraction, which was finished in 1993, is the moving war memorial sculpture dedicated to the women who served in Vietnam. Before it went to its final location in Washington, DC, it toured the USA attracting emotional crowds who found its beauty a cathartic experience.

CONTROLLING TOURISM: WHO GOVERNS AND WHO CARES?

The power of tourism to capture our imagination and shape our sense of our own identity and that of others means that the control of tourism is important. Those who sell national images, racial and gendered experiences need to be accountable to the people they affect. Unfortunately, except in very localized settings, tourism is not an issue around which votes are organized and interest groups massed. This is even more true with respect to racial and gender issues of tourism. Except for sex tours in a few Asian nations, tourism issues of primary salience to women are invisible. Even in those countries the issues remain largely unresolved and are chiefly focused on the health of the sex tourist.

In most nations, particularly developing nations, the control of the tourism industry is in the hands of the central government and is strongly influenced by major lending institutions and multinational companies. These are primarily white or Asian and almost certainly male enclaves of influence (Richter 1989a, 1991). Even in the United States where the pyramid of *governmental* control is inverted, that is, where cities often spend more on tourism than states, and where the central government's influence is divided among some forty agencies, control is in white male hands. In only a few states are there female tourism directors (Richter 1985). The *tourist industry* is also overwhelmingly in white, male control. While much of the industry is composed of small businesses, and many travel agencies are in female hands, little policy decision making rests with women.

International bodies dealing with tourism are similarly male-dominated. For example, only in 1993 has the Pacific Asia Travel Association welcomed its first female President; the Travel and Tourism Research Association has had only five female Presidents; the World Tourism Organization has had few females among its leadership cadre, and the list goes on. Change can be startling when it comes, however. Earlene Causey, the American Society of Travel Agents' first female CEO and President in its sixty-two-year history, currently has an all-female executive board (Kelley, 1993: 17).

Minorities are also underrepresented relative to their numbers and their economic role in the industry, both as management and tourists. There is, however, encouraging evidence of greater sophistication and a willingness to mobilize economic strength for political access among the African-American community and it appears to be paying off. Increasingly convention tourism decisions are being made on the basis of many other factors besides price. For example, black convention organizers are selecting cities on the basis of the attractions they offer for blacks, on the percentage of blacks in positions of political and economic responsibility and on the kinds of facilities that are provided for the conventioneers (Hayes 1983; Hayes 1990: 22–24; Hayes 1991: 52–56; Mills 1993; 'Black tourist boycott of Miami called off' 1993: 3A).

American women tried such methods once in conjunction with male conventioneers over the issue of the Equal Rights Amendment (ERA). Then, many professionals refused to hold their conventions in states that had not ratified the ERA – a costly and controversial decision negatively impacting such cities as Atlanta, St Louis, Chicago and Miami. Boycotts are blunt tools and hurt in this case the more liberal parts of some traditional states, but their effect is substantial. Such boycotts have been challenged as illegal restraints of trade; but US courts have held them to be legal. The pluralist history of the United States suggests that the only way to gain access to the political and economic goods of the society is to organize. In other nations culture and religion may afford legal access or barriers for women and minorities.

CONCLUSION

Issues of race and gender over the last twenty years have altered the way many disciplines discuss their core concepts or evaluate and assess quality and performance. That dialogue is only beginning to occur with respect to travel and tourism. The delay is understandable in some respects – tourism has been one of the last major policy sectors to attract social science scrutiny. Moreover, the subject of tourism has no obvious single disciplinary home in which to focus the discussion. In the 1990s, however, as this chapter has demonstrated, there are numerous research issues surrounding race and gender that are central to tourism and tourism development. Some are a part of the more general dialogues on race and gender, simply extended to this industry. These include issues of ownership, control, economic opportunity, harassment and discrimination. The cultural milieu in which gender and race are constructed also reflect societal variations around the globe that permeate whole cultures, not simply specific policy areas.

Still, there are other facets surrounding race and gender which *do* impact travel and tourism in ways unique to this policy area. Foremost among these is the essential *interaction* and *contact* between server and served, host and guest, national and international visitor. The central ways gender and race are structured are critical not only in terms of the destination, but in terms of the visitors' backgrounds and expectations.

Space does not permit this writer to do more here than raise some gender and race issues that particularly impact on the industry – harassment, biases in advertising, impact on attraction development and the both negative and positive characteristics of tourism employment patterns.

Much more research needs to probe how societal attitudes towards race and gender have shaped the tourism 'product'. It may be reflected in more attractions aimed at African-Americans in Africa and the Caribbean, more women-only adventure tours or the development of Las Vegas into a more family-oriented destination. (Although not discussed here, the appearance of cruises and destination resorts specifically for the homosexual and lesbian markets may also be representative of such new attractions reflecting changing attitudes towards aspects of gender (Editors' note).) Nor are such attitudes static. Places once 'meccas' for tourists are finding their presence a source of local political struggles. Consider the current and bloody struggles in Egypt and Kenya over the very desirability of a tourism industry (Richter 1993). Some of that struggle is over the role of women in the industry and the role models of the female tourist.

More research needs to determine the educational and socialization role of travel in terms of the gender and racial learning that takes place. Clichés that 'travel is broadening' and 'tourism is a force for peace' do not take tourism very far. Do historical tourist attractions subtly infer men did everything worth remembering? That the dominant racial group or successful imperialists 'civilized' the colonized? That some races or women are 'natural' waiters, maids and bellhops? Are some racial groups' burial grounds sacred sites, or historical landmarks exploited or protected more than others? Are there gender and racial implications to political control? What techniques or strategies will encourage communities, promoting agencies and the industry to critique at such a fundamental level, the way travel and tourism are organized?

It is encouraging to this writer to see how rapidly the industry and governments have begun to embrace other critiques and issues like ecotourism, terrorism, carrying capacity of destinations and visitor facilitation. Tourism is a vital and resilient sector that has absorbed and adapted the work of earlier scholars in ways that have enhanced tourism. There is good reason to expect that issues of race and gender when explored more fully will have a similar impact on the future of tourism.

ACKNOWLEDGEMENTS

Financial support from the Kansas State University Graduate School, the Arts and Sciences Dean's Office, the Women's Studies Office and the Department of Political Science was deeply appreciated. The author is also indebted to Bernetta Hayes, Jeanne Gay, William Richter, Douglas Pearce and Richard Butler for their substantive information and suggestions.

REFERENCES

Altman, J. (1989) 'Tourism dilemmas for aboriginal Australians', *Annals of Tourism Research* 16, 4: 456–476.

Bella, L. (1989) 'Women and leisure: Beyond androcentric', in E.L. Jackson and T.L. Burton (eds) *Understanding Leisure and Recreation: Mapping the Past, Charting the Future*, State College, Pa.: Venture Publishing, 151–180.

Belluccio, E. (1983) 'Sexual harassment: A long dormant demon', *Hospitality Review* 1, 2: 66–86.

'Black tourist boycott of Miami called off' (1993) *Wichita Eagle*, 13 May: 3A.

'Boholano women resist tourism project' (1992) *Contours* 5, 5/6, March–June.

Brownwell, J. (1993) 'Addressing career challenges faced by women in hospitality management', *Hospitality and Tourism Educator* 5, 4: 11–15.

Cohen, P. (1987) *Christian Science Monitor*, 15 October: 8.

Colley, A. (1984) 'Sex roles and explanation of leisure behaviour', *Leisure Studies* 3: 335–341.

Collins, P.H. (1990) *Black Feminist Thought*, Boston: Unwin Hyman.

Cottingham, J. (1981) 'Sex included', *Development Forum* IX, 5: 16.

de Beauvoir, S. (1953) *The Second Sex*, New York: Alfred A. Knopf.

Deem, R. (1982) 'Women, leisure and inequality', *Leisure Studies* 1: 29–46.

Del Rosso, L. (1992) 'Study shows women handle business travel better than men', *Travel Weekly* 51, 61, 30 July: 30–31.

Edgell, D.L. Sr (1990) *International Tourism Policy*, New York: Van Nostrand Reinhold.

—— (1993) *World Tourism at the Millennium*, Washington, DC: US Department of Commerce.

Edgell, D.L. Sr and Hayes, B. (1988) 'Cultural richness in the US black community offers great potential for tourism development', *Business America* 26 September: 8–9.

Eller, M.E. (1989) 'Sexual harassment: Prevention not protection', *The Cornell Hotel and Restaurant Administration Quarterly* 30, 4: 84–89.

Elmendorf, M. (1981) 'Changing role of Maya mothers and daughters', in R. Dauber and M.L. Cain (eds) *Women and Technological Change in Developing Countries*, Colorado: Westview, 149–162.

Enloe, C. (1990) *Bananas, Beaches, and Bases*, Berkeley: University of California Press.

Fiefer, R. (1986) *Tourism in History*, New York: Stein & Day.

Friedan, B. (1964) *The Feminine Mystique,* New York: Dell Books.

—— (1985) *It Changed My Life*, New York: W.W. Norton.

Gutek, B.A., Cohen, A.G. and Konrad, A.M. (1990) 'Predicting socio-sexual behavior at work: A contact hypothesis', *Academy of Management Journal* 33, 3: 560–577.

Hayes, B. (1983) 'Is tourism black people's business?', *Black Convention News* May: 6.

—— (1989) 'Travelling the African diaspora at home and abroad', *The 1989 African-American Blackbook International Reference Guide* January: 26–42.

—— (1990) 'What's so special about Atlanta?', *Dollars and Sense* October/November: 22–24.

—— (1991) 'The economics of travel: Do African-Americans get their share of the travel dollar?', *Dollars and Sense* December/January: 52–56.

—— (1993) 'African-Americans and tourism: Reaching new horizons', *Dollars and Sense* January: 46–48.

Hayes, B. and Lawson-Burke, F. (1990) 'An interview with Wylie Whisonant Jr, Deputy Under-Secretary for Travel and Tourism', *Dollars and Sense* February/March: 62–64.

Hayes, B. and Lawson-Evans, F. (1988) 'Cultural sites of black Americans: A cornucopia of black history around the globe', *Dollars and Sense* August/September: 50–64.

Hill, H. and Jones Jr, J.E. (eds) (1993) *Race in America: The Struggle for Equality*, Wisconsin: University of Wisconsin Press.

Hooks, B. (1981) *Ain't I A Woman?*, Boston: South End Press.

Horne, D. (1984) *The Great Museum*, Pluto: Australia.

Ireland, M. (1993) 'Gender and class relations in tourism employment', *Annals of Tourism Research* 20, 4: 666–684.

'Japanese tourists abroad top 10 million' (1993) *Contours* 4, 8, December: 23.

Kelley, T. (1993). 'A little R-E-S-P-E-C-T', *Asia Travel Trade* March: 16–17.

Maruff, P. (1993) 'Fledgeling women's movement in Korea', *Asia Travel Trade* March: 20–21.

Matsui, Y. (1984) 'Why I oppose kisaeng tours', in K. Barry, C. Bunch and S. Castley (eds) *International Feminism: Networking Against Female Sexual Slavery*, New York: International Women's Tribune Center, Inc., 64–72.

McConnell, J. (1985) 'Bare trap: The legal pitfall of requiring scanty costumes', *The Cornell Hotel and Restaurant Administration Quarterly* 26, 3 November: 78–82.

Melis, A. (1986) 'The lure of island villages', *Ms* April: 22.

Militante, G. (1993) 'Japanese women are going places', *Asia Travel Trade* March: 17–19.

Mills, H. (1993) 'Taking it to the cities: Top convention sites', *Dollars and Sense* January: 50–52.

Moreau, R. (1992) 'Sex and death in Thailand', *Newsweek* 20 July: 50–51.

Norris, J. and Wall, G. 'Gender and tourism' (forthcoming).

Nozar, R. (1990) 'Winking at sexual harassment demeans lodging', *Hotel and Motel Management* 205, 7: 6–7.

PBS (1978) 'Who pays for paradise?', PBS Television.

—— (1993) 'Travels', PBS Television.

Pearce, D. G. (1989) *Tourist Development*, London: Longman.

Pruette, L. (1924) *Women and Leisure: A Study of Social Waste*, New Hampshire: Ayer Co. (reprinted 1972).

Richter, L.K. (1982) *Land Reform and Tourism Development: Policy-Making in the Philippines*, Cambridge, Mass.: Schenkman Publishing Co.

—— (1984) 'The potential pitfalls of tourism planning in Third World nations: The case of Pakistan', *Tourism Recreation Research* 9, 1: 9–13.

—— (1985) 'State-sponsored tourism: A growth field for public administration?', *Public Administration Review* November–December: 832–839.

—— (1989a) *The Politics of Tourism in Asia*, Honolulu: University of Hawaii Press.

—— (1989b) 'Action Alert', *Contours* 4, 4 December: 4.

—— (1991) 'The impact of American tourism policy on women', in M.L. Kendrigan (ed.) *Gender Differences and Public Policy*, Colorado: Greenwood Press, 201–222.

—— (1993) 'Political instability and tourism in the Third World', in D. Harrison (ed.) *Tourism and the Less Developed Countries*, London: Belhaven Press, 35–46.

—— (1994) 'Exploring the political role of gender in tourism research', in W. Theobald (ed.) *Critical Issues in Tourism*, Indiana: Purdue University Press, 146–157.

Robinson, J. (1990) *Wayward Women: A Guide to Women Travellers*, Oxford: Oxford University Press.

Rothenberg, P.S. (1988) *Racism and Sexism*, New York: St Martin's Press.

Rybezynski, W. (1991) *Waiting for the Weekend*, London: Viking Penguin.

Smith, M. (1989) *Behind the Glitter: The Impact of Tourism on Rural Women in the Southeast*, Kentucky: Southeast Women's Employment Coalition.

Smith, V. (1979) 'Women: The taste-makers in tourism', *Annals of Tourism Research* 6, 1: 49–60.

Swain, M. (1993) 'Women producers of ethnic arts', *Annals of Tourism Research* 20, 1: 32–51.

Thanh-Dam, T. (1983) 'The dynamics of sex tourism: The case of Southeast Asia', *Development and Change* 14, 4: 533–552.

'Travelling the globe: The economics of travel: Do African-Americans get their share of the travel dollar?', *Dollars and Sense* (1990–1): 52–57.

Van den Berghe, P. (1992) 'Tourism and the ethnic division of labor', *Annals of Tourism Research* 19, 2: 234–249.

Van Houts, D. (1983) 'Female participation in tourism employment in Tunisia: Some economic and non-economic costs and benefits', *The Tourist Review* 38, 1 January/March: 28–30.

West, P.C. (1993) *Race Matters*, Boston: Beacon Press.

Wilson, W. (1973) *Power, Racism and Privilege*, New York: Free Press.

Chapter 6

Tourism between quasi-states
International, domestic or what?

Richard W. Butler and Baodi Mao

One of the most dramatic features of the second half of the twentieth century has been the pattern of political change. While human history has been a story of constantly changing political units, western society has tended to anticipate significant political change only in the context of war and revolution, or the end of major empires, also often caused by war and revolution. A somewhat different situation has emerged since the end of the last global conflict in 1945. At the beginning of World War II there were some seventy independent political units, but some forty years later this number had more than doubled to around 160 members of the United Nations and a further forty or so anomalous political units. In the first three years of the 1990s approximately twenty additional political units have appeared on the map of Europe and Asia, with the break up of the former Soviet Union and Yugoslavia. This process drew a strong expression of concern from the Secretary of the United Nations, Boutros-Ghali, who warned 'A new danger is micronationalism. You will have the risk of moving from 180 countries to 500 countries in the next 20 years' (Maclean's 1993: 30).

Not all of these political units are universally recognized as sovereign states, although most claim such status. The former Soviet Union has been divided into fifteen independent states, linked in an uneasy Commonwealth format, and Yugoslavia has been fragmented into a number of political units, some still in conflict among themselves. While these two countries are perhaps the most dramatic cases of political change in recent years, one might also look at the cases of Korea, Germany, Vietnam and China, all of which have been split into two or more segments since 1945. Two, Vietnam and Germany, have since been reunited, one by war and one by peace, while the others remain separate and to some degree anomalous. There are in total some fifty such political units around the world, with differing backgrounds and reasons for their subdivision.

Despite the often unsettled political climate which surrounds many of these units, there is often considerable travel between them. Herein lies a significant conceptual and methodological problem for researchers in travel and tourism, which this chapter discusses and for which it endeavours to provide some definitions and models. Tourism, by definition, involves travel between an origin and destination. In many cases this travel is classified into two basic types for analysis, convenience, and statistical collection, using political boundaries as the criterion. Tourism which involves travel between political units or countries is termed international tourism, while tourism within an individual's own country is termed domestic tourism. In almost every case where international tourism is involved, this refers to travel between two officially recognized independent political units or states. Where then does travel between political units which are not universally recognized or fully independent fit? A number of related questions arise. Is there such travel? Are these travellers similar in characteristics to travellers between 'normal' political states? Are their impacts, patterns and linkages the same as those of other tourists? Do the conventional tourism models, concepts and theories apply to such travellers and travel, or are new approaches and theories necessary?

Clearly there are too many questions and too many variations to be able to answer or even discuss them all in this chapter. Accordingly, attention will be given to what is defined here as the 'quasi-state', and tourism between such political units. The chapter proceeds through a conceptual and definitional discussion, a commentary on the nature of quasi-states, an initial analysis of tourism between such units, comments on the dynamic nature of such tourism and some general conclusions and implications.

CONCEPTS AND DEFINITIONS

Anomalous political units take on a variety of forms relating to their reasons for establishment and continuation, and many other factors. In this chapter attention is focused on states which, at some point in their history, were separated into a number of political units.

A quasi-state is defined here as a currently separate political unit, once part of a larger unit, subdivided by internal (religion, ethnic origin, etc.) or external (colonization/decolonization, occupation, war, etc.) forces. Although possibly possessing many of the attributes of statehood such as territory, permanent population, organized economy, government, armed forces, language and culture, a quasi-state may still be in the process of becoming a conventional state in terms of accepted sovereignty, diplomatic relations and universal recognition.

It is important to note that the term quasi-state is not used in a pejorative sense in any way, nor is it meant to perpetuate or support claims for recognition or non-recognition of the particular political units discussed. In some of the situations noted below, all or parts of some of what are termed quasi-states are claimed by another unit. In some cases units which are now universally recognized as independent political units at the global scale still behave or are regarded as quasi-states by those units from which they originated, while in other cases the relationships are regarded as temporary on one side, for example, China, Hong Kong, Macao and Taiwan. In almost all cases, the current international political boundaries were created, in some cases imposed, after the development of some or all of the cultural, linguistic, religious and economic patterns had developed.

Considerable attention has been paid in the political science literature to the problems of anomalous political units. Glassner and de Blij note that:

> Although the European state system has spread around the world during the past several hundred years, resulting in the creation of over 170 states, by no means has all the earth's land area been organized in such a neat and seemingly definitive manner. . . . Here we are concerned with types of territorial organization that fall between these two extremes – or outside them altogether. Some of these anomalies are remnants of the period before the organization of nation-states; some are simply ad hoc arrangements resulting from war or decolonization.
>
> (1989: 7)

Boal and Douglas (1982) developed an explanatory model to describe the process of integration and division of a society and to evaluate the internal cause of integration and division. They claim that these two phenomena are recognized both as attributes and process, and set the position of anomalous political units on an integration–division spectrum. There has, however, been little study of the combination of tourism and such political change, or indeed of the relationship of tourism with political aspects of life generally. Richter (1989) has been one of the few to stress the significance of political influences on tourism, especially in an international context, and drew attention in particular to Indian tourist arrivals in Pakistan, and travel from Hong Kong and Taiwan to China as the result of international politics in these areas. More recently, Mowlana and Smith (1991), in their paper on tourism and international relations, noted the appearance of many new participants on the international scene, although these authors were generally more concerned with institutions beyond the normal nation-state level, rather than below it.

Tourism between quasi-states is significant, however, not just because of the possible unique characteristics which it involves. Quasi-state tourism is considerable in size: at least thirty-five million tourists travelled between states conforming to the above definition of a quasi-state in 1990 (World Tourism Organization (WTO) 1991), and these flows are a major facet of tourism in specific parts of the world, East Asia in particular. Little attention has been paid to this topic in the literature, although the nature of tourism in and between quasi-states has been noted in the *International Tourism Reports* of The Economist Intelligence Unit (1988, 1990, 1992). However, this specific aspect of tourism was not treated explicitly in those reports. Edwards (1990) in his study *Far East and Pacific Travel in the 1990s* did recognize quasi-state tourism as a unique feature but, again, did not study such tourism in a systematic manner.

Thus tourism between these units does not fit easily into the literature or models dealing with conventional tourism. There is little theoretical discussion about the nature and scope of such tourism, along with an absence of comprehensive theoretical models or foundations dealing with the spatial aspects of this type of tourism. Pearce (1987, 1989) has made significant efforts to address some of these deficiencies and suggested possible approaches to the study of the spatial aspects of international tourism; however, such reviews and discussion represent only a first step towards the formulation of more widely accepted comprehensive theories and models relating to tourism patterns and effects. The rapid proliferation of quasi-states in the late 1980s and early 1990s, along with the disappearance of others, would suggest that this issue is likely to increase in significance rather than decline.

The description and definition of tourism has received considerable attention, of course, and tourism is often subdivided on the basis of factors such as length of stay of visitors, motivations, expenditure, nationality, group characteristics and trip characteristics (Dann 1993). In addition, perhaps the most common categorization is that relating to the political aspect of the trip, that is, whether or not an international boundary is crossed during the course of the trip. If that is the case, then the tourist is defined as an international tourist, while those travellers who remain within their country of residence will be defined as domestic tourists. Dann (1993) has already commented critically upon the limitations of relying on nationality as a criterion for defining tourism, and the over-simplified categorization into domestic and international is similarly vulnerable to criticism because this categorization also ignores a significant element of tourism, namely, that between quasi-states. As long as one political unit has claim to, or feels entitled to regard another unit as part of itself, it may choose to disregard visitors from that unit as foreign, and treat them as domestic tourists (as was the case of visitors from the former East Germany to West Germany before reunification), if it even records their visitation at all.

To appreciate why this may occur, it is necessary to consider briefly what a political boundary is. A political boundary is generally thought of as a static line on a map which bounds a homogeneous area and separates it from one or more different areas. In reality, a political boundary, especially an international one, is both a set of complicated attributes and a process of culture, economics, and politics, rather than a static line. Boundaries in many cases tend to be dynamic, indeed in some cases the feature used as a boundary, such as a river, may have the potential to move rapidly and significantly. It may be more appropriate to think of a boundary as a continuum:

Boundary —— semi/quasi-boundary —— non-boundary.

Between the two extremes there may exist the often temporary boundary denoting a quasi-state. This boundary may evolve in either direction: it may become a permanent international boundary (as much as these are ever permanent), or it may disappear if and when the quasi-state(s) become(s) part of another unit. A comprehensive and dynamic classification of tourism should, therefore, include this indeterminate form of tourism, that is, tourism between anomalous political units, or tourists crossing a semi/quasi-boundary. Figure 6.1 illustrates the dynamic political nature of tourism involving quasi-states, and the three types of tourism suggested, international, domestic, and what for the moment might be called transitional.

One of the characteristics of quasi-states as noted above is the establishment of boundaries *after* a pattern of economic, cultural and other activities has been established. The superimposition of such a boundary may or may not interfere with such established patterns, among them, travel and tourism. Tourists and other travellers may have to modify their previous behaviour because of the establishment of one or more quasi-states. In some cases previous travel patterns may become prohibited and travel between the new political units may cease or be rerouted. In other cases travel may begin or grow between the new units because of new economic or cultural opportunities which appear. There is

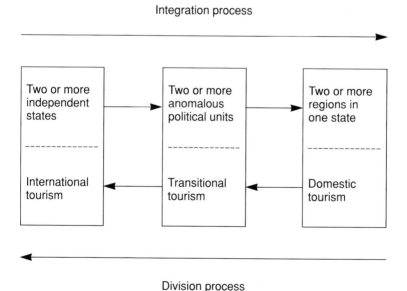

Figure 6.1 The political process and tourism classification

certainly little likelihood that travel will be symmetrical and reciprocal between such political units, as one characteristic of many quasi-states is the artificial and forced nature of their establishment, and quite often aggrievement on at least one side, if not both.

The aspect of reciprocity in tourism between political units is a topic which has received some attention in the literature. Williams and Zelinsky (1970) discussed this at some length in their article on tourist flows, and it is implicit in some multiorigin and destination models on international tourist flows, as for example the one produced by Thurot (1980) cited in Pearce (1989: 2–3).

> Thurot distinguishes between supply and demand and between domestic (or internal) and international tourism. Part of the demand for tourism generated in country B, probably the larger part, will be fulfilled by that country's tourist facilities with the remainder being distributed to countries A and C. At the same time, part of the demand from country A will be channelled to country B (and to country C), which thereby becomes an international destination as well as a source of international travellers. In contrast, no international demand is shown to emanate from country C, although it may generate domestic tourists and receive tourists from countries A and B. Country C is said to represent certain Third World countries where standards of living may generally be insufficient to generate international tourism (although often a small élite may indulge in a large amount of such travel) and Soviet bloc countries where severe restrictions on international travel may exist.

The basic supposition of Thurot's argument was that while developed countries generated both domestic and international tourist flows, with their international tourists going to both developed and undeveloped countries, the developing countries and communist bloc countries generated only domestic tourism because of a lack of economic ability to create surpluses necessary to sustain international external tourism. However, there is clear evidence that this supposition, which was first proposed in 1980, has become less accurate since its conception, as some developing countries and certainly several communist countries (even before the break up of the Soviet Union) have, in fact, produced significant numbers of international tourists (WTO 1991). It is true, however, that much of this international travel was traditionally confined to travel between developing countries, or with other member states of the communist bloc. Lower, and often subsidized travel costs between these countries explain much of this pattern of travel. It should be borne in mind also that much of the world's religious travel emanates from and is destined to developing countries (Richter Chapter Five), in particular, the mass travel of Muslims from primarily developing countries to Mecca and other religious sites. In the specific context of quasi-states, considerable travel may occur from the less developed unit to the more developed one. It should be noted also that it was not only the communist bloc which imposed restrictions upon travel, as many developed countries still have restrictions upon the granting of even tourist visas to some tourists from developing countries, and some developing countries have strict controls on outbound travel of their residents.

It is necessary to consider in a little more detail some of the assumptions about travel from developing countries. It is not unreasonable to agree with Thurot's supposition that it is primarily economic factors which keep travel from developing countries to developed ones at a low level. Distances involved are often considerable, travel is therefore expensive, and may be even more expensive for those wishing to travel the 'wrong way', that is, against the predominant flow of traffic. Travel costs in developed countries are frequently far higher, in relative, and in some cases absolute terms, than in developing countries. However, travel between developing countries also may follow different rules to those between developed countries. Motivations of tourists between developing countries may be much more heavily biased towards pilgrimage, visiting friends and relatives, shopping, business and culture, rather than the more blatantly hedonistic pursuits of mass tourists from developed countries. A modified model of mass tourist flows can be suggested, therefore, and is illustrated in Figure 6.2, which shows four hypothetical countries (A, B, C and D) divided into two basic groups (developed-core, and developing-periphery).

Three basic types of tourism flows are depicted, domestic tourism (within a country's own boundaries), tourism *within* the basic group, that is, developed or developing countries, and tourism *between* the basic groups. At the level of mass tourism, developed countries generate all three types of tourism, while developing countries generate only the first two types. Given the

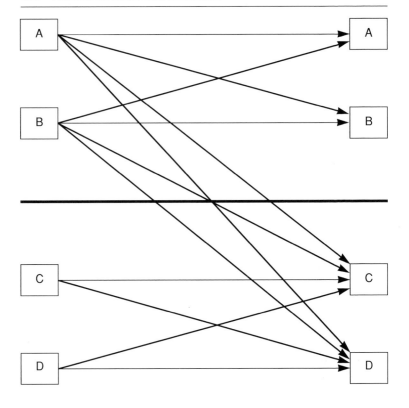

Figure 6.2 Tourism flows in a world system
Source: After Thurot 1980

dynamic nature of the political process and of tourism, any particular state may change position within such a model at relatively short notice, and the flows become altered accordingly. While Williams and Zelinsky (1970) showed that in 1970 there was remarkable consistency in the patterns of global tourist flows, it is likely that changes in the political scene and in technology, especially in the field of transportation, have not only altered some of these earlier patterns, but also made them less static and more dynamic, as noted earlier in this volume (Butler Chapter One). Pearce (1987) elaborated and analysed the geographic dimensions of tourism, and explored further the nature of international and domestic tourist flows, and the role of factors in shaping these flows, including the effect of gateways, a feature which is of considerable importance in the context of some quasi-states.

CHARACTERISTICS OF QUASI-STATES

In a discussion such as this, where the focus is upon tourism rather than political processes, it is only possible to describe briefly the principal characteristics of what have been termed quasi-states. The term itself may cause problems in some quarters, particularly in those cases where a state has been established and received general recognition for a considerable time. However, as noted earlier, it is meant to imply that the political units concerned betray signs of incongruency with some or all aspects of economic, cultural, linguistic, religious and racial significance. It is unwise to attempt to generalize too broadly as each quasi-state has its own unique historical context, but there are some characteristics which would appear to be most common to, and perhaps characterize, quasi-states:

1 Adjacent Location; many quasi-states are located adjacent to one another, reflecting the fact that, in many cases, they were part of the same larger political unit, for example Ireland and Northern Ireland, South and North Korea.
2 Shared Culture and Language; political and often military separation does not automatically remove a shared cultural and linguistic history, and many quasi-states share either or both of these features, especially when they are adjacent and have a common 'parent' unit.
3 Kinships; family relationships often transcend the boundaries of quasi-states, and indeed, may be a major factor in the development or continuation of travel and tourism between units.
4 Recency; many of the quasi-states currently in existence are relatively recent creations, the vast majority appearing after the end of World War II, and as noted earlier, many of them are the direct results of that conflict. A few, especially in Europe, for example Northern Ireland, have a considerably longer history.
5 Different Political Systems; related quasi-states quite frequently have differing political systems, and this difference may account for the creation of the individual units. It may also be the cause of continued non-recognition or hostility between units, for example South and North Korea.
6 Different Religious Affiliation; as with the political factor, this may be a key aspect for the establishment of the units, and a major reason for the continued separate identities, for example in the case of India and Pakistan.

7 Different Economic Levels of Development; this aspect is normally a result of other differences rather than a cause of the establishment of one or more quasi-states, for example, in the case of East and West Germany before reunification, although severe inequality in regional development may make the case for separation stronger.
8 Travel Restrictions; a frequent characteristic of quasi-states is the existence of restrictions upon movement of people into and/or out of the states, and such restrictions are quite often aimed specifically at residents of, or visitors to, related quasi-states. Again, in many cases the existence of restrictions may be one sided and not reciprocal, for example between Cyprus and the Turkish Republic of North Cyprus (Lockhart 1993).

Clearly, these features are not confined to quasi-states. Many states have travel restrictions, although considerably fewer than in the past, and the other similarities and differences noted above can apply to many neighbouring countries. However, it is a characteristic of quasi-states that many of these features are common to them.

TOURISM BETWEEN QUASI-STATES

It was suggested earlier that tourism between quasi-states may be different to what is thought of as conventional tourism between conventional states. As noted above, the existence of travel restrictions is a common occurrence between quasi-states and this can give rise to unusual and distinctive travel patterns. Figure 6.3 illustrates five of these patterns in a diagrammatic fashion.

The first case illustrated is that of the Republic of Ireland and Northern Ireland, where there is no restriction on tourism and travel between the two neighbouring quasi-states, despite the political and civil unrest which exists in Northern Ireland. Since the creation of the Republic of Ireland (Eire) in 1923, travel between the North and South has remained virtually restriction free and is reciprocal, and as Wilson (1993: 142) has noted, 'tourism developments in Northern Ireland and the Republic of Ireland are not independent of one another'. However, Eire has a separate category for visitors from Northern Ireland, listing visitors as 'overseas', 'domestic' and 'Northern Ireland' (Bord Failte 1989).

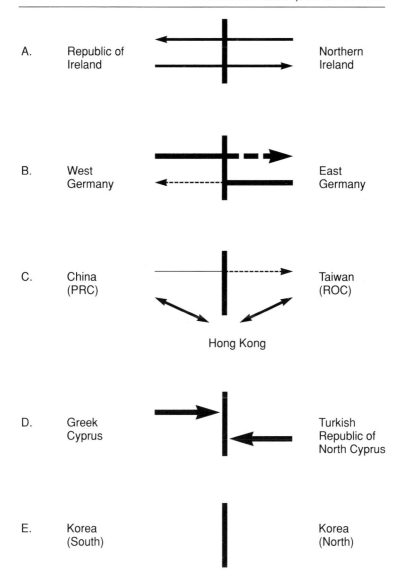

Figure 6.3 Tourist flows in quasi-states

The second case is the example of the former West Germany and East Germany before reunification. Following World War II, Germany evolved into two states, both of which proclaimed sovereignty and the constitutional right to establish common institutions throughout Germany. The superimposed military cease-fire line of 1945 became a physical and political boundary and served as the front line between the communist and non-communist forces. The freedom of travel within the former Germany was suspended with the closing of most zonal frontiers and the establishment of a security zone, epitomized by the construction of the Berlin Wall. In the initial years of division immediately following the end of World War II, both countries restricted travel between each other.

Their relationship improved in 1972 after the signing of the Basic Treaty and agreement was reached on cross-border tourist movement, although with differing policies. The more developed of the two quasi-states (the Federal Republic of Germany, or West Germany) was open to visitation and for visitation abroad by its residents, while the less developed partner (the German Democratic Republic, or East Germany) had severe travel restrictions for all of its existence. In other words, West Germany allowed its residents to visit East Germany and East Germans to visit West Germany without restriction, while East Germany placed restrictions upon all visitors from outside the communist bloc, allowing West Germans to visit East Germany only using a Forced Currency Exchange. East German travel to the Federal Republic, far from being a universal right, was granted only with a high degree of selectivity, generally only to those of pensionable age or those on urgent family business, and then rarely to all members of a family at the same time. Thus before reunification one state was an open system and one effectively a closed system for tourism, with the flow of tourists being primarily one way, from West to East, between the two quasi-states.

In the 1960s and 1970s around 1.4 million West Germans visited East Berlin annually, and some 3.3 million visits were made by West Berliners to East Germany (Whetten 1980). In contrast, only around 42,000 non-pensioners and one million pensioners visited West Germany annually from East Germany. When the Berlin Wall came down in 1989, and the communist regime toppled along with it, the number of tourists from East to West rose dramatically, with overnight visitation from East to West rising by over 55 per cent in

1989 from the 1988 figure (WTO 1991). In the first three months of 1990 alone, over four million people from East Germany visited West Germany. The Federal Republic of Germany, as the Republic of Ireland (see above), never did formally recognize visitors from what it viewed as the other part of the country as foreigners. Tourists were classified as 'visitors from the Democratic Republic of Germany', and 'foreign' and 'domestic' tourists (Federal Republic of Germany 1989). Since reunification in 1991, *de facto* international tourism has ceased between what were two quasi-states.

The third case illustrated in Figure 6.3 is that of China and Taiwan. In 1949 communists achieved power in mainland China, and the nationalists withdrew to Taiwan and other islands, establishing a separate state. Since 1949 China has been separated into two quasi-states, the People's Republic of China (PRC) on the mainland, and the Republic of China (ROC), the island of Taiwan, each refusing to recognize the other and each claiming to be the official and only Chinese government. Tourist relations did not exist between the two states until 1978. In that year PRC allowed Taiwanese residents to visit the mainland, but few could take advantage as ROC restricted travel by its residents to mainland China until 1987. In 1987 ROC allowed its residents to travel to mainland China but only via a third country gateway, and still did not allow PRC residents to visit Taiwan. In this case, therefore, there is a non-direct flow of tourists from ROC to PRC via a gateway, but no reciprocal flow. Hong Kong has emerged as the primary gateway in this situation because of its location, cultural background and political organization (Chow 1988). Exactly what will happen in 1997 when Hong Kong reverts from British rule back to PRC remains to be seen. In the short term Macao, the Portuguese territory, may take over as the principal gateway for ROC residents travelling to mainland China, and will have an international airport completed by 1995, but its future in that role will presumably change in 1999 when it too reverts back to PRC control. Thus in this situation, as in the case of Germany, *de facto* international tourism will become domestic tourism once the political reunification is complete.

The fourth case illustrated in Figure 6.3 is that of Cyprus, which was a British colony until it received independence in 1963, and continued as a separate state until 1974 (Frendo 1993). In that year the unrest between the Greek and Turkish segments of the population erupted into civil war, resulting in an invasion by Turkish troops and *de facto* partition of the island. This partition has remained in effect since then, peace being maintained by United Nations troops. Since 1974 tourism has been developed extensively in the southern (Greek) portion of the island (Andronikou 1988), but disappeared to almost nothing in the northern, Turkish segment, although this was originally the site of most tourism development prior to partition (Lockhart 1993). Travel between the two parts of the island is almost non-existent owing to the restrictions imposed. Travel by visitors from the Greek side to the Turkish side is allowed if no overnight stop is involved and return must be through the same crossing point. Entry to the Turkish Republic of North Cyprus from any other location results in prohibition of return to both the Greek part of Cyprus and Greece itself, and probable prohibition of future visitation to both the Greek part of Cyprus and Greece. On the other hand, there are no restrictions on entry to the Turkish Republic of North Cyprus, although that state is only recognized by Turkey. The pattern of visitation between the two quasi-states is therefore minimal, although both are now pursuing aggressive tourism development policies to attract visitors from other countries (Lockhart 1993).

The final example of tourism between quasi-states is that between South and North Korea. Korea has been divided into two parts since 1945, and governments of both parts refuse to issue visas to nationals of the other part, as both view the division as temporary and do not recognize the validity of the other regime. There is, therefore, currently no tourism between this pair of quasi-states, although recently both sides have agreed to discuss the possibility of tourist travel between themselves (Kim and Crompton 1990). International tourist visitation to South Korea has grown rapidly in recent years, spurred by the Olympic Games, hosted in 1988. However, tourist visitation to North Korea is low and mostly confined to communist bloc residents (WTO 1991).

THE DYNAMICS OF QUASI-STATE TOURISM

The level of dynamism of quasi-states has already been emphasized. The disintegration of the former Soviet Union and Yugoslavia, and the reunification of Germany, are dramatic examples within the last five years. In some cases, however, the changes in status of political units are planned and predictable, even if the effects of such changes on tourism are not. In 1997 Hong Kong will revert to Chinese control under the Sino-British agreement, and Macao will follow in 1999. While the disappearance of these two quasi-states is widely known and anticipated, the likely effects upon tourism as a result are much less certain. One obvious effect will be that from the point of view of official statistics, international tourism in the region will decline, as travel by residents of Hong Kong, Macao and PRC between these areas will become technically domestic tourism.

The above example also illustrates another aspect of tourism between quasi-states, which reflects relationships between former imperial powers and their dependencies, both past and present. These relationships vary in character but affect the nature of tourism and the way travel is recorded in some instances. In many cases, while there may be few restrictions on tourism in either direction, the classification of tourists may differ markedly between the dependency and the imperial power, with the dependency tending to classify tourists from its 'protector' as foreign, while the imperial power tends to classify tourists from its dependencies as domestic. For example, the Pacific island of Guam, a dependency of the USA, records visitors from the USA as 'foreign' tourists, while the USA records visitors from Guam as 'non-foreign' tourists. As former imperialist powers such as France, Great Britain and the USA eventually relieve themselves of their remaining colonies and dependencies, further changes in the recording, and perhaps the pattern, of tourism can be expected.

The example of the Chinese states serves to emphasize that most quasi-states are temporary units only, although some may have a longer lifespan than is often anticipated. Others can find their status suddenly and violently changed, as with the armed acquisition of Kuwait by Iraq, which prompted the Gulf War in order to restore the *status quo*. Given this temporary status, one may argue that all quasi-states are transitional, evolving in one of two directions; either they will become completely independent and gain universal recognition, or they will integrate again, either peacefully or through military action. As a result of these processes of separation and integration, quasi-state tourism will similarly evolve into two categories, international tourism if the quasi-states become fully independent, or domestic tourism if they integrate into one unit. These processes are illustrated in Figure 6.4.

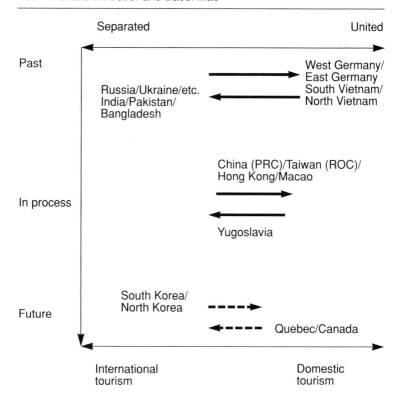

Figure 6.4 The dynamic process of quasi-state tourism

Eight examples serve to illustrate the process. As noted above, in the case of Germany, two independent quasi-states emerged after World War II, and the tourist flows between them developed in a non-reciprocal manner. With the collapse of communism and the Berlin Wall, tourism between the two units reached an all time high in early 1990. Reunification has meant that all tourism within Germany by Germans is now domestic tourism, rather than international. A similar situation, resolved in this case by war, has occurred in Vietnam. The next examples in Figure 6.4 are of quasi-states which have normalized their relationships and to all intents and purposes have become fully fledged independent states. These include India, Pakistan and Bangladesh and the former Soviet Union. In such cases the tourist flows tend to become regular as international relations have been stabilized. Even in such cases, however, anomalous situations still exist. A large proportion of the

tourist traffic between India and Pakistan is not recorded as international tourism, and visitors between these countries often do not
show in the visitor statistics of either country. It is unclear what, if
anything, is recorded on tourist arrivals in the disputed territory of
Kashmir. The exact nature of tourism between the now independent elements of the USSR remains to be seen, but will be
recorded as international tourism.

In the case of China, which split into the four segments noted
above (PRC, ROC, Hong Kong and Macao), international tourism
has gradually grown between most of the segments, albeit with the
use of third states as gateways in one case. With the return of Hong
Kong and Macao to PRC in 1997 and 1999 respectively, a considerable portion of PRC's international tourist numbers will be
replaced by domestic tourism, and as ROC engages in talks with
PRC, travel between these two segments may increase markedly
(Guangrui 1993). If such talks break down, however, no ROC
residents will visit PRC because their currently required third state
gateways (Hong Kong and Macao) will no longer be available. On
the other hand, Yugoslavia is still in the process of its final subdivision, and when peace is finally attained one can assume
considerable travel will develop between its newly independent
parts.

The example of South and North Korea illustrates a potential
starting point for tourism between two quasi-states. However,
whether such travel, when it begins, will be regarded and recorded
as international or domestic remains to be seen. Under normal
conditions it would be regarded as international until such time as
the two Koreas reunite, whence it would become domestic. In the
case of Canada, where there is the possibility of a division of
the country with the current province of Quebec becoming a
separate state, tourism between Quebec and the rest of Canada
would likely continue but become classified as international, rather
than domestic.

CONCLUSIONS AND IMPLICATIONS

This discussion has endeavoured to show that the conventional
breakdown of tourism into the categories of international and
domestic does not deal adequately with the considerable numbers
of tourists between quasi-states. Conventional models of tourism
also tend to ignore the extremely dynamic nature of tourism

between such political units. In the context of the Middle East, at the end of 1993 considerable progress had been made in securing a lasting peace between Israel and its Arab neighbours. To many of the Arab states, Israel is at best a quasi-state, and this is reflected in a number of ways. One which has particular relevance to this discussion is the insistence of some states that visitors holding Israeli passports, or even those foreigners whose passports carry Israeli immigration stamps, are not allowed admittance to their countries. As a result, some visitors to Israel, especially frequent business visitors, either hold two passports, one for use in entering Israel, and one for use elsewhere, or request that their passport not be stamped by Israeli immigration officials, a request which is regularly honoured. In either case visitors are recorded by Israeli authorities as having entered Israel, but their documents do not reveal this. If a permanent peace is secured in the Middle East, and Israel loses its quasi-state status with its neighbours, such subterfuge will not be necessary.

Other issues arise, however, which bear further investigation. Given the nature of the origin and establishment of many of the quasi-states, it is likely that the motivations of at least some of the tourists themselves are different from those of tourists between more conventional political units. A significant proportion of the tourists between quasi-states may be motivated by ties of kinship and be involved in visiting friends and relatives, with a much lower proportion than normal being purely pleasure- and recreation-seeking visitors. Pearce (1992) notes that 54 per cent of all visitors to the Republic of Ireland stay with friends and relatives, and that this proportion is over 70 per cent in the case of visitors from Britain. Wilson (1993: 143) quotes figures which suggest that half of the reasons given for visiting Northern Ireland relate to 'visiting friends and relatives', a figure more than twice the level given by visitors to Great Britain or the Republic of Ireland, and the next most common reason given was 'business', with the conventional reason 'holiday' only reaching third in popularity. In addition, other motivations would appear to include a higher proportion of business trips, often reflecting traditional economic linkages developed prior to separation, and shopping trips, and associated with these is a higher level of repeat and regular visitation (Edwards 1990: 48–49; The Economist Intelligence Unit 1992; Wilson 1993).

If these suggested differences in motivations and types of

tourists are accurate, then there are significant implications for the impacts of such tourists and the facilities which they require and use. Little demand on conventional tourist facilities is made by many tourists whose motivation is to visit friends and relatives, especially in quasi-state situations, where there may be great disparities between living standards and political regimes in the two states. Costs for many of the tourists will be low, and because of this, the average income level of such tourists can be significantly lower than that of the average international tourist. Lengths of stay can be expected to be longer than for the average international tourist, although in the case of frequent business tourists, as elsewhere, these are likely to be short. Clearly, many of these points are conjecture at this time, and considerably more research needs to be done on the types of tourists between and to quasi-states, their motivations and activities.

Given the dynamic nature of the quasi-states themselves, it would be expected that the tourists generated by and attracted to these anomalous political units are also likely to change over time. Indeed, the possibly temporary nature of quasi-states, for example the limited future of Hong Kong and Macao, or the reappearance of former states, for example Estonia, Latvia and Lithuania, may prompt tourist visitation, first out of curiosity or a desire to visit before they disappear, and then for more conventional, hedonistic reasons. The existence of borders in themselves would also appear to be a tourist attraction, and this is perhaps even more the case where political anomalies such as quasi-states exist. At the height of the Cold War, Checkpoint Charlie in Berlin, perhaps the most infamous of the crossing points of the Berlin Wall, was a popular tourist feature. A major tourist attraction in Korea is the De-Militarized Zone (DMZ), where the border or cease-fire line between North and South Korea can be visited, albeit with some slight potential element of risk. So popular is the site at Panmunjon that regular tours operate from Seoul to the DMZ on most days of the week, in conjunction with American and United Nations forces. Crossing borders, as opposed to merely visiting them, is also appealing to some tourists, perhaps more so when there is an element of snobbery, uncertainty, challenge, or even, within acceptable limits, risk. Certainly some of the appeal of visiting places such as East Germany by non-Germans, or North Vietnam before reunification, was the excitement and difficulty of such an expedition.

This discussion has only begun to explore one aspect of tourism which has been given little attention in the past. As the world's political situation seems unlikely to suddenly assume a static form, given its highly chaotic nature since 1945, and especially since 1985, it is reasonable to conclude that tourism between quasi-states is likely to increase in the future and continue to be at odds with the established categories of tourism, suggesting the need for revision or elaboration of recording and classifying visitation between countries. It therefore becomes all the more important to determine where tourism to and between such states fits in the accepted models and theories of tourism.

REFERENCES

Andronikou, A. (1988) *Development of Tourism in Cyprus: Harmonization of Tourism with the Environment*, Nicosia: Cosmos.

Boal, F. and Douglas, N. (1982) *Integration and Division: Geographic Perspectives on the Northern Ireland Problem*, London: Academic Press.

Bord Failte (1989) *Tourism Facts 1988*, Dublin: Bord Failte.

Chow, W.S. (1988) 'Open policy and tourism between Guangdong and Hong Kong', *Annals of Tourism Research* 5, 2: 205–218.

Dann, G. (1993) 'Limitations in the use of "nationality" and "country of residence" variables', in D.G. Pearce and R.W. Butler (eds) *Tourism Research: Critiques and Challenges*, London: Routledge, 88–112.

The Economist Intelligence Unit (1988, 1990, 1992) *International Tourism Reports*, London: The Economist Intelligence Unit.

Edwards, A. (1990) *Far East and Pacific Travel in the 1990s*, London: The Economist Intelligence Unit.

Federal Republic of Germany (1989) *Statistiches Bundesamt*, FRG Bonn.

Frendo, H. (1993) 'The legacy of colonialism: The experience of Malta and Cyprus', in D.G. Lockhart, D. Drakakis-Smith and J. Schembri (eds) *The Development Process in Small Island States*, London: Routledge, 151–160.

Glassner, M and de Blij, H. (1989) *Systematic Political Geography*, New York: John Wiley & Sons.

Guangrui, Z. (1993) 'Tourism across the Taiwan Straits', *Tourism Management* 14, 3: 228–231.

Kim, Y. and Crompton, J.L. (1990) 'Role of tourism in unifying the two Koreas', *Annals of Tourism Research* 17, 3: 353–366.

Lockhart, D. G. (1993) 'Tourism and politics: The example of Cyprus', in D.G., Lockhart, D. Drakakis-Smith and J. Schembri (eds) *The Development Process in Small Island States*, London: Routledge, 228–246.

Maclean's (1993) 3 August, Toronto: Maclean's.

Mowlana, H. and Smith, G. (1991) 'Tourism as international relations: Linkages between telecommunications, technology and transnational banking', *World Travel and Tourism Review* 1: 215–218.

Pearce, D.G. (1987) *Tourism Today: A Geographic Analysis*, New York: Longman.
—— (1989) *Tourism Development*, London: Longman.
—— (1992) *Tourist Organization*, London: Longman.
Richter, L. (1989) *The Politics of Tourism in Asia*, Honolulu: University of Hawaii Press.
Thurot, J.M. (1980) 'Capacité de charge et production touristique', *Études et Mémoires* No. 43, Aix-en-Provénce: Centre des Hautes Études Touristiques.
Whetten, L.L. (1980) *East and West: Conflicts, Collaboration, and Confrontation*, New York: New York University Press.
Williams, A.V. and Zelinsky, W. (1970) 'On some patterns in international tourist flows', *Economic Geography* 46, 4: 549–567.
Wilson, D. (1993) 'Tourism, public policy and the image of Northern Ireland since the troubles', in B. O'Connor and M.Cronin (eds) *Tourism in Ireland: A Critical Analysis*, Cork: Cork University Press, 138–161.
World Tourism Organization (1991) *International Tourism Statistics*, Madrid: WTO.

Chapter 7

A socio-linguistic approach towards changing tourist imagery

Graham Dann

The projection of an appropriate destination image has been described as a vital element in tourism marketing (Ryan 1991: 170). At the same time, 'image' is reckoned to be 'a critical factor in a traveller's decision to visit an area' (Gartner and Hunt 1987: 16). Generally speaking, positive images result in increased visitation, and the latter in turn affects destination imagery (Gartner and Shen 1992: 47).

Essentially three processes are at work: image projection/ formation; selection of the destination from competing images; and image reinforcement or modification as a result of the travel experience. The first is a dual process since it relates to image formation in the tourist and how this is effected by various agents. Gunn (1972) distinguishes the latter into 'organic' and 'induced' according to whether they are based on visitation experience (either of self or of others) or on external factors linked to the tourism industry which project selective images of the destination (Nash Chapter Three; Graburn Chapter Four). Gartner (1993) proposes a more sophisticated scheme in which he subdistinguishes 'induced' agents into 'overt 1' (that is, travel advertising, brochures), 'overt 2' (information from tour operators), 'covert 1' (testimonies from celebrities and satisfied customers) and 'covert 2' (independent endorsement through travel writing). 'Organic' agents, on the other hand, are either based on visitation by self or of others. In the latter case they are subdistinguished into 'solicited' (sought out information from friends, relatives and other visitors) and 'unsolicited' (information provided by tourists other than self). He also introduces 'autonomous' sources such as independent news stories, documentaries and TV sitcoms, since these often have significant impacts on image formation and image change. While 'induced' agents, with the occasional exception of travelogues (Dann 1992a), present positive images, 'organic' and 'autonomous' sources are additionally capable of providing neutral and negative images.

The second process (Gartner 1993) assumes a funnel-like structure through which the potential tourist narrows down the options from a universe of all possible destinitions to a final holiday choice (Goodall 1991). Critically informing this decision are the various 'pull' motives linked to the destination's attractions and the extent to which these correspond to the 'push' motives of the potential traveller (Dann 1981).

The third process, and the one most pertinent to the general theme of this volume, focuses on image change and the degree to which such modification can occur as the result of the vacation experience. Thus, Gartner and Hunt (1987), for instance, found that respondents who had visited the state of Utah in the past were more impressed with its current attributes and attractions than those who had never been there. At the same time, they reported that persons who resided in areas closest to Utah (where most of the promotion had been targeted) also tended to hold the most favourable images of that state. Consequently, the authors concluded, an amelioration of image may involve a combination of induced and organic factors (that is, process one).

For the latter reason, there are a number of studies which relate image change to the projection and formation stage (Gartner and Shen 1992), for example, the effect of the adverse publicity surrounding the Tiananmen Square episode on subsequent images of the People's Republic of China. Indeed, it is probably true to say that most of the research on tourism imagery can be found dealing with this initial process with a corresponding strong emphasis on Gartner's (1993) 'overt 1' sources, for example Cohen's (1989) study of jungle tour advertisements in Thailand, and a number of works on brochures from a variety of theoretical perspectives (for example, Buck 1977; Thurot and Thurot 1983; Uzzell 1984; Selwyn 1992). Research on 'overt 2' sources (for example, Gartner and Bachri in press) is less frequent, as indeed is that relating to 'covert 1' and 'covert 2' sources (Dann 1992a). While 'autonomous' and 'organic' agents have generally been examined more in relation to image change than initial formation (Phelps 1986), there are also some studies such as by Paradice (1985) which have explored the importance of 'word of mouth' advertising on image formation.

However, and in spite of these worthwhile attempts to understand the complexities of tourism imagery, there are some methodological problems which remain unresolved. Gartner (1993), for instance, complains that adequate baseline data are not always unearthed by researchers, thereby rendering problematic investigations of image formation and image change. More specifically, Gartner and Hunt (1987: 15) maintain that it is not sufficient simply to measure the comparative advantages and disadvantages of destinations as assessed by prospective travellers. The perceptions and images underpinning these evaluations must also be explored. Chalfen (1985) makes a similar point when he argues that much of the content analysis of promotional material disregards the groups to which it has been targeted, together with the various cognitive processes of the potential tourist in responding to the stimuli of messages sent by operators, advertisers and the designers of brochures. He thus calls for an ethnographic semiotic approach along the lines proposed by Worth (1977) in order to remedy the situation.

Of course, there are some exceptions to the above charges of methodological weakness, for example Gottlieb (1982: 166–168) who argued in favour of direct conversations and interviews with vacationers in order to gain a participant point of view rather than imposing *a priori* categories of the researcher on respondents. Pearce (1982), too, preferred to generate his qualitative data inductively from tourists themselves and how they defined their own situations, as opposed to measuring their responses to the preconceived stimuli of a survey instrument. He later justified his 'emic' perspective with reference to a career model of tourist motivation (Pearce 1993). Other works in this vein include studies by Weaver and McCleary (1984), Marsh (1986) and Olsen *et al.* (1986).

However, while all of the immediately foregoing are interested in what tourists are saying, few seem as concerned about the ways in which tourists articulate imagery. More pertinently, there seems to be a gap in the literature between the content of attitude and its socio-linguistic form. Yet, with a growing emphasis on niche marketing and various sophisticated types of segmentation (Mazanec Chapter Eight), one surely needs to know a lot more about the language of the tourist if the discourse of promotion is to target successfully. When one realizes at the same time that such language is constantly changing on account of real or virtual

experiences (Cohen Chapter Two), it becomes increasingly important to monitor such change. Indeed, tourism research in the 1990s
may well switch attention to how the travel trade organizes its
imagery in order to fit the growing and rapidly changing imagery
produced by the consumer. In this sense, early studies by Boorstin
(1987) on the hyping of pseudo events, Buck (1977) on the tauto-
logical messages of brochures and their function in preserving
exotic groups such as the Amish from the prying gaze of visitors,
and the works of Gritti (1967) and Mohamed (1988) on tourism's
language of social control, should assume renewed significance.
So also should research conducted by McCullough (1977) and
Andrew (1977) which respectively examined variation in image
articulation by tourists and travel agents, and the effects of holiday
brochure format on the image descriptions of their audiences.

A further justification for concentrating on the neglected
area of language is derived from the theoretical position that
images (whether mental, verbal or pictorial) are articulated socio-
linguistically. Not only do the induced images of tourism's promotional photographs have meanings through the anchorage and
relay provided by accompanying commentaries (Barthes 1982),
they also enjoy a semiotic autonomy with a pictorial grammar
and messages of their own (Lindekens 1971; Eco 1979; Nöth
1990: 450–455). On the one hand, such pictures evoke a closed or
focused discourse which draws on selective and sometimes exag-
gerated cultural markers in order to provide a mental grid for
tourists to filter their perceptions and expectations (Albers and
James 1988; Nash Chapter Three). On the other, they are open
texts with several layers of meaning ranging from metanymic to
metaphorical (Cohen 1993), denotative to connotative. It thus
becomes important to analyse the different levels of decipherment
and interpretation offered by potential tourists towards whom
these pluriform messages have been transmitted (Cohen et al.
1992). Moreover, since the appeal of the image is primarily
addressed in terms of life's major problems (Langholz-Leymore
1975), personality (Mayo and Jarvis 1981) and the socio-
psychological needs of the consumer (Uzzell 1984), or what
Urbain (1989) describes as 'the narrating consciousness of the
leisure traveller', it becomes crucial to focus on the multiple
ways in which responses to such imagery are articulated. The additional recognition that images may arise subjectively as illusory
devices to replace reality with more extravagant expectations of

strangeness than the world naturally offers (Boorstin 1987) suggests that there is a need to investigate how such illusions are created and socio-linguistically framed.

In spite of the many advantages of concentrating on touristic discourse, there are nevertheless a few dangers associated with socio-linguistic analyses which require a brief comment. The first of these difficulties relates to the high dross rate often encountered in conversation analysis and the recurrence (in English at least) of such verbs as 'to be' and 'to have', along with the frequent appearance of personal pronouns and possessive adjectives. One way of minimizing this problem (and a strategy followed in the current investigation) is to restrict the content analysis of articulated touristic imagery to nouns and adjectives, together with respective gerunds and gerundives. Also, for reasons of simplicity, where respondents are unable or unwilling to verbalize images, such replies can be conveniently treated as absent data.

A second area which may be methodologically hazardous is the measurement of language change as a result of one or more intervening factors. Here it can be objected that to ask tourists about a situation in the past (for example, what image they had of a destination prior to visitation) is to rely too heavily on memory, and this in turn could lead to distorted replies. Some researchers (for example Phelps 1986) attempt to reduce this difficulty by conducting their studies longitudinally. In contrast, this writer takes the view that such multiphasing is not only complex and expensive, but is also quite unnecessary in the current context. As Boulding (1956: 5–6) points out, one's stock of knowledge is based on personal history through which images of the world are fashioned. It is, therefore, quite legitimate to pose even hypothetical questions about the past. After all, if people can be asked where they would like to live (permanently), and the replies are framed within the context of recalled pleasant experiences (Gould and White 1970: 18), surely a similar strategy can be employed in relation to the temporary relocation associated with travel.

A third problem area surrounds the evocation of images and language by induced stimuli, particularly where these occur in a pre-trip setting. Here it is maintained that the use of induced material to call forth past images can be justified by Urbain's (1989) observation that the very essence of tourism advertising is grounded in individual and collective memory. Moreover, the images portrayed by advertisers in which sights are recreated and reproduced for the consumer are effective precisely because they can be preserved for moments or centuries (Berger 1972: 9–10). Alternatively stated, if a past experience has been found to be rewarding, it is this approach behaviour which is projected into the future by the advertiser to remedy dissatisfaction with the present (Dann 1993a).

THE PRESENT STUDY

Having noted the potentials and pitfalls of examining tourists' definitions of the situation through language, the present study seeks to build on and complement earlier research by exploring tourism imagery from a socio-linguistic participant standpoint. More specifically, the inquiry focuses on some 535 tourists visiting Barbados during the winter season of 1989. While other facets of the same study have been reported elsewhere (Dann 1992b, 1993b, forthcoming), including details concerning the representativeness of the sample, this section of the interview schedule sought to investigate:

(a) the ways in which respondents articulated open-ended images they held of the destination prior to arrival and without the benefit of pictorial stimuli,

(b) the effect of visitation on the foregoing internalized mental images (that is, whether or not socio-linguistic changes had taken place as a result of the travel experience),

(c) the formation of images in response to the introduction of induced agents (external pictorial stimuli) in a pre-trip setting,

(d) the modification of induced imagery in an on-trip setting.

Whereas points (a) and (c) refer to the process of image projection/formation, points (b) and (d) relate to image reinforcement or modification as a result of the travel experience. However, for purposes of presentation, (a) and (b) are treated as 'the socio-linguistics of images *without* pictorial stimuli' and (c) and (d) as 'the socio-linguistics of images *with* pictorial stimuli'.

The socio-linguistics of images without pictorial imagery

Mental images constituted unaided open-ended replies which tourists supplied in response to questions seeking information on images of Barbados (a) before they ever came to the island, and (b) now that they were there.

The transcripts of mental images comprised 521 pre-trip and 531 on-trip descriptions. With corresponding high response rates of 97.4 per cent and 99.2 per cent, the slight elevation in the latter figure is probably attributable to the effect of the travel experience.

Use of nouns

The first row of Table 7.1 shows the distribution of nouns employed. Here it can be seen that 162 nouns were common to both sets of descriptions (303–141; 358–196), a figure which exceeded the number of nouns specific to the pre-trip image, but one which was less than that registered for nouns specific to the on-trip image. In other words, the effect of travel resulted in richer imagery than did the lack of such experience. The point is reinforced with the realization that the mean frequency of use of the combined pre-trip nouns was 5.0, whereas in the second scenario it had dropped to 4.3. Alternatively stated, there was a greater linguistic limitation in the first instance, to the extent that a smaller number of words was being used with a higher frequency.

Table 7.1 Nouns and adjectives featured in pre-trip and on-trip mental images

	Pre-trip image			On-trip image		
	Number specific to pre-trip image	Total number employed	Overall frequency of total number	Number specific to on-trip image	Total number employed	Overall frequency of total number
Nouns	141	303	1506	196	358	1527
Adjectives	112	300	1616	259	447	1991

From the first column in Table 7.2, the total percentages reveal that the ten most frequently employed nouns accounted for over half of all description content in the case of pre-trip images and a still considerable, though lesser, amount with respect to on-trip images. When one recalls that the respective total number of nouns for each was 303 and 358 (Table 7.1), the usage of these ten words becomes highly significant. Furthermore, the first four nouns – 'island', 'people', 'place' and 'beach' – accounted for 34.8 per cent of all usage in the first situation and 31.4 per cent in the second.

Table 7.2 Top ten nouns with percentage frequencies

Pre-trip

Image	Picture 1	Picture 2	Picture 3	Picture 4	Overall
Island (10.4)	Place (11.1)	Service (12.7)	Church (19.6)	Rasta (6.7)	People (8.4)
People (9.0)	Island (7.7)	People (11.0)	People (14.8)	Jamaica (4.9)	Island (5.6)
Place (8.4)	Beach (7.1)	Woman (5.9)	Children (7.4)	Barbados (4.4)	Place (5.2)
Beach (7.0)	Sunset (7.0)	Person (4.5)	Religion (4.0)	Rastafari (4.1)	Church (3.7)
Weather (4.8)	Romance (6.0)	Motel (4.3)	School (3.3)	Rastaman (4.0)	Beach (3.5)
Sun (2.7)	Honeymoon (4.2)	Smile (3.6)	Community (3.2)	Person (4.0)	Barbados (2.7)
Lots (2.6)	Paradise (3.5)	Hospitality (2.8)	Barbados (2.8)	People (3.8)	Service (2.1)
Climate (2.3)	Couple (3.3)	Lady (2.7)	Place (2.2)	Reggae (2.6)	Weather (1.7)
Barbados (2.1)	Barbados (3.3)	Native (2.6)	Island (2.1)	Island (2.3)	Person (1.5)
Country (1.8)	Lover (3.2)	Food (2.0)	Family (2.1)	Mair (2.3)	Children (1.4)
Totals (51.1)	Totals (56.4)	Totals (52.1)	Totals (61.5)	Totals (39.1)	Totals (35.8)

On-trip

Image	Picture 1	Picture 2	Picture 3	Picture 4	Overall
People (14.1)	Sunset	People (11.2)	Church (15.7)	Beach (18.1)	People (11.0)
Place (7.5)	Beach	Service (9.2)	People (13.5)	People (12.4)	Beach (4.3)
Island (5.1)	Barbados	Hotel (8.0)	Children (6.0)	Rasta (7.5)	Place (4.2)
Beach (4.7)	Place	Woman (7.7)	Religion (3.7)	Barbados (4.0)	Church (3.7)
Weather (3.3)	Picture	Person (5.1)	Island (3.0)	Guy (3.9)	Barbados (3.6)
Barbados (2.3)	Romance	Smile (4.9)	Sunday (2.9)	Rastaman (3.9)	Island (3.4)
Country (2.0)	Island	Picture (4.9)	Barbados (2.4)	Vendor (2.9)	Service (2.3)
Lots (2.0)	People	Barbados (2.4)	School (2.1)	Drugs (2.7)	Sunset (2.3)
Climate (1.4)	Honeymoon	Worker (2.3)	Life (2.0)	Jamaica (2.4)	Picture (1.7)
Ev'thing (1.2)	Lover	Food (2.2)	Picture (1.8)	Person (1.6)	Children (1.6)
Totals (43.6)	Totals (38.1)	Totals (57.9)	Totals (53.1)	Totals (59.4)	Totals (37.5)

A further comparison of the before and after accounts showed the salience of the image of Barbados as an 'island' in the first setting, one which was downplayed in favour of its 'people' in the second; similarly, whereas 'sun' featured in the pre-trip's ten most frequently used words, it was replaced by the generalized expression 'everything' in the on-trip descriptions. In the first scenario 'beaches', 'weather' and 'climate' were considered more important. In the second situation 'place' became less anonymous and 'Barbados' as a 'country' was slightly more pronounced. The change in emphasis thus switched from the physical attractions of almost anywhere in the Caribbean to a greater identification with the destination as a host society.

Use of adjectives

Turning to the adjectives (and gerundives), the second row in Table 7.1 shows that there were 188 adjectives common to both image descriptions. When these data are compared with those pertaining to nouns (first row), several observations can be made.

First, the total number of adjectives featured in both sets of mental images, that is, 559 (112 + 259 + 188), exceeded the number of nouns, which was 499 (141 + 196 + 162) by 60.

Second, while the number of specific adjectives and total number of adjectives were both greater than their corresponding counterparts for nouns in relation to on-trip image, the reverse situation obtained with respect to pre-trip image. Alternatively stated, pre-trip images relied to a greater extent on words denoting objects or things, whereas on-trip images depended more on descriptive or evaluative words.

Third, and as noted for nouns, there was also a higher usage of a smaller number of adjectives in the articulation of pre-trip images (mean frequency 5.4) than was the case for on-trip images (mean frequency 4.4), both averages marginally exceeding their noun counterparts of 5.0 and 4.3 respectively.

Fourth, when the top ten adjectives according to frequency of use were examined, the following distribution was recorded as shown in column one of Table 7.3. Here the ten most utilized adjectives still accounted for a substantial percentage of the overall frequency of the 559 adjectives featured (41.1 per cent for pre-trip images and 31.5 per cent for on-trip images), neverthe-

Table 7.3 Top ten adjectives with percentage frequencies

Pre-trip

Image		Picture 1		Picture 2		Picture 3		Picture 4		Overall	
Friendly	(6.5)	Romantic	(31.5)	Friendly	(26.3)	Religious	(23.0)	Looking	(9.0)	Friendly	(7.7)
Nice	(6.2)	Beautiful	(7.8)	Happy	(8.5)	Going (to)	(10.6)	Friendly	(3.2)	Nice	(4.9)
Beautiful	(4.8)	Nice	(6.4)	Serving	(8.0)	Dressed (up)	(5.4)	Different	(2.8)	Romantic	(4.6)
Good	(4.5)	Peaceful	(6.1)	Nice	(4.3)	Coming (from)	(3.2)	Happy	(2.6)	Religious	(3.5)
Warm	(4.1)	Tropical	(5.9)	Pleasant	(3.0)	Nice	(2.9)	Barbadian	(2.4)	Beautiful	(3.5)
Thought	(4.1)	Lovely	(3.7)	Barbadian	(2.9)	Happy	(2.1)	Good	(2.1)	Warm	(2.3)
Tropical	(3.0)	Quiet	(3.7)	Typical	(2.6)	Small	(2.0)	Scary	(2.1)	Tropical	(2.2)
Sunny	(2.7)	Typical	(2.8)	Caribbean	(2.1)	Typical	(2.0)	Mean'less	(2.1)	Good	(2.2)
Small	(2.7)	Young	(2.2)	Warm	(1.9)	Important	(2.0)	Nice	(1.9)	Happy	(2.1)
Relaxing	(2.5)	Relaxing	(1.7)	Hospitable	(1.7)	Local	(1.8)	Never seen	(1.9)	Thought	(1.7)
Totals	(41.1)		(71.8)		(61.5)		(55.0)		(30.1)		(34.7)

On-trip

Image		Picture 1		Picture 2		Picture 3		Picture 4		Overall	
Friendly	(7.2)	Romantic	(23.4)	Friendly	(22.6)	Religious	(19.2)	Friendly	(5.8)	Friendly	(7.7)
Beautiful	(5.5)	Beautiful	(9.8)	Happy	(7.5)	Going (to)	(11.2)	Looking	(4.5)	Nice	(4.4)
Nice	(5.1)	Nice	(5.7)	Serving	(6.6)	Dressed (up)	(4.6)	Nice	(4.3)	Beautiful	(3.9)
Good	(3.9)	True	(5.1)	Barbadian	(4.4)	Typical	(3.4)	Selling	(3.4)	Religious	(2.9)
Liking	(1.9)	Lovely	(4.9)	Typical	(4.2)	Barbadian	(3.2)	Happy	(2.1)	Romantic	(2.7)
Lovely	(1.8)	Peaceful	(4.5)	Pleasant	(3.7)	Many	(3.1)	Good	(2.1)	Good	(2.1)
Warm	(1.8)	Typical	(3.7)	Nice	(3.5)	Important	(2.2)	Religious	(2.1)	Happy	(2.1)
Loving	(1.6)	Tropical	(3.5)	True	(2.3)	Nice	(2.0)	Reminded	(2.1)	Typical	(1.7)
Relaxing	(1.4)	Quiet	(3.2)	Helpful	(2.3)	Strong	(1.9)	Different	(1.9)	Lovely	(1.6)
Thought	(1.3)	Relaxing	(2.0)	Warm	(2.0)	Coming (from)	(1.7)	Bothered	(1.9)	Going (to)	(1.6)
Totals	(31.5)		(65.8)		(59.1)		(52.5)		(30.2)		(30.3)

less these percentage totals were lower than those respectively calculated for nouns (51.1 per cent and 43.5 per cent). Even so, in both cases percentage totals were higher in the pre-trip situation, thereby indicating a heavier reliance on frequently occurring words.

Fifth, and as was the case for noun ranking, Table 7.3 shows that the first four adjectives were the same in both the pre-trip and on-trip situations. On this occasion, however, there was a change of order in the second and third rankings. Here the rather vague descriptions of 'nice' and 'good' became marginally less frequent in the on-trip image descriptions, while there were corresponding slight increases in the usages of 'friendly' and 'beautiful'. Since in the respondents' accounts the quality of friendliness was almost exclusively attributed to 'people' or 'persons', its re-appearance as an epithet in open-ended replies is surely evidence that tourists' images of destinations are more focused on members of the host society than might have been contemplated by the tourism establishment (McCullough 1977). The fact that people were considered more friendly in the on-trip than in the pre-trip situation suggests that already some benefits had been derived from inter-cultural exchanges. The appearance of the people-oriented adjectives of 'liking', 'loving' and 'lovely' in the second situation, as opposed to the place-oriented epithets of 'tropical', 'sunny' and 'small' in the first scenario, tends to reinforce such an interpretation. While the featuring of the gerundive 'thought' denotes a comparison between mental image and reality, the shared description 'relaxing' is probably indicative of the motivation associated with recreational forms of mass tourism (Cohen 1979).

The socio-linguistics of images with pictorial stimuli

After respondents had articulated their spontaneous mental images of Barbados in a before and after format, they were subsequently asked to identify the meanings which they attached to four photographs of the island. These latter subjective interpretations thus represented responses to visual induced material (again with reference to the two time periods of pre- and on-trip), and could, therefore, be compared socio-linguistically to the first set of replies which lacked such pictorial stimuli.

The visual stimuli

As far as the four pictures shown to the respondents are concerned, these had all featured in 'official' promotional material (Barbados Board of Tourism: nd; Official Guide 1988/89: 89). In this sense they approximated the type of photograph described by Chalfen (1979) which portrays a preferred image of the host society, as opposed to the photograph produced by tourists for their own purposes (Bourdieu 1990; Cohen *et al.* 1992). Furthermore, even though these pictures were selective as to their choice of subject matter, colour and composition, the realization that they contained many layers of meaning, ranging from literal to symbolic, meant that they were capable of multiple interpretation by those at whom they were targeted.

The four photographs were chosen according to anticipated decreasing levels of familiarity to the visitor. The first portrayed a young Caucasian couple on a beach at sunset, and typified the majority situation of brochure photographs in which only tourists are featured (Dann 1988). The next three pictures showed only local people. The second photograph depicted a maid serving in a hotel, the third photograph showed a group of children coming out of a rural church, and the final photograph showed a Rastafarian. That increasing strangerhood was operating could be gauged both in terms of the settings and experiences (Cohen 1979) evoked by these visual stimuli.

Responses to pictorial stimuli

Table 7.4 shows that response rates with pictorial stimuli were slightly lower than those without such visual aids. Apart from unlikely respondent fatigue (these items occurred near the beginning of the interview), perhaps some of the relative percentage shortfall in the two rates can be explained in terms of the question wording ('what *image* did/do you have of Barbados?' as opposed to 'what did/does this picture *mean* to you?'). Alternatively, variation could be attributed to the presence or absence of a pictorial medium, analogous to the situation recorded by Andrew (1977) in which subjects respond differently to brochure material according to whether or not they are exposed to written or visual messages. Equally, however, such differences could have been due to the fact that, even though the former situation lacked an accompanying visual aid, it may have been considered less problematic to verbalize an open-ended reply from an amalgam of such elements as attitudes, perceptions and motivations (Mayo and Jarvis 1981) which had *already been internalized,* than to *begin* articulating a response to a fixed *external* stimulus supplied by the researcher. Moreover, and given that the pictures had been selected according to increasing degrees of unfamiliarity, it is interesting to observe that (with the exception of the picture of children (3)) the response rates progressively declined.

Table 7.4 Percentage response rates with and without pictorial stimuli

	Pre-trip	On-trip	Difference
Without pictorial stimulus			
Mental image	97.4	99.2	1.8
With pictorial stimulus			
Picture 1 (couple at sunset)	96.3	97.6	1.3
Picture 2 (maid serving)	92.9	96.3	3.4
Picture 3 (children at church)	89.5	93.4	3.9
Picture 4 (Rastafarian)	90.1	93.3	3.2

n = 535

In all cases, too (as indeed with the question on mental imagery), on-trip reactions to pictorial stimuli achieved higher response rates than those relating to the pre-trip situation. A probable explanation for this state of affairs is that, whereas on-trip attitudes are informed by actual experiences, pre-trip attitudes rely on analogous vicarious experiences. In other words, empirical differences in response reinforce Gartner's (forthcoming) theoretical distinction between organic and induced sources.

Finally it can be seen from Table 7.5 that, as the transition was made from the articulation of mental images to the reaction to pictorial stimuli, so too was there a decline both in the number of words employed and in their corresponding frequencies.

Top ten nouns – frequency of use

From the last column in Table 7.2, it can be seen that 'people' headed the list in terms of frequency of noun usage, accounting for 8.4 per cent of all descriptions at the pre-trip stage and 11 per cent in the on-trip situation. Taking both sets together, this means that

Table 7.5 Overall response patterns

Trip stage stimulus	Pre nil	On nil	Pre P1	On P1	Pre P2	On P2	Pre P3	On P3	Pre P4	On P4
Respondents	521	531	515	522	497	515	479	500	482	499
Nouns used	303	358	104	124	134	145	144	190	198	246
Frequency of nouns	1506	1527	718	740	739	764	847	974	728	776
Mean nouns per resp.	0.6	0.7	0.2	0.2	0.3	0.3	0.3	0.4	0.4	0.5
Mean freq. nouns per resp.	2.9	2.9	1.4	1.4	1.5	1.5	1.8	1.9	1.5	1.5
Adjectives used	300	447	88	105	119	137	129	141	181	206
Frequency of adjectives	1616	1919	542	491	624	651	556	589	469	534
Mean adjectives per resp.	0.6	0.8	0.2	0.2	0.2	0.3	0.3	0.3	0.4	0.4
Mean freq. adjectives per resp.	3.1	3.7	1.0	0.9	1.2	1.3	1.2	1.2	1.0	1.1

Stimulus Nil = mental image without pictorial stimulus
Stimulus P1, P2, P3, P4 = with pictorial stimulus of Pictures 1–4

approximately 10 per cent of the occurring and recurring nouns in respondent accounts were taken up with the use of this one word. Again this socio-linguistic finding lends further support to McCullough's (1977) view that tourists are more attracted to the host population than the various sites of the destination area. Additionally, with the exception of the picture of children (3), the evidence shows that 'people' featured more in on-trip than in pre-trip descriptions. Only in the first picture, and then just in the pre-trip situation, was there an absence of 'people' in the top ten items. This significant omission is quite understandable when one recalls that that photograph portrayed a young couple of tourists in a romantic beach setting devoid of locals.

The nouns 'island' and 'place', by contrast, tended to occur more frequently in pre-trip accounts. While 'island' has been treated by Cohen (1982), a comprehensive interpretation of 'place' has been offered by Relph (1976). However, in the present study it is interesting to note that there was an increasing use of 'Barbados' as one moved from the pre-trip to the on-trip situation, that is, there was a heightened identification of place with local culture. Only in one instance (the pre-trip image of the maid in the hotel (2)) did Barbados not feature in the top ten nouns. Yet overall it accounted for 2.7 per cent of all nouns used in pre-trip and 3.6 per cent in on-trip descriptions. In the last picture – that of the Rastafarian – there was a fascinating tension between Jamaica and Barbados, one which was eventually resolved in favour of the latter.

Apart from the foregoing communalities of image, there were several nouns which dominated the proceedings on account of their image specificity. The first picture, for example, evoked 'sunset', 'romance', 'honeymoon', 'couple' and 'lover', words which hardly featured elsewhere. Similarly the second picture produced descriptions which contained 'woman', 'lady', 'hotel', 'smile', 'native', 'hospitality', 'worker' and 'food'; the third picture yielded particular references to 'church', 'children', 'religion', 'school', 'community', 'Sunday', 'family' and 'life'; and the last picture specifically conjured up 'Jamaica', 'Rasta', 'Rastafarian', 'Rastaman', 'guy', 'reggae', 'drugs', 'hair' and 'vendor'. Moreover, some of these top ten nouns, such as 'church', 'service' and 'children', had such a high specific frequency of usage that they appeared in the overall listings at both the pre-trip and on-trip level. This is not to say that they did not occur at all outside the range of their specific pictorial stimulus. Rather it indicates that their usage elsewhere was far less systematic and pronounced.

The data therefore reveal that two levels of evocation are in operation. One calls forth connotative images regardless of stimulus. The other simply yields denotative images which mirror the visual content of the reality presented. The challenge for the creator and selector of pictorial material surely lies in being able to produce level one responses from specific photographs.

Top ten adjectives – frequency of use

With the exception of the picture of children, the combined percentage use of the top ten nouns showed a gradual decline in the totals as one moved from the first picture to the last. Alternatively stated in socio-linguistic terms: the less familiar the scene, the stronger the reliance on a greater variety of words.

The same sort of configuration occurred with respect to adjectives, as can be seen from Table 7.3. On this occasion, however, the above patterning was even more pronounced and the third picture was not an exception to the general trend. Here there was a steady and uninterrupted transition from the first picture (where the top ten adjectives accounted for 71.8 per cent of all descriptions) to the last (where their combined total was only 30.1 per cent).

The salience of the epithet 'friendly' was associated with the prominence of 'people' among the nouns (Table 7.2) since in most accounts the two words were combined at the general level. However, whereas the adjective 'friendly' occurred without the benefit of a visual stimulus in the articulation of mental images, its appearance among the top ten pictorial descriptions tended to be more associated with individual relationships. In practice, 'friendly' featured predominantly in the second and fourth pictures where there was just one local (maid and Rastafarian respectively) but not in the first and third pictures (absence of locals and group of local children respectively).

While it has already been noted that there was a marginal increase in the use of 'friendly' in mental image descriptions from the pre-trip to the on-trip situation, the same trend could also be observed in the last picture. However, in the second picture (the maid) there was a decline in friendliness and the emergence of 'true' and 'helpful' to take up the relative percentage shortfall. Such a counter trend can perhaps be explained by reference to the respective picture contents. Whereas the Rastafarian (in the fourth picture) at first was often deemed as 'scary', 'meaningless' and 'never seen', once he was actually encountered such descriptions yielded to the more functional and less hostile epithets of 'selling' and 'religious'. The transition from negative (pre-trip) to neutral or positive (on-trip) thus became predicated on experience and a presumably parallel diminution of strangerhood. By contrast, the maid in the hotel (in the second picture) was initially considered to be a more familiar and less threatening person. Instead of later becoming more friendly she came to be viewed as more 'typical', more 'pleasant' and 'helpful'. At the same time, there was a transference in the descriptions from 'Caribbean' to 'Barbadian'.

Looking at some of the remaining adjectives in Table 7.3, it can be seen that 'beautiful', 'typical' and 'pleasant' increased their percentage frequency share as the transition was effected from the pre-trip to the on-trip stage. By contrast, 'nice', 'good', 'thought', 'tropical', 'peaceful', 'quiet', 'romantic', 'happy' and 'religious' generally diminished in relative significance as one moved from the first to the second situation. Only 'warm' and 'relaxing' did not fall into either pattern, and their percentage variations were minimal. A possible key to the foregoing trends may hinge on the word 'typical'. Somehow the actual experience of a vacation tended to heighten the authenticity content (Cohen Chapter Two), and the emergence of 'true', together with the increased attribution of 'Barbadian', further reinforced such an interpretation.

Just as there were nouns which were stimulus specific, so too one encountered level two denotative adjectives which almost exclusively pertained to the contents of individual photographs. In picture 1, for instance, 'romantic' so dominated the situation that the epithet became third and fifth respectively in the pre-trip and on-trip rankings. 'Quiet', 'peaceful', 'young' and 'lovely' were also closely associated with this scene. In picture 2, 'serving', 'pleasant', 'Caribbean', 'hospitable' and 'helpful' were image specific, as were 'going to', 'dressed', 'coming from', 'small', 'many', 'important', 'strong' and 'local' with respect to picture 3, and 'looking', 'different', 'selling', 'scary', 'meaningless', 'reminded', 'never seen' and 'bothered' in relation to picture 4.

Interestingly, of all the adjectives in Table 7.3, only three were negative in nature – 'scary', 'meaningless' and 'bothered' – and all of them were evoked by picture 4 where maximum strangerhood would have been experienced.

CONCLUSION

According to Boulding (1956: 16), 'the development of images is part of the culture or sub-culture in which they are developed'. Moreover, in promotional material these images 'talk to one culture about another culture'. The current study has attempted to focus on the culture of the destination by listening to what tourists have to say about it as they structure their responses sociolinguistically with and without the assistance of visual stimuli. In this sense, the investigation contributes to an understanding of the images which are constructed for and perceived by tourists, and can be considered as forming part of a 'recentering of research on interpretation and communication links between cultures' (MacCannell 1979: 156) and as a first step towards 'a semiotic phenomenology of transcultural materials' (MacCannell 1979: 161). The present work also, by examining some of the relationships between photography and its touristic interpretation, has tried to respond to Chalfen's (1985: 103–104) objection that such an issue is often neglected or treated as unproblematic.

Whereas Gartner (1993) may claim with some justification that 'most tourism image research has been piecemeal without a theoretical basis for support', this presentation has sought a grounding in semiotics. While tending to side with cultural relativists, who, like Hall (1982: 64) maintain that 'photographs are the result of an active signifying practice' and that 'photography is not simply the transmission of an already existing appearance', but rather 'the more active labour of making things mean', one may also share Eco's (1979) view that pictures can and do have a message of their own. Nevertheless, the full interactive process of induced image speech on touristic response and touristic articulation on the language of image formation requires a more systematic theoretical treatment which limitations of space preclude here.

At the methodological level, some originality is claimed to the extent that tourists were questioned not only regarding their reactions to pictorial stimuli but also about their articulation of mental images which had already been internalized. Furthermore, by making socio-linguistic comparisons between pre- and on-trip accounts, it was possible to gauge differences which were respectively attributable to hypothetical variation in vicarious and actual experiences.

However, due to the preliminary nature of the investigation, one was unable on this occasion to explore several questions for which the data set offered further potential. The first of these avenues of inquiry which could constitute a useful future agenda is the analysis of language by tourist categories. Thus one could, for instance, examine the incidence and frequency of words according to such profile variables as age, sex and class. Additionally, it would be interesting to analyse choice of vocabulary according to a number of tourist typologies.

A second area with enormous potential would be to introduce the various media to which tourists had been exposed prior to their visit and to assess the separate and cumulative effects of such induced and organic sources of information on the socio-linguistics of imagery. Thus, for example, existing data could establish the respective influences of variables such as previous visits, travel agents, advertising and travelogues on the formation of pre-trip mental images and how these in turn relate to on-trip images. Already one interesting relationship was noted, namely the tension between descriptions containing references to people and places. However, a more extensive analysis of this topic, which includes various bases for the formation of pre-trip imagery, would provide a more rigorous testing of the proposals put forward by McCullough (1977).

Third, in relation to pictorial stimuli, no analysis was undertaken as regards the use of shape and colour (Andrew 1977), and how these and other dimensions feature in linguistic accounts. Yet such a possibility still exists within the 200 or so pages of transcripts yielded by the open-ended responses to the two items on image and meaning which formed only a small part of the wide-ranging interview schedule.

Fourth, this writer has already commenced an analysis (Dann 1993b) according to the cognitive, affective and connotative components (Gartner 1993), of expressions used by tourists and how these relate imagery to the process of destination selection. This avenue of inquiry leads naturally to a more detailed study of motivation and the various socio-linguistic devices used by tourists to articulate such vocabulary of motive in all its complexity.

Fifth, another line of investigation which has already been initiated is a more detailed analysis of words by their initial letter. Interestingly, it has been found in this study that tourists use a disproportionate number of words beginning with the letter 'S' in their images of the destination area. What needs to be determined is whether such accentuation is a mere response to the 'sun-sand-sea-sex' formula of the travel trade (Rivers 1972) or a socio-linguistic determinant of induced imagery.

It can therefore be seen that such a rich qualitative data set is almost limitless in scope. One could look at the valency of expressions, that is, their evaluative content. One could also examine their touristic authenticity content and whether there is any language change in descriptions which distinguish between natural and contrived attractions (Cohen Chapter Two). At the same time, the before and after format permits an interesting alternative to the study of tourist satisfaction than that normally provided by the check list of items in a traditional questionnaire.

It should also soon be possible to gauge the goodness of fit encompassing the imagery constructed by the media makers, those about whom it has been prepared and those at whom it has been targeted. Only by bringing in all three parties, and by looking at the various subgroups within (Cohen 1993), will the socio-linguistics of tourism imagery ever be complete. When that moment comes, when the language of promotional material reflects the realities of the host society and edges closer to the mindset of the post-modern consumer than the discourse and visual stimuli of the advertiser, only then will it be possible to speak about a comprehensive framework for socially responsible tourism. Indeed, such an agenda may well constitute one of the most important research issues of the 1990s.

Finally, this chapter, by highlighting an alternative approach to the analysis of touristic phenomena, is implicitly arguing that, since tourism itself is both an agent and an object of change, it calls forth respective pro-active and re-active treatments from those who study tourism. Moreover, if it is true that we live in the age of the 'simulacrum' (Baudrillard 1983), where increasingly life comes to be dominated by images and hyperreality (Cohen Chapter Two), then tourism clearly will become more and more emblematic of this 'time of the age' (MacCannell and MacCannell 1982). Whether or not tourism will continue to expand or come to an end in Virtual Reality (Urry 1991), there will always be a need to examine its changing messages, together with the various ways these are received and sent by participants. It is language which is and will always be the medium for such communication, and hence analyses grounded in semiotics and socio-linguistics will have a guaranteed future in a changing world of visiting the Other.

ACKNOWLEDGEMENTS

Gratitude is expressed to Richard Butler, Erik Cohen, William Gartner and Douglas Pearce for a number of useful suggestions which were incorporated into the revised version of this chapter.

REFERENCES

Albers, P. and James, W. (1988) 'Travel photography: A methodological approach', *Annals of Tourism Research* 15: 134–158.

Andrew, C. (1977) 'An investigation into package holiday brochure design', unpublished MSc. dissertation, University of Surrey.

Barbados Board of Tourism (nd) *Barbados*, Hastings, Barbados: Cot Printery.

Barthes, R. (1982) *Image, Music, Text*, London: Fontana.

Baudrillard, J. (1983) *Simulations*, New York: Semiotext(e), Foreign Agent Press.

Berger, J. (1972) *Ways of Seeing*, Harmondsworth: Penguin.

Boorstin, D. (1987) *The Image. A Guide to Pseudo-Events in America*, 25th anniversary edn, New York: Atheneum.

Boulding, K. (1956) *The Image. Knowledge in Life and Society*, Ann Arbor: University of Michigan Press.

Bourdieu, P. (1990) *Photography. A Middle-brow Art*, Cambridge: Polity Press.

Buck, R. (1977) 'The ubiquitous tourist brochure. Explorations of its intended and unintended use', *Annals of Tourism Research* 4, 2: 195–207.

Chalfen, R. (1979) 'Photography's role in tourism', *Annals of Tourism Research* 6, 3: 435–447.

—— (1985) 'An alternative to an alternative. Comment on Uzzell', *Annals of Tourism Research* 12, 1: 103–106.

Cohen, E. (1979) 'A phenomenology of tourist experiences', *Sociology* 13: 179–201.

—— (1982) 'The Pacific Islands from utopian myth to consumer product: The disenchantment of paradise', *Cahiers du Tourisme*, série B no. 27.

—— (1989) 'Primitive and remote. Hill tribe trekking in Thailand', *Annals of Tourism Research* 16, 1: 30–61.

—— (1993) 'The study of touristic images of native people. Mitigating the stereotype of the stereotype', in D. Pearce and R. Butler (eds) *Tourism Research: Critiques and Challenges*, London: Routledge, 36–69.

Cohen, E., Nir, Y. and Almagor, U. (1992) 'Stranger–local interaction in photography', *Annals of Tourism Research* 19, 2: 213–233.

Dann, G. (1981) 'Tourist motivation: An appraisal', *Annals of Tourism Research* 8, 2: 187–219.

—— (1988) 'The People of Tourist Brochures', Paper presented to the First Global Conference – Tourism, A Vital Force for Peace, Vancouver, October.

—— (1992a) 'Travelogs and the management of unfamiliarity', *Journal of Travel Research* XXXI Spring: 59–63.

—— (1992b) 'Predisposition towards alternative forms of tourism among tourists visiting Barbados: Some preliminary observations', in V. Smith and W. Eadington (eds) *Tourism Alternatives. Potentials and Problems in the Development of Tourism*, Philadelphia: University of Pennsylvania Press, 158–179.

—— (1993a) 'Advertising in tourism and travel', in M. Khan, M. Olson and T. Var (eds) *Encyclopaedia of Hospitality and Tourism*, New York: Van Nostrand Reinhold, 893–901.

—— (1993b) 'A socio-linguistic analysis of the cognitive, affective and connotative content of images as an alternative means to gauging tourist satisfaction, motivation and experience', Paper prepared for the conference on Decision Making Processes and Preference Changes of Tourists: Interpersonal and Inter-Country Perspectives, Innsbruck: Leopold-Franzens-Universität, November.

—— (forthcoming) 'De higher de monkey climb, de more 'e show 'e tail – tourists' knowledge of Barbadian culture', *Journal of International Consumer Marketing* 6, 4: 1994.

Eco, U. (1979) *A Theory of Semiotics*, Bloomington: Indiana University Press.

Gartner, W. (1993) 'Image formation process', *Journal of Travel and Tourism Marketing* 2, 2/3: 191–215.

Gartner, W. and Bachri, T. (in press) 'Tour operators' role in the tourism distribution system: An Indonesian case study', *Journal of International Consumer Marketing*.

Gartner, W. and Hunt, J. (1987) 'An analysis of state image change over a twelve year period (1971–1983)', *Journal of Travel Research* 26, 2: 15–19.

Gartner, W. and Shen, J. (1992) 'The impact of Tiananmen Square on China's tourism image', *Journal of Travel Research* 30, 4: 47–52.

Goodall, B. (1991) 'Understanding holiday choice', in C. Cooper (ed.) *Progress in Tourism, Recreation and Hospitality Management*, London: Belhaven Press, 58–77.

Gottlieb, A. (1982) 'Americans' vacations', *Annals of Tourism Research* 9, 1: 165–187.

Gould, P. and White, R. (1970) *Mental Maps*, New York: Penguin.

Gritti, J. (1967) 'Les contenus culturels du *Guide Bleu*', *Monuments et Sites à Voir Communications* 10: 51–64.

Gunn, C. (1972) *Vacationscape: Designing Tourist Regions*, Austin: Bureau of Business Research, University of Texas.

Hall, S. (1982) 'The rediscovery of "ideology": Return of the repressed in media studies', in M. Gurevitch, T. Bennet, J. Curran and J. Woollacott (eds) *Culture, Society and the Media*, London: Methuen, 56–90.

Langholz-Leymore, V. (1975) *Hidden Myth: Structure and Symbolism in Advertising*, London: Heinemann.

Lindekens, R. (1971) *Eléments pour une Sémiologie de la Photographie*, Paris: Didier.

MacCannell, D. (1979) 'Ethnosemiotics', in I. Winner and J. Umiker-Sebeok (eds) *Semiotics of Culture*, The Hague: Mouton, 149–171.

MacCannell, D. and MacCannell, J. (1982) *The Time of the Sign*, Bloomington: Indiana University Press.

McCullough, G. (1977) 'Tourist holiday images with specific reference to tropical destinations', Unpublished MSc. dissertation, University of Surrey.

Marsh, J. (1986) 'Advertising Canada in Japan and Japanese tourism in Canada', in J. Marsh (ed.) *Canadian Studies of Parks, Recreation and Tourism in Foreign Lands*, Peterborough, Ontario: Department of Geography, Trent University, 83–110.

Mayo, E. and Jarvis, L. (1981) *The Psychology of Leisure Travel*, Boston, Mass.: CBI.

Mohamed, M. (1988) 'Moroccan tourism image in France', *Annals of Tourism Research* 15, 4: 588–591.

Nöth, W. (1990) *Handbook of Semiotics*, Bloomington: Indiana University Press.

Official Guide (1988/89) *Barbados*, vol. 9, Bridgetown: Tourist Promotions.

Olsen, J., MacAlexander, J. and Roberts, S. (1986) 'The impact of the visual content of advertisements upon the perceived vacation experience', in W. Benoy Joseph (ed.) *Proceedings of Marketing Sciences Conference*, Ohio: Cleveland State University.

Paradice, W. (1985) 'Recreation information dissemination and the visitor choice process in Australian natural environments', *Tourism Recreation Research* 10, 2: 19–27.

Pearce, P. (1982) *The Social Psychology of Tourist Behaviour*, Oxford: Pergamon.

—— (1993) 'Fundamentals of tourist motivation', in D. Pearce and R. Butler (eds) *Tourism Research: Critiques and Challenges*, London: Routledge, 113–134.

Phelps, A. (1986) 'Holiday destination image: The problem of assessment. An example developed in Menorca', *Tourism Management* 7, 3: 168–180.

Relph, E. (1976) *Place and Placelessness*, London: Pion.

Rivers, P. (1972) *The Restless Generation. A Crisis in Mobility*, London: Davis-Poynter.

Ryan, C. (1991) *Recreational Tourism. A Social Science Perspective*, London: Routledge.

Selwyn, T. (1992) 'Peter Pan in South-East Asia. Views from the brochures', in M. Hitchcock, V. King and M. Parnnell (eds) *Tourism in South-East Asia*, London: Routledge, 117–137.

Stringer, P. (1984) 'Studies in the Socio-environmental psychology of tourism', *Annals of Tourism Research* 11, 1: 147–166.

Thurot, J. and Thurot, G. (1983) 'The ideology of class and tourism: Confronting the discourse of advertising', *Annals of Tourism Research* 10, 1: 173–189.

Urbain, J. (1989) 'The tourist adventure and his images', *Annals of Tourism Research* 16, 1: 106–118.

Urry, J. (1991) 'Tourism, travel and the modern subject', *Vrijetijd en Samenleving* 9, 3/4: 87–98.

Uzzell, D. (1984) 'An alternative structuralist approach to the psychology of tourism marketing', *Annals of Tourism Research* 11, 1: 79–99.

Weaver, P. and McCleary, K. (1984) 'A market segmentation study to determine the appropriate ad/model format for travel advertising', *Journal of Travel Research* 22, 1: 12–16.

Worth, S. (1977) 'Toward an ethnographic semiotic', Paper presented to the Conference on Utilisation de l'Ethnologie par le Cinéma/Utilisation du Cinéma par l'Ethnologie, Paris: UNESCO.

Chapter 8

Constructing traveller types
New methodology for old concepts

Josef A. Mazanec

This chapter examines the construction of traveller types from a marketing research perspective. This is not a restriction since all social science disciplines have generated traveller typologies over the past years. The data techniques employed are of universal interest and methodological improvements should be stimulating from whatever discipline they may originate, particularly in view of current trends and changes in the tourist market.

Traveller types are potential market segments. In the language of marketing research they are identified through a process called *aposteriori* segmentation. Segment sizes and structures are unknown in advance. Initially, there is no more than a simple hypothesis expecting that travellers may be broken down into homogeneous subgroups in terms of benefits sought or other psychographics depending on the underlying explanatory model ('active' variables). Various techniques of cluster analysis, frequently in conjunction with discriminant analysis, assist in the construction of segments (types). A particular profile in psychographics alone does not warrant a distinction in behavioural and consumption patterns. Additional attributes ('passive' variables) must step in to complete the segment/type description.

In most cases the active variables are subject to data reduction during measurement, that is, many individual items or statements in a questionnaire are combined to form constructs like an attitude, a state of motivation, a lifestyle or a vacation style. The (passive) descriptors usually stand for themselves: a first-time versus a repeat visitor, a tourist with high or low daily expenditure, a traveller on a main holiday, a traveller on a short trip. Until recently there were no measurement and data processing techniques capable of mastering the double job of reduction and description all at once. Encouraging results, however, have been obtained with neural networks modelling. These procedures may approximate any continuous mapping function; they are undisturbed by non-linearities and interactions, thus offering several advantages over traditional multivariate methods. In the case of this discussion, empirical results of such analysis will be demonstrated for a sample study of tourists staying in Austria during summer 1991.

TRAVELLER TYPOLOGIES IN TOURISM AND IN MARKETING RESEARCH

The construction of traveller typologies is neither a new undertaking in tourism research nor in marketing research. Reports published in the proceedings of the Travel and Tourism Research Association have covered this issue regularly (Darden and Darden 1976) and social science approaches to tourism research repeatedly touched upon typological issues (Pearce 1982; Cohen 1988; Dann *et al.* 1988). It is also common practice to consider traveller types as potential market segments for travel and tourism marketing (Smith 1989; Vavrik and Mazanec 1990).

Market segmentation research in tourism denies the existence of a unique, all-encompassing and universally satisfying traveller typology. It is rather inspired by the vision that typologies are bound to be situation-specific and dependent on a particular research objective. Typology construction remains a continuous effort for each competitor in the travel market. Tourist destinations and providers of tourist services facing the competitive challenges of the 1990s have become aware of market segmentation as a strategic tool. By redefining and reselecting market segments they manage to evade the competitive pressure at least temporarily and act as quasi-monopolists in highly specialized segments (niche marketing). To some extent, competitive advantage rests on a thorough behavioural foundation and on the methodological sophistication of segment and type construction.

Market segmentation has been a strategic issue in marketing planning for decades, stimulating research and industry practices alike. From the beginning it was evident that marketing managers need decision support regarding segmentation depth (number and size of segments) and segmentation criteria (Frank 1968: 40). The process of determining the number and size of segments may still be governed by (qualitative) reasoning about segment attributes (Kotler 1967: 45) or may be subject to an optimization model (see Claycamp and Massy 1968 for one of the earliest examples). A wealth of segmentation criteria have been proposed and explored (to the benefit of the commercial market research institutes). Sometimes, vigilant observers raised criticism concerning a lack of theory in criteria selection (Hustad and Pessemier 1971; Arndt 1974; Mazanec 1978). Since the 1970s psychographics have gained an ever increasing share among segmentation criteria. Lifestyle and AIO (activities, interests, opinions) variables, and personality traits have become popular (Wells and Tigert 1971; Wells 1974, 1975) and remain so today. Tourism and leisure research followed suit (Mayo and Jarvis 1981; Bernard 1987; see Veal 1989 for a critical comment). Travel activities are particularly typical of segmentation studies in tourism (Hsieh *et al.* 1992). Sometimes tourists are referred to as 'role players' but a set of activities remains the raw material for role definition (Yiannakis and Gibson 1992).

Consumer values or value systems (Kamakura and Novak 1992) are the latecomers in the list of innovations to the psychographic segmentation toolkit. To cite a recent example of a successful commercialization, the Europanel group of market research institutes offers a standardized value system and lifestyle typology called EUROSTYLES in fifteen European countries (Cathelat 1985; Winkler 1991). Its application to tourism marketing has been examined by Mazanec and Zins (1993).

Marketing theory distinguishes between *a priori* and *aposteriori* market segmentation, or criterion versus similarity segmentation (Bagozzi 1986: 229) and *a priori* and factor-cluster segmentation (Smith 1989). The segment-defining variables and their values are either predetermined (*a priori*) or fixed during the construction of previously unknown segments or types. *A priori* segmentation commences with a single variable (or a combination of a few attributes) directly related to purchasing behaviour. Typical examples are buyer vs non-buyer, quantity purchased, trial or repeat purchase, brand loyalty and other visible outcomes of buying behaviour. The consumers' segment affiliation is clearly defined. Either they are heavy or occasional users, trial or repeat buyers.

In *aposteriori* segmentation neither the number nor the composition of segments is known in advance. The process sets out with a hypothesis that consumer subgroups may be homogeneous with

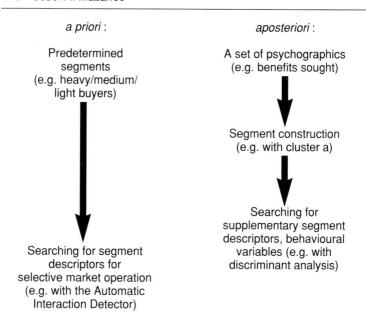

a priori :

Predetermined
segments
(e.g. heavy/medium/
light buyers)

aposteriori :

A set of psychographics
(e.g. benefits sought)

Segment construction
(e.g. with cluster a)

Searching for
supplementary segment
descriptors, behavioural
variables (e.g. with
discriminant analysis)

Searching for segment
descriptors for
selective market operation
(e.g. with the Automatic
Interaction Detector)

Figure 8.1 The logical structure of *a priori* and *aposteriori* segmentation

respect to a major explanatory construct of buying behaviour. Typical examples are psychographics such as benefits sought, motives, attitudes or values.

Psychographics are multidimensional constructs. They are made up of a list of items and need a measurement design which includes a data reduction step. Once the segments have been identified (for example, through cluster analysis) *aposteriori* segments require an additional description with 'passive' variables in just the same manner as their *a priori* counterparts (Figure 8.1).

Contemporary marketing theory seems to accept a division between *a priori* and *aposteriori* segmentation. It shifts the responsibility to the marketing manager, who is supposed to take the right option with either a predetermined classification of consumers or with an attempt to detect a new partition of the market. The new methodology introduced in the next section handles *a priori* and *aposteriori* variables simultaneously and enables the manager to couple both segmentation approaches in the same analysis.

In marketing research even the fanciest typology is not an end in itself. Finally it has to serve a sales target. All psychographic segments or consumer types must be examined with respect to their consumption patterns. They are conducive to reaching marketing goals if significant behavioural differences (purchasing, media usage) emerge.

SEGMENTATION AND TRAVELLER TYPOLOGY CONSTRUCTION WITH A NEURAL NETWORK MODEL

As this is not the first application of neural network (NNW) modelling to market segmentation (cf. Mazanec 1990, 1992; Hruschka and Natter 1992, 1993) it is not necessary to discuss NNW modelling principles starting from scratch here. Aleksander and Morton (1990) and Wasserman (1989) are recommended as introductory texts; Freeman and Skapura (1991) provide an introduction for readers with some background in engineering and Simpson (1990) succeeds in compressing an outline of the major NNW paradigms into less than 200 pages. The discussion here is limited to drafting a version of a feedforward network which accommodates all types of variables inherent in a combined *a priori/aposteriori* segmentation project.

A neural network is made up of data processing units (or elements), layers (usually between two and four) and connections. The segmentation network developed in this study consists of three layers of processing units. Figure 8.2 (see the following section) exhibits the architecture. The processing elements on the bottom layer represent the demographic, socio-economic, psychographic and behavioural attributes of the travellers under study. Only those variables intended to fulfil the *a priori* mission are excluded. They are located on the top (i.e. output) layer where they deliver each traveller's segment affiliation predicted by the network. The intermediate layer is made up of 'hidden' elements with no direct relationship to the outside world. The flow of information runs from the bottom (i.e. input) to the top layer (feedforward network). In the standard version of a three layer feedforward network adjacent layers are fully connected to each other. Hence it is the purpose of m hidden units to extract and to compress the information arriving from n input units (m < n).

The segmentation network restricts the number of connections as it is guided by a set of hypotheses. In fact, the number of connections is greatly reduced. The hidden units share responsibility for only a subset of input units (see Figure 8.2). They fulfil a function similar to unobservable constructs in a causal model (of the LISREL type; Bagozzi 1980; Jöreskog 1982). For example, a hidden unit representing a travel motive type has connections to a series of motivational variables itemized and measured in a questionnaire. Generally, a number of m_1 hidden elements are interconnected with a number of n_1 input units ($m_1 < n_1$), m_2 hidden elements to n_2 input units ($m_2 < n_2$), etc., where $m_1 + m_2 + \ldots = m$ and $n_1 + n_2 + \ldots = n$.

Data processing occurs in each unit (*parallel* processing). The inbound flow of information arriving at a unit's input edge consists of the weighted output values of the connecting units on the preceding layer. The input gets accumulated (usually by a simple summation function) to represent a unit's activation potential. A unit's actual state of activation and, therefore, its outbound information depends on how it treats the summated input, that is, on the type of transfer function employed. If this transfer function is non-linear (a logistic curve, or a hyperbolic tangent), the unit's state of activation varies between the boundaries 0 and 1 or –1 and 1. A hidden layer in conjunction with a nonlinear transfer function enables the network to mimic any continuous mapping function of any (unknown) complexity. Non-linearities and interactions are implicitly taken into account and need not be modelled separately as in conventional multivariate analysis.

In more rigorous notation, for the elements on the hidden layer,

$$(1)\ p(i) = \sum_{j=1}^{n} w(i, j) \times (i, j)$$

with p(i): activation potential of unit i
    w(i): weight for input from preceding unit j
    x(i): activation transferred from unit j
      n: number of units on the preceding (input) layer connected to unit i,

$$(2)\ a(i) = \frac{1}{1 + \exp(-p(i))}$$

with a(i): actual state of activation of unit i.

The 'knowledge' a network acquires about the outside world rests in its associative memory made up of the weight vectors. The network learns by adapting its weight structure. The adjustment of the weights occurs through training, that is, repetitive exposition to training examples (travellers with their *a priori*, *aposteriori* and accompanying descriptive attributes). A very powerful method of network training and weight estimation is called *backpropagation*. It is based on teaching or supervision by feeding the network with input data and comparing the network's response to the known output. On the top layer the difference between a desired output $o(i)$ and an actual output $a(i)$ of unit i enters a least-squares error function

$$(3) \ E = \frac{1}{2} \sum_k (o(i, k) - a(i, k))^2.$$

Then a weight update amounts to

$$(4) \ \Delta w \, (i, j) = -\eta \, \left(\frac{\delta E}{\delta w(i, j)} \right)$$

with learning constant $0 <$ eta < 1 and
the derivative dE/dw of the error function.

The *delta rule* in formula 4 corresponds to the gradient procedure (steepest descent principle) employed in many optimization routines. In simple terms this means that the weights are altered in the direction promising the largest amount of improvement in the network response.

A problem arises for the layer with the hidden elements. As the hidden layer has no direct links to observable values, a difference $o(i,j) - a(i,k)$ is not available. A more general updating principle is required. It is called the *generalized delta rule* and relies on the accumulated error involving all output units connected to a hidden unit (Rumelhardt *et al.* 1986: 322 ff.). Each training cycle entails a forward pass through the network (from bottom to top) for calculating (trial) output and errors and a subsequent backward pass (top to bottom) for the weight updates (hence the term *back*propagation). Convergence has been proven for infinitesimally small corrections of the weights. For weight updates with reasonable magnitude to be achieved within a finite number of iterations, various variants of the basic estimation procedure have been suggested to prevent the gradient procedure from getting trapped in local minima and to accelerate convergence (see Wasserman 1989: 55ff.).

In traditional classification terminology, the network estimates the *aposteriori* probabilities of a traveller belonging to an output class given the input attributes (Wan 1990), thereby approximating the Bayes optimal discriminant function (Ruck *et al.* 1990). This means that the activation of the output units indicates the degree of confidence in class membership (Shoemaker 1991). The classification ambiguity for each respondent becomes apparent. An input vector resulting in one dominant output unit reveals a high degree of confidence. A rather uniform activation level on the output layer is typical for a respondent with a weak relationship to any class.

To examine a network's performance and practical relevance the same prediction criteria which are customary in discriminant analysis may be applied. The contextual interpretation refers to the weights denoting the strength of connections between input variables (input units), constructs (hidden elements) representing types or clusters, and the network output. In contrast to the traditional segmentation methodology all the weight estimates serve one final purpose: to reproduce the desired *a priori* classification. The *aposteriori* portion of the network makes no exemption to this rule; it is also governed by the overall input–output mapping principle. Thus, the results do not just correspond to a data reduction or clustering solution derived from an external optimality criterion (for example, to render travellers homogeneous within and heterogeneous between types/clusters). Typological results (the *aposteriori* part) are not attained through the network model unless they relate to traveller attributes relevant for selective market operation. The typology formation turns out to be 'goal-oriented'. Unlike many other social science applications of type detecting methods (where 'unbiased' typologies might be desired) this is characteristic for research in marketing.

PSYCHOGRAPHICS, IDENTIFIERS AND REPEAT VISITATION

Background

The database of the Austrian National Guest Survey serves the National Tourist Office (ANTO) and other tourist organizations and businesses in optimizing their marketing decision making. In 1991–92 the study was commissioned for the fourth time. Special emphasis lay on guest attributes related to lifestyles and vacation styles. These concepts require a mixture of psychographic and behavioural variables. The traditional approach towards constructing vacation types implies a set of psychographics and/or activities subject to a clustering or factorization procedure (Darden and Darden 1976; Smith 1989: 52–62). Only afterwards, once the typology is complete, are the resulting types (*aposteriori* segments) evaluated as potential target markets. In contrast to the standard procedure this study attempts to perform the data reduction task while simultaneously maintaining the relation to a marketing objective.

Objectives

The ANTO management was primarily concerned about the guests' intention to repeat their visit. The examination of potential vacation styles is not an end in itself but part of a strategy to identify and to understand better travellers with a high likelihood to return to their summer 1991 destination.

The *a priori* part of the network model demands a classification into travellers with a strong ('almost certainly') versus a weak ('probably not') intention to repeat their visit within the next three years. The intermediate category ('probably') is skipped in order to accentuate the contrast (4,557 cases remain in the sample). Cherishing customer loyalty is a prominent objective in the marketing of services and an outstanding characteristic of the breakthrough companies (Heskett *et al.* 1990). Also in this example the 'probably not'-repeaters were not considered a target group. They only serve the purpose of detecting excitatory and inhibitory relationships. One should emphasize, however, that tourism marketing for an entire receiving country may be slightly different in its treatment of fluctuating demand. The 'once-and-never-again' guests have their merits. They spend significantly more than the repeaters and their seasonal prefer-ences are more balanced. Thus, the tourism industry also has to cater to the presumable non-repeaters and a National Tourist Office is expected to include them in some of its marketing strategies.

Model specification and data

The *aposteriori* part of the network model rests on two sets of items, travel motives and activities ('relevant things to do on a summer holiday'). That is where data reduction must step in to account for the mutual dependencies within each variable set. Motives as well as activities arrive in symptomatic combinations. Looking into them individually may be misleading. Given a number of six motives and eight activities it was hypothesized that not more than three motivational types and four activity types would emerge. Therefore, seven hidden elements ('constructs') are specified. The three motivational elements are fully connected to the six input units for motive items (main 'reasons for staying here'). The same applies to the four activity units and their eight observables (see Figure 8.2).

In addition to the multi-item attributes eight univariate descriptors were admitted. They fulfil the role of 'identifiers' (Day 1990: 103). These criteria correspond to the 'passive' variables in the traditional terminology. They are helpful in converting segmentation strategy into action. Their main purpose is to characterize repeaters and non-repeaters for selective exposure to marketing influence. One single hidden element is specified to absorb the predictive power of these attributes. All input variables are dichotomous. Table 8.1 contains the complete list with the abbreviations employed in the network graphs.

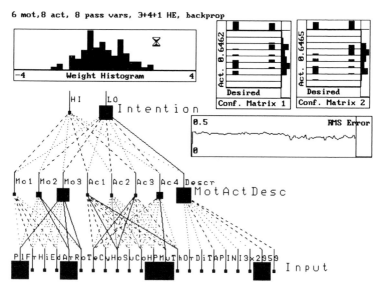

Figure 8.2 A neural network 'hybrid' model

Table 8.1 Variables, hidden units and weight estimates (before network pruning)

Input variables (abbreviation)	Connection weights for hidden units (types)							Descriptive variable group unit
	Mo1	Mo2	Mo3	Ac1	Ac2	Ac3	Ac4	
INPUT to HIDDEN LAYER								
Motives/ reasons:								
Pleasure, fun (Pl)	−1.04	−0.55	1.01					
Visit friends (Fr)	1.00	−0.69	−0.72					
Hiking (Hi)	0.37	−1.51	−0.97					
Education/ studies (Ed)	0.10	−0.61	−0.55					
Seeing works of art (Ar)	−1.29	1.14	1.00					
Tour, Round trip (Ro)	−0.90	1.48	2.08					
Activities:								
Playing tennis (Te)				0.36	−0.14	1.07	0.54	
Cycling (Cy)				0.22	−0.16	0.70	−0.55	
Horseriding (Ho)				1.14	−0.04	1.49	−0.48	
Sunbathing (Su)				0.57	−0.38	−0.57	−2.10	
Visiting historical sites/places (HP)				−0.74	−0.63	−1.34	−0.43	
Going to concerts (Co)				0.53	−0.02	0.38	−0.42	
Visiting museums (Mu)				0.07	−0.35	−0.42	1.44	
Going to the theatre (Th)				1.76	−0.06	0.51	−0.77	
Descriptors:								
Country of origin, Germany + Austria vs rest (Or)								−0.38
Advance arrangement directly with the place of accommodation (Di)								−0.86
Information from travel agent (TA)								0.43
Personal informants (PI)								−0.50
No information required (NI)								−0.22
Frequency of past visits, 2 or more (3x)								−2.14
Age, < 30 years (29)								0.98
30–59 (59)								0.65
HIDDEN LAYER to OUTPUT								
Connection weights for *a priori* classes:								
intention HI	0.62	−0.59	−0.14	0.65	−0.22	0.63	−0.93	−2.12
intention LO	−0.61	0.59	0.16	−0.64	0.24	−0.65	0.91	2.11

Comparison with discriminant analysis

All subsequent analyses are based on a random split of the sample, with 2,285 out of 4,557 cases retained for validation purposes. The remaining 2,272 cases are subject to discriminant as well as network estimation procedures. A linear discriminant analysis (DA) including all twenty-two variables (canonical correlation = 0.62, Wilks' lambda = 0.61) leads to an overall percentage of cases correctly classified (in the hold-out sample) of 75.4 per cent. Travellers with a low intention to repeat their visit are recognized more easily (81.2 per cent) than those with strong intentions (69.7 per cent; Table 8.3). Not surprisingly, the variables highly correlated with the canonical discriminant function are frequency of past visits (0.79) and direct prior arrangements/booking at the place of accommodation (0.51). Motivational criteria like 'seeing works of arts' (−0.26), going on a 'tour/round trip' (−0.23), and activities such as 'visiting museums' (−0.23) or 'visiting historical sites/places' (−0.23) follow next. The DA results are of practical value compared to a proportional chance (and also a maximal chance) criterion of 50 per cent correctly classified (Morrison 1969).

Network model results

The improvement expected here from a neural network model does not primarily relate to classification performance. As the network involves more parameters and a (nonlinear) mapping function of arbitrary complexity it should never perform worse than a traditional linear model. The innovative aspect is a conceptual one. The DA specification cannot accommodate the '*aposteriori* task' of typology formation. In the DA the motivational and activation variables are treated separately without exploiting their interrelationships for the generation of traveller types. The network model is expected to demonstrate how the individual motive and activity items unite or force out each other in favouring or impeding repeat visitation.

A NNW model is constructed with the Backpropagation Builder of the NeuralWorks Professional II/Plus Package (NeuralWare 1991a). Considering the experience collected in many other applications a hyperbolic tangent is chosen as transfer function squeezing the output of the processing elements into the [−1, 1] interval; the learning constant decreases gradually with the number of iterations and the hidden layer makes greater adjustments than the output layer in the early stages of the learning process (NeuralWare 1991b). Figure 8.2 and Table 8.1 present NNW results after 200,000 iterations. The Weight Distribution showing the magnitude of the weight values spreads out over a range from –2 to +2. The Root Mean Square Error (showing the goodness of fit between the expected and the predicted network output) moves downward continuously and the Confusion Matrices show a reasonable degree of correlation between the observed and predicted affiliation of the travellers with the 'hi' or 'lo' intention subgroups.

If the NNW model is fed with the cases in the hold-out sample 75.2 per cent are classified correctly (Table 8.3). It is easier to detect non-repeaters (82.4 per cent) than repeat travellers (67.9 per cent). Without the demographic and trip-related descriptors (age, country of origin, frequency of past visits, arrangements made prior to starting the trip, information behaviour) the percentage correctly classified drops to 62.4 per cent. This means that the two sets of motives/activities variables and 'passive' descriptors contribute roughly the same amount to the overall percentage correctly classified.

An examination of the weight structure (large values in Table 8.1 or solid connections in Figure 8.2 vs small values or dotted lines) reveals that the motivational and activity units Mo1, Ac1 and Ac3 are closely linked to a strong intention to repeat the visit. Elements Mo2, Ac2 and Ac4 are likely to be activated for non-repeaters. If the descriptive hidden unit becomes highly activated (indicated by a 'fat' box) it enforces a 'lo'-intention judgment.

Compared to the other units Mo3 and Ac2 have only weak connections to the output layer. The corresponding elements are candidates for elimination during a 'pruning' exercise. A less complex network is expected to generalize better when exposed to novel input data (Karnin 1990; NeuralWare 1991a: 78). In two pruning phases connection weights falling 10 per cent (up to 400,000 iterations) and then 20 per cent (until 440,000 iterations) below the maximum (absolute) weight value are removed (see Table 8.2 and Figure 8.3 with the weight histogram after removal of small weights around zero). The classification power slightly improves (Table 8.3). Conclusions are based on robust relationships and easily verified. Only two motive bundles ('types') are important in terms of repeat behaviour. A strong interest in 'works

Table 8.2 Variables, hidden units and weight estimates (after network pruning)

Input variables (abbreviation)	Connection weights for hidden units (types)					Descriptive variable
	Mo1	Mo2	Ac1	Ac3	Ac4	group unit
HIDDEN LAYER						
Motives/reasons:						
Pleasure, fun (Pl)	−1.18					
Visit friends (Fr)	0.91					
Hiking (Hi)		−1.65				
Education/studies (Ed)		−0.84				
Seeing works of art (Ar)	−1.25	1.25				
Tour, Round trip (Ro)	−0.97	1.69				
Activities:						
Playing tennis (Te)				1.28	0.76	
Cycling (Cy)				0.86	−0.60	
Horseriding (Ho)			1.19	1.68	−0.60	
Sunbathing (Su)			0.53	−0.58	−2.00	
Visiting historical sites/ places (HP)			−0.49	−1.30		
Going to concerts (Co)			0.64			
Visiting museums (Mu)					1.27	
Going to the theatre (Th)			1.70	0.49	−0.86	
Descriptors:						
Country of origin, Germany +Austria vs rest (Or)						
Advance arrangement directly with the place of accommodation (Di)						−0.93
Information from travel agent (TA)						0.56
Personal informants (PI)						
No information required (NI)						
Frequency of past visits, 2 or more (3x)						−2.00
Age, < 30 years (29)						0.84
30–59 (59)						0.60
HIDDEN LAYER to OUTPUT						
Connection weights for *a priori* classes:						
intention HI	0.64	−0.70	0.68	0.77	−0.89	−2.27
intention LO	−0.64	0.71	−0.67	−0.79	0.87	2.25

of art' in conjunction with a 'round trip' characterizes the non-repeater, in particular if it is not accompanied by a 'hiking' motive. By contrast, a single dominant purpose to 'visit friends and relatives' motivates a repeater.

At the same time the travellers are subject to a classification in

Table 8.3 Percentage correctly classified (hold-out sample)

Observed group membership	Predicted group membership							
	Discriminant analysis with all variables		Network without descriptors before pruning		Network with descriptors		Network with descriptors after pruning	
	HI	LO	HI	LO	HI	LO	HI	LO
Intention								
HI	69.7	30.3	61.4	38.6	67.9	32.1	70.2	29.8
LO	18.8	81.2	36.9	63.1	17.6	82.4	19.0	81.0
Percentage correctly classified	75.4		62.4		75.2		75.7	

terms of activities. There are two activity patterns or types prone to repeat their visit. Ac1 prefers to 'go to the theatre' (and concert); horseriding is the only sports activity worth mentioning. Travellers who arouse the Ac3 unit are 'sports-lovers'; tennis and cycling add to their list; sunbathing – more a 'passiveness' than an activity – and 'historical sites' do not fit into the activity pattern capable of increasing repeat visitation. Arousal of unit Ac4 characterizes a 'non-repeater' mostly occupied with 'visiting museums'; playing tennis would fit into the pattern but a typical preoccupation of a main-holiday maker such as sunbathing would definitely not.

Deriving guest types by a winner-takes-all classification

The arousal levels of the motive and activity units caused by each respondent's input data vector may be analysed separately. To portray the interrelationships among the Mo and Ac elements on the hidden layer of Figure 8.3 the activation values are extracted and processed in several ways. First they are correlated over all respondents. Then, according to the winner-takes-all principle, the highest element in its group is determined for each case leading to a classification into two Mo- and three Ac-types. After that the activation values are recoded into 'weak' and 'strong' with the mean value of each element serving as the cutting point. This procedure will assist in clarifying the amount of ambiguity in type affiliations.

With regard to Table 8.4, 37 per cent and 63 per cent of the

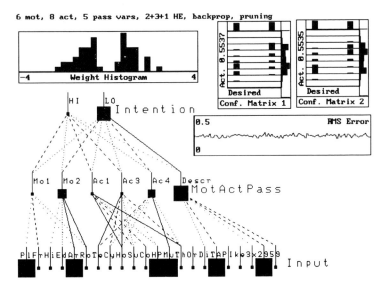

Figure 8.3 Network model after pruning

respondents (2,285 cases) appear to be Mo1 and Mo2 types arousing the respective element to win the competition against the rivals in its group. Two frequent types Ac1 and Ac4 and one minority type Ac3 result in the activities section. All the correlations between Mo and Ac activation values are small. Mo1 and Mo2 are rather unrelated; Ac1 is more similar to Ac3 than to Ac4.

Table 8.5 reports some indeterminacy of type affiliations. Sixty-one per cent of the cases produce a high loading either on Mo1 or Mo2 and a low activation on the other motive unit. Only 9 per cent

Table 8.4 Motive and activity bundles ('types'): size and interrelations

Hidden elements (types)	Mean activation value	No. of cases with highest activation on		Correlations with . . .			
				Mo2	Ac1	Ac3	Ac4
Mo1	.14	846	(37%)	−.47 *	.02	.08 *	−.18 *
Mo2	.24	1439	(63%)		−.02	−.10 *	.22 *
Ac1	.23	1066	(47%)	−.02		.36 *	−.37 *
Ac3	.12	169	(7%)	−.10 *	.36 *		−.14 *
Ac4	.18	1050	(46%)	.22 *	−.37 *	−.14 *	

* Signif.(2–tailed) < = .01

Table 8.5 Indeterminacy of motive and activity bundles ('types')

Motive and activity bundles (types)	Per cent of cases with high/low loading on . . .							
	Mo1		Mo2		Ac1		Ac3	
	hi	lo	hi	lo	hi	lo	hi	lo
Mo2								
hi	30	33						
lo	28	9						
Ac1								
hi	21	14	22	13				
lo	37	28	41	24				
Ac3								
hi	28	13	25	16	16	25		
lo	30	29	38	21	19	40		
Ac4								
hi	30	25	36	18	6	48	26	29
lo	28	17	27	19	29	17	15	30

produce weak activations on both units; 30 per cent are indeterminate with high loadings on either unit. Ac1 and Ac4 are least ambiguous but a considerable portion of Mo2 travellers overlap with Ac4 tourists.

To some extent the motive and activity bundles reinforce or neutralize each other. Mo1 (the 'visitor to friends', if not 'for fun' or for 'works of art' or on a 'round trip') is a minority type. If this motivational pattern is accompanied by an above average Ac3 profile ('sports with no historical interest') or by an Ac1 ('sports and theatre lover') rather than by an Ac4 profile ('museum visitor') a stronger tendency towards repeat visitation will result. Ac3 rarely wins the activity type arousal contest, but, in conjunction with a Mo1 motive profile, may contribute to produce a potential repeat visitor. By contrast, a strong non-repeating Mo2 activation tends to strengthen the Ac4 activity pattern in blocking repeat visitation.

To conclude, there are synergistic as well as counteracting effects within and between motivational and activity-oriented classifications not easily pursued in conventional multivariate analysis. The neural network approach, however, may prove capable of accommodating the *multimotive* aspect of travel behaviour emphasized by Pearce (1993).

Passive variables

'Frequency of past visits' among the complementary descriptors exerts a considerable influence strong enough to override the psychographic and lifestyle effects. 'Direct booking' and 'age' are also well represented in the compound descriptive unit. 'Information from a travel agent' and the younger age brackets coincide with low intention; 'two or more past visits' and 'direct arrangements' with the place of accommodation inhibit the descriptive unit in getting activated, thus preventing it from 'firing' 'lo'-intention ammunition.

CONCLUSIONS

Suggestions for future research

The foregoing connectionist findings differ from traditional typology construction in several ways. On the hidden layer of typology formation (the *aposteriori* subsystem) travellers are not classified into exhaustive and mutually exclusive clusters. In fact a person may be ambiguous with respect to motivational and/or activity types. In network terminology this means that more than one hidden element gets activated and induced to 'fire' into the output layer. No information is lost if a case does not fit nicely into a typological straitjacket.

Compared to traditional methodology the typological information extracted is not complete. The hidden units (as type equivalents) cannot survive a pruning process unless they contribute to the final classification target (the *a priori* subsystem). There, on the output layer, the amount of excitation of the 'lo' and 'hi' intention units may be interpreted as *aposteriori* probabilities (not yet normalized) in the Bayesian sense. The allocation of travellers follows the maximum probability rule (winner-takes-all).

A next step in exploring NNW models for typology formation will be to detach the *aposteriori* subsystem from the *a priori* classification during an initial stage and to combine the two subsystems afterwards. In particular, the so-called 'self-organizing maps' (SOM) (Kohonen 1984) are worth experimenting with. Under the SOM paradigm a two-dimensional layer of hidden units performs the typology formation of the *aposteriori* segmentation task. This 'Kohonen layer' accomplishes a data reduction by transforming input vectors of arbitrary dimensionality into a two-dimensional mapping. The transformation preserves order in such a way that input vectors (cases) similar to each other tend to stimulate neighbouring units on the hidden layer. The second phase of weight estimation relates typology results and complementary descriptive attributes to an output layer of desired *a priori* classes. Compared to the NNW model outlined above the typology formation will not be 'disturbed' by any pre-determined partitioning. The idea sounds very familiar to analysts normally applying a clustering approach: first let the types evolve themselves and then have them assessed in terms of consumption criteria (but in the same network).

Outlook for travel marketing practice

The neurocomputing methodology arrives just in time for managers to cope with travel market segmentation in the 1990s. What are the expectations for the foreseeable future? With the increasing saturation of the mass markets more destinations and tour operators will experience the need for selective market operation. The simple-minded approaches to segmentation exclusively relying on demographics or socio-economic criteria are becoming obsolete. They will be complemented by a finer tapestry of psychographic typologies (involving motives, values and lifestyles, or benefits) and activity bundles.

Tourism marketing research will have to put more effort into exploring *vacation styles* as the appearance of tourist products continues to shift from *'place and service'* to *'temporary escape into another lifestyle'*. The empirical analysis of all sorts of psychographics and activity variables automatically requires large data sets and appropriate data reduction methods for typology construction. The traditional techniques of typology formation run the risk of constructing types that are nicely different in terms of psychographics but rather homogeneous behaviourally (or vice versa). Neural networks attempt to incorporate both aspects.

Currently, NNW model specification may be regarded 'more an art than science'. New methodology such as genetic algorithms will contribute to rendering the specification process more objective and analytically tractable. Network training on sequential machines takes a lot of computing time. With optical computers and massively parallel processing schemes implemented in hardware the computing time for network training will become almost negligible.

There are some caveats: as the statistical properties of neural networks presently are not very well understood the method favours exploratory research over inferential reasoning. Advanced methodology further broadens the gap between tourism marketing research and practice. Greater emphasis will have to be laid on involving managers and on the didactic value of analytical results. The Austrian National Tourist Office, for example, has successfully employed the EUROSTYLES lifestyle typology (Mazanec and Zins 1993) to educate local tourism managers. A visualization of the individual types, their personal attributes, their consumption and vacation patterns or media habits greatly helps in demonstrating that markets are made up of distinct target groups calling for specialized offerings and promotional treatment. Based on changes and developments in tourism in the last decade or so, the diverse nature of the tourism market may be expected to continue and probably become even more specific in its requirements in the future.

REFERENCES

Aleksander, I. and Morton, H. (1990) *An Introduction to Neural Computing*, London: Chapman & Hall.

Arndt, J. (1974) *Market Segmentation*, Bergen: Universitetsforlaget.

Bagozzi, R. P. (1980) *Causal Models in Marketing*, New York: Wiley.

—— (1986) *Principles of Marketing Management*, Chicago: Science Research Associates.

Bernard, M. (1987) 'Leisure-rich and leisure-poor: Leisure lifestyles among young adults', *Leisure Sciences* 10, 131–149.

Cathelat, B. (1985) *Styles de vie*, vols 1 and 2, Paris: Éditions d'organisation.

Claycamp, H. J. and Massy, W. F. (1968) 'A theory of market segmentation', *Journal of Marketing Research* 5, 388–394.

Cohen, E. (1988) 'Traditions in qualitative sociology of tourism', *Annals of Tourism Research* 15, 1: 29–46.

Dann, G., Nash, D. and Pearce, P. (1988) 'Methodology in tourism research', *Annals of Tourism Research* 15, 1: 1–28.

Darden, W. and Darden, D. (1976) 'A study of vacation life styles', in Travel and Tourism Research Association, *Proceedings of the 7th Annual Conference*, Salt Lake City: TTRA, 231–236.

Day, G. S. (1990) *Market Driven Strategy, Process for Creating Value*, New York: Free Press.

Frank, R.E. (1968) 'Market segmentation research: Findings and implications', in F.M. Bass, C.W. King and E.A. Pessemier (eds) *Applications of the Sciences in Marketing Management*, New York: Wiley, 39–68.

Freeman, J. A. and Skapura, D. M. (1991) *Neural Networks, Algorithms, Applications, and Programming Techniques*, Reading: Addison-Wesley.

Heskett, J.L., Sasser, W.E. and Hart, C.W.L. (1990) *Service Breakthroughs*, New York: Free Press.

Hruschka, H. and Natter, M. (1992) *Using Neural Networks for Clustering-Based Market Segmentation, Research Memorandum No. 307*, Vienna: Institute for Advanced Studies.

—— (1993) 'Analyse von Marktsegmenten mit Hilfe konnexionistischer Modelle', *Zeitschrift für Betriebswirtschaft* 63, 425–442.

Hsieh, S., O'Leary, J.T. and Morrison, A.M. (1992) 'Segmenting the international travel market by activity', *Tourism Management* 13, 209–223.

Hustad, T. P. and Pessemier, E. A. (1971) *Segmenting Consumer Markets with Activity and Attitude Measures*, Paper no. 298, Krannert Graduate School of Industrial Administration, Purdue University.

Jöreskog, K.G. (1982) 'The LISREL approach to causal model-building in the social sciences', in K.G. Jöreskog and H. Wold (eds) *Systems Under Indirect Observation*, Part I, Amsterdam: North-Holland, 81–99.

Kamakura, W.A. and Novak, T.P. (1992) 'Value-system segmentation: Exploring the meaning of LOV', *Journal of Consumer Research* 19, 119–132.

Karnin, D.D. (1990) 'A simple procedure for pruning back-propagation trained neural networks', *IEEE Transactions on Neural Networks* 1, 239–242.

Kohonen, T. (1984) *Self-Organization and Associative Memory*, Berlin: Springer.

Kotler, P. (1967) *Marketing Management, Analysis, Planning, and Control*, Englewood Cliffs: Prentice-Hall.

Mayo, E. J. and Jarvis, L. P. (1981) *The Psychology of Leisure Travel*, Boston, Mass.: CBI.

Mazanec, J. (1978) *Strukturmodelle des Konsumverhaltens*, Vienna: Orac.

—— (1990) 'Market segmentation once again: Exploring neural network models', in *Association Internationale d'Experts Scientifique du Tourisme, Tourist Research as a Commitment*, St Gall: AIEST, 36–53.

—— (1992) 'Classifying tourists into market segments: A neural network approach', *Journal of Travel & Tourism Marketing* 1, 39–59.

Mazanec, J. and Zins, A. (1993) 'Tourist behaviour and the new European lifestyle typology', in W. Theobald (ed.) *Tourism in the 21st Century*, Oxford: Butterworth-Heinemann.

Morrison, D. G. (1969) 'On the interpretation of discriminant analysis', *Journal of Marketing Research* 6, 156–163.

NeuralWare Inc. (1991a) *Reference Guide, NeuralWorks Professional II/Plus*, Pittsburgh: Technical Publications Group.

—— (1991b) *Neural Computing, NeuralWorks Professional II/Plus*, Pittsburgh: Technical Publications Group.

Pearce, P. L. (1982) *The Social Psychology of Tourist Behaviour*, Oxford: Pergamon Press.

—— (1993) 'Fundamentals of tourist motivation', in D.G. Pearce and R.W. Butler (eds) *Tourism Research: Critiques and Challenges*, London/New York: Routledge, 113–134.

Ruck, D.W., Rogers, S.K., Kabrisky, M., Oxley, M.E. and Suter, B.W. (1990) 'The multilayer perceptron as an approximation to a Bayes optimal discriminant function', *IEEE Transactions on Neural Networks* 1, 296–298.

Rumelhardt, D.E., Hinton, G.E. and Williams, R.J. (1986) 'Learning internal representation by error propagation', in D.E. Rumelhart and J.L. McClelland (eds) *Parallel Distributed Processing, Vol. I: Foundations*, Cambridge: MIT Press, 318–362.

Shoemaker, P. A. (1991) 'A note on least-squares learning procedures and classification by neural network models', *IEEE Transactions on Neural Networks* 2, 158–160.

Simpson, P.K. (1990) *Artificial Neural Systems*, New York: Pergamon Press.

Smith, S.L.J. (1989) *Tourism Analysis, A Handbook*, New York: Wiley.

Vavrik, U. and Mazanec, J. (1990) 'A-priori and a-posteriori travel market segmentation: Tailoring automatic interaction detection and cluster analysis for tourism marketing', *Cahiers du Tourisme*, Série C No. 62, Aix-en-Provence: Centre des Hautes Études Touristiques.

Veal, A.J. (1989) 'Leisure, lifestyles and status', *Leisure Studies* 8, 141–153.

Wan, E.A. (1990) 'Neural network classification: A Bayesian interpretation', *IEEE Transactions on Neural Networks* 1, 303–305.

Wasserman, P. D. (1989) *Neural Computing, Theory and Practice*, New York: Van Nostrand Reinhold.

Wells, W.D. (ed.) (1974) *Life Style and Psychographics*, Chicago: American Marketing Association.

Wells, W.D. (1975) 'Psychographics: A critical review', *Journal of Marketing Research* 12, 196–213.

Wells, W.D. and Tigert, D.J. (1971) 'Activities, interests and opinions', *Journal of Advertising Research* 11, 27–35.

Winkler, A.R. (1991) 'EURO-STYLES in panel analyses', *Europanel Marketing Bulletin* 8–11.

Yiannakis, A. and Gibson, H. (1992) 'Roles tourists play', *Annals of Tourism Research* 19, 2: 287–303.

Chapter 9

The emergence of casino gaming as a major factor in tourism markets
Policy issues and considerations

William R. Eadington

By the 1990s in the United States, Canada, the European Community, Australia and New Zealand, as well as in various developing countries, there had emerged a substantial increase in the legal and social acceptance of gambling and commercial gaming. Gaming industries had become increasingly sophisticated and legitimate to reflect this new reality and change in attitude in society.

From a consumer's perspective, gambling had transformed itself over the previous thirty years from an inappropriate 'sinful' endeavour to a mainstream participatory activity. From the perspective of governments, gaming seemed to hold the potential to create certain economic and fiscal benefits that were otherwise elusive. Furthermore, as acceptability increased, various special interests, ranging from charities to churches to private enterprises to government agencies, lobbied for the right to earn the franchise to offer commercial gaming services to the general public – or at least be the passive benefactor – so as to capture the resultant economic benefits, often for some higher stated purpose than merely their own self-interest.

The type of emerging commercial gaming activity which has the greatest relevance to tourism issues is casino gaming, especially destination resort casino gaming. Casinos have been historically identified with exotic venues such as Las Vegas, Monte Carlo, Baden Baden, Australia's Gold Coast or The Bahamas. However, increasingly by the 1990s, casino legalization and authorization had become part of broader tourism development strategies in locations not commonly associated with destination resort casinos, such as Sydney, Australia; Biloxi/Gulfport and Tunica County, Mississippi; Windsor, Ontario; Athens, Greece; Auckland, New Zealand; and Amsterdam, Holland.

For the most part, public policy attitudes towards gambling throughout the world – perhaps with the exception of most Asian countries – shifted from viewing gambling as a vice to treating it as an opportunity to be exploited. This is perhaps the main reason why there developed such a strong trend towards legalization of new forms of commercial gaming and the relaxation of constraints on existing commercial gaming activities from the 1980s onward. Based on the events leading up to the mid-1990s, these trends promise to continue and perhaps even accelerate by the turn of the twenty-first century.

This analysis looks specifically at the issue of casino gaming and its relationship to tourism development in various settings. Since the dominant motivation of casino legalization in most jurisdictions deals with the objective of capturing the economic benefits that such legalization can bring about, jurisdictions must realistically assess the likelihood that casinos can indeed be the economic catalyst they expect or hope them to be. This, in turn, depends upon a number of circumstantial issues, such as interjurisdictional competition, the general appeal of casinos to both local markets and potential tourism markets, and the constraints that regulation and statute might place upon the gaming operations. All of these issues will be dealt with below.

VARIATIONS IN THE CHARACTERISTICS OF CASINOS

There are a variety of types of casinos that have emerged with the proliferation of legal gaming that provide insight into the directions future trends may take. Casinos can be categorized according to their general physical structure and characteristics; with regard to their geographic placement; with regard to their size, exclusivity and other market structure aspects which are dictated by statutory or regulatory edict; by competitive market conditions or by private or public sector ownership.

Casino structures

Often casinos are authorized or developed with the idea of harking back to a more idyllic era, or of creating a striking visual or fantasy experience for the customer (see Cohen Chapter Two; Graburn Chapter Four). This is often reflected in the physical structures in which casinos are located. Thus casinos – old and new – can be divided into the following forms:

1 casinos in historic or refurbished structures;
2 casinos on riverboats;
3 casinos in purpose-built facilities with limited non-gaming amenities; or
4 casinos in purpose-built facilities with extensive non-gaming amenities and attractions.

At the stage of legalization, there are many reasons why governmental bodies or private sector companies might choose any one of the above alternatives. In practice, where casinos are allowed, the choices are often limited by statutory or regulatory constraints placed upon gaming operators. The following discussion sheds light on the strengths and weaknesses of each of these various types of venues.

Historic or refurbished structures

Casinos in various parts of the world can be found in historic buildings or buildings that were initially constructed for purposes other than housing casinos. For example, most of the casinos in London (UK) – legalized by the Gaming Act of 1968 – are quite small, being located in former residences or in space that was originally built for other purposes, such as offices or restaurants. Many continental European casinos follow the same pattern. In Winnipeg, Canada, an exclusive franchise government-owned casino opened in 1990 on the top floors of an early-twentieth-century railroad hotel, and in Atlantic City, New Jersey, where the first legal casino opened in 1978, two of the initial casinos developed were placed in structures that were originally early-twentieth-century Boardwalk hotels. In Australia, the casino in Adelaide that opened in 1985 was adapted from a former railway station, and the Brisbane casino – scheduled to open in 1995 – is housed in the former Treasury Building, a late-nineteenth-century heritage structure.

Though the motivation for developing casinos in historic or refurbished structures is often to preserve the building because of its architectural or historic significance, there are usually design difficulties, shortcomings or challenges associated with such projects. These are either dictated by the physical limits of the facility or the rigidity of rules regarding alterations to heritage structures. Frequently, such buildings are quite limiting in terms of the allowable size or placement of a casino. For example, because of size constraints, most London casinos have fewer than fifteen gaming tables and no more than two slot machines – though the limit on slot machines is a legal constraint. The casino in Winnipeg has limited ingress and egress with only three elevators as the alternative to a ten storey stairway ascent or descent, and the casino itself is quite small, constrained by the square footage available. The Adelaide casino and public facilities are spread over three levels and the setting is not conducive to easy customer flow through the building.

Furthermore, casinos in refurbished buildings are often at a disadvantage – especially in comparison to purpose-built casinos – in the provision of various non-gaming amenities for visitors to the facility. Based on the size and configuration of the original structure, there may be significant limitations on space availability for restaurants, parking, entertainment venues or other facilities that are complementary to a successful casino operation. Finally, historic buildings are not always geographically located at the best physical site for a casino. Generally speaking, it might not be possible to develop a casino in a refurbished building which is of adequate size or meets the entertainment demands of its potential customer base. This is often due to the fact that the design requirements of a building in its original use may have been quite different from the needs and demands of a casino facility. Architects and engineers might be able to make such structures more 'user-friendly' through creative – and perhaps expensive – remodelling, but some limitations of the original building might be insurmountable.

Of course, some of the earliest European casinos were placed in purpose-built structures which themselves were quite elegant and have since become buildings of historic significance. The old casino at Monte Carlo fits this description, as do the German casinos at Baden Baden, Aachen and Wiesbaden.

Riverboat casinos

Riverboat casinos emerged in the early 1990s in the United States as a politically palatable, though not necessarily a logical or efficient, venue for casino gaming. The justification was usually couched in a nostalgic recreation (not unlike that discussed by Graburn Chapter Four) of *ante bellum* nineteenth-century riverboats which carried professional gamblers among their passengers between ports on the Mississippi. For various reasons, including lobbying by riverboat interests, they have been legislatively successful. However, the limitations of casinos on riverboats point out – by their absence – some of the fundamentals needed for successful gaming operations in increasingly competitive environments.

By 1993, riverboat casinos were approved or operating in the American states of Iowa, Illinois, Mississippi, Louisiana, Missouri and Indiana. In all these jurisdictions – with the exception of Mississippi and some sites in Missouri which permit dockside riverboat gaming – enabling legislation required that riverboats would sail, that is, they have to leave their docks and sail on rivers or other bodies of water. (In some jurisdictions, exceptions would be allowed in winter or during inclement weather.) Riverboat casinos that must make excursions have the following characteristics that make them 'customer unfriendly' in comparison to land-based or dockside casinos:

1 they typically require customers to pay admission fees;
2 they have to hold to fixed schedules for departure and return, and such schedules might not coincide with customer desires on how long to gamble;
3 they require certified maritime crews and incur operating costs for sailing that are unrelated to gaming operations;
4 they incur various safety risks that are not present with land-based casino operations, that is boats can sink;
5 they are unable to operate as a casino as many hours per day as a comparable land-based facility because of schedule limitations; and
6 there can be serious problems of ingress and egress, and queuing for parking and admission because of the fixed departure and arrival schedules.

Many of these limitations can be overcome by allowing riverboats to offer dockside gaming, as has been done in Mississippi and parts of Missouri. Dockside legislation has permitted the development of casinos on permanently docked and non-seaworthy vessels. Indeed, in Mississippi, this has led to construction of casino facilities which often are not even on boats, but are rather the equivalent of land-based buildings built over authorized waterways.

Clearly, cross-border competition for tourism and gaming revenues will tempt other states to authorize new laws that will not require riverboats with casinos to sail, or, alternatively, states might approve land-based casinos which are clearly more cost competitive and 'user friendly' than casinos on sailing riverboats. If this emerges as a dominant trend, then riverboat casinos will have difficulty competing against nearby land-based casinos.

Purpose-built casinos with limited non-gaming amenities

In some North American jurisdictions, especially where competition for casino gaming is limited, purpose-built casinos have been constructed that provide gaming opportunities, but little else. This has been the case with some of the gaming jurisdictions on Indian lands in such locales as Connecticut, Wisconsin, Minnesota, California, Arizona and Washington State in the early 1990s. Usually, such facilities have no hotel or motel accommodation, limited restaurant or buffet outlets, and no entertainment venues. They are able to satisfy some of the demand for gaming, but they offer little else in terms of meeting customer needs and demands for complementary activities, such as restaurants, lodging and entertainment venues. Often, they exist in monopoly or quasi-monopoly situations in undersupplied gaming markets and are able to operate quite profitably in spite of an absence of complementary activities. In competitive environments, such as Nevada, such single purpose casinos have become increasingly uncommon because they have difficulty competing against more 'full service' casino facilities.

However, in some newly authorized gaming jurisdictions, such as New Orleans and Windsor, legislation mandates casinos cannot be full service, for fear that they will provide unfair competition for existing hotel or restaurant businesses. In particular, the legislation authorizing the only land-based New Orleans casino requires that the facility cannot have hotel or significant restaurant facilities, and in Windsor the planned exclusive franchise casino will only have limited restaurants and cannot open its hotel facilities until the hotel occupancy rate for the city's other hotels exceeds 75 per cent.

Purpose-built casinos with extensive non-gaming amenities and attractions

The casino development trend in many jurisdictions throughout the world is towards the construction of purpose-built casino–hotel complexes which offer a variety of non-gaming amenities such as hotel, restaurant, entertainment facilities and amusement areas, along with architecturally unique features. Such has certainly been the case with new casinos developed in the 1990s in Las Vegas, Nevada, such as the MGM Grand, the Luxor, Treasure Island, the Mirage, and the Excalibur; and in South Africa, with the Lost City and the Carousel Casinos. In many cases their styles and designs reflect the 'inauthentic' discussed by Cohen (Chapter Two). The major Australian casinos in Perth and the Gold Coast (Queensland) meet this description, as do most of the casinos in Atlantic City, New Jersey, and in other Nevada locations such as Laughlin, Reno and Lake Tahoe.

There are a variety of advantages to such facilities. First, since the casinos are purpose-built, they can be developed with the anticipated size and preferences of the customer market in mind. Thus, they can address ingress and egress issues, availability and amount of parking and floor plan design and customer flow aspects, as well as hotel, restaurant and entertainment facilities. They can be tailored to the particular needs of specific markets or market niches. Their ultimate success depends on how well they are able to match the preferences of their customers.

Casino locations

Casinos also can be classified in terms of where they are located. The following categories can be used to classify types of location:

1 distant from urban population concentrations in areas with natural touristic attractions (for example, Monte Carlo, Deauville, the Gold Coast, The Bahamas, Lake Tahoe, Baden Baden);

2 outside of urban population concentrations in settings that may or may not have natural touristic attractions, but which are conveniently located relative to urban concentrations (for example, Las Vegas, Reno, Atlantic City, Sun City in Bophuthatswana, the Highlands outside Kuala Lumpur, Malaysia);

3 in major urban centres, but established in such a manner that access by the local population is discouraged, constrained or prohibited (for example, London, Berlin, Seoul, Cairo, Istanbul); or

4 in major urban centres, and which are openly accessible to local

and regional populations (for example, Adelaide, Perth, Melbourne, Sydney, Montreal, Windsor/Detroit, Kansas City, St Louis).

Clearly, the historic pattern had been to isolate casinos from urban population concentrations. This was often motivated by a system of belief that suggested casinos by their very nature are predatory and therefore dangerous to the indigenous working-class population. France, for example, prohibits the offering of casino 'wheel' games, such as roulette, within 100 kilometres of Paris. Legislators of the day (1907) apparently believed that it would be impossible for a person to travel 100 kilometres in a day in order to gamble in a casino, and return home the same day. If casino gaming is to be allowed, such attitudes proclaimed, it should only be made available to those who can afford it, during their leisure time away from their 'real' lives.

Often, some locales with natural touristic settings either allowed casinos to cater to the appropriate socio-economic classes who could afford to frequent such vacation spots, or encouraged casinos to play an important role in developing and supporting the local economy or infrastructure of the area. Such a description would certainly fit such historic casino sites as Baden Baden, the French Riviera, Monaco and Lake Tahoe.

The most recent trend has been the emergence of urban casinos. These are casinos located in the centre of major population centres. Prior to the mid-1980s, the only types of casinos to be found in cities anywhere in the world were relatively invisible or highly restrictive in terms of who could enter them. Thus, one could visit any of more than twenty casinos in London, but only if one were a member of the casino club, and only if one had declared one's intention forty-eight hours prior to one's first visit to that club that one desired to gamble. However, beginning in the mid-1980s, easily accessible casinos in urban areas have started to emerge. The Australian cities of Perth and Adelaide – each with a population of about one million – were the first to have easily accessible urban casinos in major metropolitan areas, when they opened exclusive franchise casinos in 1985. By the early 1990s, easily accessed urban casinos had opened or had been authorized in the cities of Brisbane, Melbourne, Sydney, Auckland, Christchurch, Amsterdam, Rotterdam, New Orleans, Kansas City, St Louis, Montreal, Windsor and Winnipeg. Some of these are land-based, some on riverboats; some are developed in historically significant buildings, whereas others are purpose built.

Perhaps of greatest significance in this process of change has been the decline in the belief that casinos in cities would create substantial social damage. In light of the fact that, for the most part, urban casinos are just beginning to appear on the scene in the early 1990s, this may turn out to be an erroneous position. The issue of social problems linked to casinos – in urban areas in particular – may once again become a major concern, reflecting the changing role and place of leisure and tourism in society (Nash Chapter Three).

Market structure

Another characteristic difference of note between casinos from one jurisdiction to another has to do with the market structure conditions that prevail. This can be due either to government or statutory edict or to the evolutionary working of competitive forces. In many jurisdictions there are no legislative or regulatory barriers to entry, so competitive forces are allowed to dictate the size, variety and extent of the casino market. However, in such circumstances, there seem to be natural economies of scale that come into play, and smaller and less diverse casino operations are generally unable to compete effectively against larger, more diverse operations. This is clearly an observable pattern in such competitive markets as Las Vegas and Reno, as well as in some of the newer emerging markets in the United States such as Colorado and Mississippi.

However, many new jurisdictions are following the so-called 'Australian approach', which is to authorize only a single exclusive franchise casino for each jurisdiction, and then to invite bids from possible owning or operating companies for the purpose of running the monopoly casino (Mossenson 1991; Neilson 1991). If done correctly, the government which passes the enabling legislation is then able to capture the lion's share of the excess rents by inducing competing bidders to offer higher and higher prices for the monopoly licence. This process has characterized all the casino bids in Australia and New Zealand, as well as in New Orleans and Windsor.

Finally, government owned and operated casinos have emerged in a number of jurisdictions. The casinos of Holland and Austria are owned by corporations which themselves are owned by the government. The casinos in Winnipeg and in Montreal are owned and operated by their respective provincial lottery companies, and the casino in Windsor is to be built and operated by a private sector company, but will be owned by a government Crown Corporation.

LEGALIZATION OF CASINOS AND POLICY CONSIDERATIONS

As more and more jurisdictions consider legal casino gaming, policy-makers will have to weigh a variety of economic, moral and social considerations. Such a process is useful to evaluate the decision whether or not to authorize casinos, and – if the decision is positive – to determine the regulatory and operational constraints to which casino operations should be subject. Traditional cost–benefit analysis can be prone to biases in evaluating the decision to legalize casinos. Benefits are usually in the form of economic impacts that accompany the introduction of casino gaming industries (and other forms of tourist development as noted by Wanhill Chapter Ten), which can be in the form of new jobs, induced investment activities and new tax revenues, offset to some extent by demands on law enforcement, fire protection, infrastructure improvements and social services. Another economic benefit is the creation of consumer surplus brought about by meeting the latent demand of potential customers for gaming facilities. Assuming consumer expenditures on gaming are rational within the standard context of economic analysis, making casino gaming available increases utility for consumers as they reallocate expenditures to gaming from other activities.

As a group, economic impacts linked to legalization of casinos tend to be tangible and quantifiable, and for the most part are positive, especially in jurisdictions where casino gaming is substantially undersupplied. On the other hand, non-economic impacts, such as social costs linked to gambling, are usually intangible, difficult to measure and – on balance – negative. Thus, if a jurisdiction relies primarily on economic considerations in approaching the decision to legalize gaming, there may be a systematic bias that overemphasizes benefits and underestimates costs. When casino gaming is legalized, substantial potential for excess profits – economic rents – can arise. Allocation of these economic rents becomes an integral part of the public policy process, even though social costs may be ignored in the process. Comprehensive policy should try to mitigate social costs associated with such legalization by tapping the economic rents – through taxes, regulatory constraints or mandated actions by operators – in order to reduce the various costs associated with the new legal status of gaming. Furthermore, since the guidelines by which casino gaming can be operated and controlled are created by a political process, the allocation of economic rents to 'deserving' parties also becomes part of the deliberation. The experience of a number of new casino jurisdictions in the 1980s and 1990s has been characterized by the following pattern of events. When casinos open, they meet a latent demand for casino-style gaming among the general public. Revenues generated by legal casino gaming typically far exceed the volume of illegal or social gambling that legalization might have displaced. This creates an interesting question of from where gaming expenditures are reallocated; that is, which industries and activities, on balance, are substituted away from when people spend in casinos? Various studies have pointed out that wagering on horse races clearly declines when casino-style gaming is made available in the same market (Syme 1992; Thalheimer 1992). However, such expenditures also have to be redistributed from other economic activities, such as restaurants, bars and taverns, and other sources of discretionary expenditure (see Nash's discussion on the necessity of surplus production or decreased consumption as a precondition for tourism and leisure to exist in a society, Chapter Three, and Wanhill's discussion on displacement in Chapter Ten).

That there is a strong latent demand for gambling – given the option, many people will choose to gamble – has not by itself been a sufficient reason for moving from prohibition to legalization. In order to be politically acceptable, the legalization of casino gaming – as well as other forms of commercial gaming – must be linked to one or more 'higher purpose' that can benefit from an allocation of a portion of the created economic rents in order to overcome the arguments against gambling. Such higher purposes may be such things as tax benefits, investment stimuli, job creation, regional economic development or redevelopment, and revenue enhancement for deserving interests. Thus, for example, casinos have been legalized in hopes of stimulating local and regional economies, and revitalizing or bolstering existing tourist industries.

Charities have been authorized to sponsor a variety of gambling activities – such as 'Las Vegas' casino nights – because the revenues extracted from gambling's excess rents allows such organizations to better fulfil their charitable objectives. Casino gaming on Indian reserves in America and Canada has received political support because of its ability to provide economic development opportunities and wealth for otherwise impoverished Indian tribes and bands.

The experience in North America in the past few years has been that seldom does casino gaming become legal without substantial public debate on its merits and its costs. The traditional arguments against legalizing gaming are that the activity is immoral and works against family and social values that directly link reward to hard work; that gambling is inseparable from disrespect for the law, political corruption and infiltration by organized crime; and that it can lead to personal and family tragedies from compulsive or pathological gambling behaviour. Policy makers considering legalization of casino-style gambling are confronted with evaluating the strength of these arguments in light of the consequences of keeping gambling in a prohibited status. Certainly, if gambling is kept illegal, it is likely it will still play a role in society. The appropriate comparison is between the amount of cost (and benefit) associated with illegal gambling in comparison to legally sanctioned gambling which is constrained through a variety of regulatory or statutory options.

General objections to legal gambling have clearly weakened during the second half of the twentieth century. Moral arguments, which in the past were most strongly put forward by churches and government bodies, have suffered partly because of the diminishing authority such institutions presently carry in comparison to previous times, and partly because many churches and governments have themselves become actively involved – through charitable gambling, church bingo and lotteries – in the provision of commercial gaming services. Also, in comparison to previous generations, the general public does not rank gambling as a significant immoral activity in the 1990s.

Perhaps the main reason why gambling has been illegal for so long – at least in America – has been its association with organized crime, political corruption and scandal. Such concerns are most likely to emerge in jurisdictions with legacies of such problems, or in environments where gambling is either prohibited or highly constrained but where public officials have considerable discretion in awarding contracts or as to whether they will enforce the law. Furthermore, much of the history of crime and corruption associated with gambling in the United States and elsewhere is linked to illegal gambling, a by-product of prohibition. There is somewhat of a chicken and egg problem associated with the legitimacy of gaming and issues of corruption. In Nevada, New Jersey, Australia and the United Kingdom, as legal commercial gaming has become more legitimate and established, and as regulatory bodies have become more professional and sophisticated, the opportunities for corruption and for organized crime infiltration into many gaming operations have diminished. However, where casinos remain prohibited or considered outside the mainstream of business activities, they can still invite problems of corruption. In light of the recent proliferation of casinos in America, there is ongoing concern that some jurisdictions – especially those which tend towards under-regulation or have a legacy of political corruption – will once again enmesh casino gaming in scandal with such problems.

The issue of compulsive or pathological gambling – problem gambling – is perhaps the most important concern of otherwise legitimate casino jurisdictions. The relation of casinos to problem gambling is not unlike the relation of the liquor industry to alcoholism. Problem gambling is, in part, a by-product of the availability of casinos, and various policies can mitigate the damage associated with problem gambling, though it is folly to act as if such problems do not exist. There are two related research questions that should be part of the public policy debate. First, how prevalent is the incidence of compulsive gambling, especially when society changes the legal status of gambling? Second, what policies will be most effective in dealing with the consequences of problem gambling, especially when gambling is made more available through legalization? Neither of these questions has been definitively answered, but there is a growing body of research that addresses them (Shaffer *et al.* 1989; Eadington and Cornelius 1993).

The issue of incidence involves both the question of definition (what constitutes being a 'compulsive gambler'?) – and measurement (how many compulsive gamblers can be expected in jurisdictions with different degrees of access to legal or illegal gambling opportunities?). Studies from the United States and elsewhere indicate an incidence of compulsive gambling of between 1 per cent and 5 per cent of the adult population (Volberg 1989). Furthermore, greater access to legal gambling – in particular, to the more exciting forms of gambling which casinos provide – seems to lead to a greater incidence of compulsive gambling.

On the question of appropriate public policy, it is instructive to compare gambling with certain other 'morally suspect' activities. In recent years with gambling, there has been a trend towards allowing adults to have greater control over their choice of activities and to allow them to be more responsible for the consequences of their actions. However, this principle has not been applied uniformly over other so-called 'vices', such as alcohol, tobacco, illicit drug use, prostitution and pornography. These vices, along with gambling, have similar economic and social characteristics. Each is characterized by strong demand for the activity, at least from select segments of the population, a belief that the activity should be constrained to some extent to control its negative social consequences, and a history of changing social and legal tolerance and acceptance.

In spite of their similarities, each of these vices seems to be at a different place on its 'social acceptance' cycle. With illicit drugs, the last three decades have been characterized by a strong drive to prohibit both use and sale, accompanied by severe penalties for violations of legal sanctions. With tobacco smoking, there has been an increase in restrictions on both users and producers, partly to protect potential consumers from being 'seduced' into smoking (thus prohibitions against certain types of advertising), and to protect non-smokers from the health and aesthetic costs of having to share space with smokers (leading to the creation of 'smoking prohibited' spaces). With alcohol, the response to social costs created by alcohol abusers has been to attempt to mitigate third party costs through deterrence by implementing stiff penalties on such things as drunken driving violations or on establishments who serve patrons who are visibly inebriated. With alcohol and tobacco, there will likely be a trend towards denial of insurance benefits associated with health costs related to use or abuse in some jurisdictions. Common perceptions of problem gambling suggest the individual has little or no control over his or her actions while gambling, and therefore cannot be held fully responsible for the consequences (Rose 1988). Because of this, it is difficult to ascribe guilt or responsibility to the adverse consequences that arise from compulsive gambling. As a result, there has arisen no clear 'best' policy. To prohibit gambling outright penalizes the majority who wish to gamble for the weaknesses of the compulsive minority. To allow gambling but require commercial gaming industries to absorb all costs and consequences of compulsive gambling places an undue burden of identification and policing upon providers of gaming services. To hold the individual fully responsible for actions done as a result of gambling ignores the compulsive nature of the activity. Thus the best policy makers can do is to try to mitigate the severity of compulsive gambling through appropriate regulatory and operational constraints placed both on operators and customers.

If legal gaming industries already exist when a jurisdiction is considering introducing new forms of commercial gambling such as casinos, the cost–benefit considerations and economic trade-offs may be more difficult to identify and the moral and social costs more ambiguous. For example, wagering on horse racing has had a considerably longer legal status than other forms of gambling in many countries. However, when new types of commercial gaming – especially casinos – are introduced, wagering on horse racing typically suffers from the new competition (Syme 1992; Thalheimer 1992). As a result of such economic threat, racing lobbies are often formidable opponents to the introduction of new forms of legal gambling in their jurisdictions. When casinos or casino-style gaming come under consideration for legalization, racing, along with other economically threatened industries, may find itself in the company of organizations who oppose gambling on more idealistic grounds. These include church groups who are morally opposed to gambling and its impact on values and the family, law enforcement agencies who are concerned about the potential for criminal spill-overs, and social services organizations who see gambling as a disruptive factor for a class of people whose lives are already somewhat tenuous.

As mentioned above, social costs linked to casinos are difficult to identify and evaluate in the legislative process. Whereas economic impacts are tangible and quantifiable – in the form of jobs, payrolls, tax revenues and new investments – negative social impacts are usually qualitative and intangible – such as increased financial distress within families, a greater incidence of spousal and family abuse and a higher propensity for embezzlements and petty theft. Because of the historic prohibitions against casinos, there are legitimate concerns about what widely available casinos might do to a previously unexposed public. Because there has been so little experience with easily accessible casino gaming in the past – especially in the form of urban casinos – introducing such gambling at the pace it has been occurring in the 1990s carries with it many risks of the unknown – of what might go wrong in society as a by-product of casinos as well as other newly available gambling opportunities.

Even when a jurisdiction makes the commitment to legalize casino gaming for whatever 'higher purpose', there is usually enough lingering doubt concerning the wisdom of such an act to induce policy makers to saddle the new industries with a variety of regulations and constraints which they hope will mitigate the potential for social damage, or protect existing economic interests. Such regulations might be directed at protecting consumers of gambling from their own folly, such as with prohibitions against the granting of credit for gambling purposes, maximum wager size limitations or maximum loss limits. They may take the form of restrictions on the ability of the gaming industry to promote itself, as with prohibitions on advertising or solicitations. They might restrict the access to or ambience of the gambling activity, as with geographic constraints, entrance fees or dress code requirements, mandated closing hours or prohibitions against alcohol or live entertainment. Or they might protect the existing competing gaming or non-gaming industries by limiting the areas in which newly legalized gaming operations might compete. Such restrictions are usually above and beyond the 'fundamental' objectives of regulation, which are: to protect the integrity of the games and wagers by regulating against cheating and fraud, to protect the integrity of tax collections by requiring acceptable accounting standards and practices, and to protect the general integrity of the gaming industry by establishing procedures to guard against infiltration by undesirables into ownership and management positions in gaming operations.

In summary, though some legislative bodies have chosen to allow casino gaming to become a legal presence within their jurisdictions, there remains enough lingering doubt about negative side-effects that such authorization is often accompanied by a wide array of restrictions and regulations to limit the overall negative impacts that might arise. Yet when placed within the context of increasing presence of casino gaming activities, such restraints might later be analysed more in terms of their adverse competitive impacts. This creates the dynamic problem that will likely influence the future policy debates among decision-makers on how best to allow casino gaming to exist within the social framework. Thus, a common theme which emerges among industrialized countries is the struggle to answer the following broad questions. If casino gambling is going to be authorized, who should be allowed to capture the economic rents associated with supplying casino gaming services? How should the general public be protected against their own potential weaknesses when confronted with the opportunity to gamble? And how should the interests of other presently legal industries, whether involved with gambling or not, be protected against the adverse competitive pressures that could arise?

CASINO GAMING AND THE LEGALIZATION PROCESS: THE US EXPERIENCE

From the mid-1960s to the 1990s, the proliferation of casino gaming took place in a variety of ways in different countries throughout the world. Yet important common patterns emerge, and many of these are reflected by the experience of jurisdictions in the United States. Furthermore, because of cross-border competitive effects in the United States among the various states and with autonomous Indian tribal nations, the process of legalization has been far more accelerated than in other parts of the world. In general, legalization of commercial gaming in the United States has tended to be directed at specific objectives, which primarily have been economic in nature. There are actually four main commercial gaming industries in America – with aggregate revenues of $30 billion in 1992 – that have emerged in the second half of the twentieth century: lotteries, casino gaming, *pari mutuel* wagering and charitable gambling (Christiansen and McQueen 1993). Though each of these industries poses interesting and related economic and policy issues, this analysis examines casino gaming in particular in the context of the policy alternatives that have presented themselves.

Casino gaming is the second largest commercial gaming industry in the United States – after lotteries – in terms of gross gaming revenues (after payment of prizes), with over $11 billion in revenues in 1992. Since 1988, many American jurisdictions have begun the process of determining how the economic opportunities that casinos promise can best be exploited. Until the mid-1970s, Nevada was the only state in the United States that allowed ongoing casino operations. In 1976, New Jersey voters authorized the development of a casino industry in Atlantic City which has since grown in terms of gross gaming revenues – over $3.3 billion – to nearly the size of Las Vegas' casino industry. However, all other attempts to bring casino gaming to the United States between 1976 and 1988 failed (Dombrink and Thompson 1989).

Beginning in the fall of 1988, three important events occurred that began a process of rapid change in the presence of casino gaming in the United States. First, a statewide ballot issue in South Dakota approving limited stakes casino gaming in the small mining community of Deadwood. Second, Congress passed the Indian Gaming Regulatory Act of 1988 (IGRA) (Eadington 1990). Third, riverboat gambling was given legislative approval in Iowa in early 1989. Since then, the presence of casino-style gaming in America has exploded, with a wide variety of new forms of casino gaming appearing in various jurisdictions.

There have been distinct patterns which have emerged from these consequential events. Both the South Dakota and Iowa authorizations began with the implicit premise that those forms of casino gaming were relatively benign and controllable in terms of their possible negative social side effects. The South Dakota referendum, for example, limited the maximum wager size to $5 and kept casino operations small by allowing no more than thirty table games or gaming devices per casino licence. Furthermore, the remoteness of Deadwood promised to minimize social problems that might be associated with casino gaming. In Iowa, casino gaming was restricted to riverboats along major waterways only. Admission fees would be charged to gain entrance onto the riverboats, wagers in excess of $5 were not permitted, and players were limited to a maximum loss of $200 per riverboat excursion. Furthermore, the state of Iowa earmarked 3 per cent of gross gaming revenues for problem gambling treatment programmes in the state.

Both South Dakota and Iowa began casino gaming with the belief that the economic benefits which casino gaming would create would be within the scale of what the affected communities could utilize. Both states devised constraints that limited casino gaming's appeal to out-of-state or major corporate interests. And Iowa established funding mechanisms to mitigate whatever social damage might occur as a result of casino gaming. Though they did not realize it at the time, South Dakota and Iowa established models for other states to follow with variations of mining town and riverboat casino gaming respectively. The pattern that emerged was for new jurisdictions to copy the legislation of their predecessors, but to be slightly less restrictive and constraining in the regulations governing their new casino industries. Thus, when Illinois authorized riverboat gaming in 1990, that state allowed credit and did not incorporate maximum wager limits or loss per excursion limits. When Mississippi legalized riverboat casinos in 1990, the legislation allowed 'dockside' casino operations. Missouri's 1992 referendum authorizing riverboat casinos also allowed boats in certain locations to remain dockside. When the voters of Colorado approved small stakes casino gaming for three mountain mining towns in 1990 based on South Dakota's approach, they did not restrict the size of the gaming operations to any pre-set number of games or devices, as had South Dakota.

Indian casino gaming in America has developed in a quite different manner since 1988 (Eadington 1990). The 1988 Indian Gaming Regulatory Act was passed in response to a 1987 Supreme Court decision, Cabazon v. the State of California. The Cabazon decision recognized that Indian tribes in America were autonomous governmental entities which existed within states but were independent from civil or regulatory control from the states. Thus, if a state allowed any person for any purpose to operate gaming within their jurisdiction, then Indian tribes with reservation land within that state could not be prohibited from operating the same type of gambling on tribal land. Furthermore, the Cabazon decision indicated the state could have no regulatory authority over the Indian gaming operations within their borders. The ruling carried the implication of the unregulated spread of a variety of forms of gambling on Indian lands, so Congress passed IGRA to create a framework for states and tribes to negotiate what forms of Indian gaming would be allowed and how the states' public policy interests might be protected through regulatory oversight. However, when IGRA was passed into law, it was certainly unclear to Congress and to many Indian tribes what its true impact would be. IGRA noted that states must negotiate in good faith with Indian tribes, and that if states did not negotiate in good faith, tribes could go to federal court for mediation or arbitration. As a result, many of the important consequences of IGRA and Indian gaming have come about as a result of lawsuits brought on behalf of Indian tribes, and court interpretations of IGRA.

Either by negotiating processes or through judicial findings, Indian casino gaming spread rapidly in the five years following IGRA's passage. Major Indian casinos appeared in the states of Connecticut, New York, Michigan, Wisconsin, Minnesota, Colorado, Washington, California and Arizona. Often, Indians were able to gain the right to operate full-service Nevada-style casinos because the state in which their tribal lands were located allowed a highly restricted form of casino-style gambling, such as charity 'Las Vegas' nights, allowed for not-for-profit organizations. Because such situations led to substantial casino gaming for Indian tribes within those states, the public policy debate was notably changed. No longer were those states debating the issue of whether or not to have casinos; Indian casinos were clearly established. Rather, the debate shifted to how many casinos a state should have, where they should be located, and who should benefit. As of the mid-1990s, it is clear that Indian casino gaming will continue to spread throughout the United States, and following closely behind it will be the continued proliferation of non-Indian casino gaming.

Another noteworthy development in American casinos has been the emergence of urban casino gaming. As noted earlier, casinos in Europe and America have always been geographically isolated from population centres, at least partly because of a belief that casinos are deleterious for urban working-class populations. Legal American casinos in operation as of the end of 1992 – whether in Nevada, Atlantic City, in mining towns, on riverboats or on Indian reservations – had all held to that general pattern. However, in 1992, New Orleans became the first American jurisdiction to legalize an urban casino, with passage of a law authorizing a monopoly casino for that city. Subsequently, St Louis and Kansas City, Missouri, authorized riverboat casinos close to their urban centres. Other American cities such as Chicago, Boston, Philadelphia, Hartford and Bridgeport actively debated the possibility in 1992 and 1993, and the Canadian cities of Winnipeg, Montreal and Windsor introduced government-owned casinos into urban locations between 1990 and 1994.

Other American cities had attempted to legalize casinos in the 1980s because they had found themselves in dire economic straits and felt that casinos offered one of the only ways out. None were successful at that time. Such cities as Gary, Indiana; Detroit,

Michigan; and East St Louis, Illinois, share an economic desperation not unlike that which prevailed in Atlantic City in 1976. There was little hope of traditional economic resurgence left for such cities, and there was a strong belief that casinos could reverse their fortunes. However, in spite of earlier failures, by 1993 a riverboat casino had opened in East St Louis, riverboat casinos had been authorized for Gary and significant efforts were under way to authorize casinos in Detroit, at least partly in competitive response to the casino authorized by the Ontario provincial government across the river from Detroit in Windsor.

However, there are harsh lessons to be learned for such cities from Atlantic City, especially as far as urban redevelopment is concerned (Sternleib and Hughes 1983). In Atlantic City, the creation of a casino industry that brought thirty million visitors to the city each year, and created nearly 50,000 jobs in the industry's twelve casinos, did not alleviate the urban blight or poverty that had plagued that city. Regrettably, because of the similarities of Atlantic City to these other cities – in terms of economic desperation and circumstances – the same general disappointing outcomes might also apply.

The past decade has also brought about significant growth and change for the major existing casino cities in the United States. In Atlantic City fifteen years after legalization, the casino industry had grown to apparent maturity, but there has been increasing concern about the future health of Atlantic City and its casino industry. Between 1988 and 1992, over half of Atlantic City's casinos went through bankruptcy, and one of them closed permanently. Atlantic City experienced its major growth in the first half of the 1980s and, as with other American industries that expanded in that period, many of the problems of Atlantic City's casinos can be traced to over-leveraging and over-reliance on debt financing for capital expansion. The Atlantic City casino industry effectively gambled that the growth it experienced through the mid-1980s would continue. It did not, and Atlantic City also failed to cure many of its fundamental problems, such as urban blight. Some of these problems may no longer be curable, and legalization of casino-style gaming elsewhere – especially in Philadelphia and Bridgeport – threatens to compete for and cut into some of Atlantic City's eastern seaboard markets. Thus there is reason to believe that Atlantic City's slowdown in growth may indeed be a harbinger of future contraction.

At the same time, however, Las Vegas has been a casino boomtown virtually without precedent. According to the 1990 census, Nevada was the fastest growing state in the United States for the decade of the 1980s, its population increasing by more than 50 per cent to 1.2 million, and Las Vegas was the epicentre for that state's growth. The causes of population growth in Las Vegas are easy to see. About 30 per cent of the labour force is employed in the gaming, hotel and recreation sector. Las Vegas has nine of the ten largest hotels in the world, all of them casino–hotels. Las Vegas has become the premier convention city in the world, in terms of convention facilities and hotel rooms, with over 88,000 hotel rooms available as of the end of 1993. In terms of variety and quality of live entertainment available, Las Vegas compares favourably with virtually all of the world's capital cities. All this has come about in the last thirty years. In the 1960s, conventional wisdom viewed Las Vegas as a city controlled by organized crime, a place filled with transients, low-lifers and opportunists (Reid and Demaris 1964; Turner 1964). The transformation of Las Vegas is a direct result of the popularity and growth of casino-style gambling, and in the mid-1990s no end is in sight for its casino-fuelled growth boom.

One of the reasons for the continued growth of Las Vegas – and of other casino centres in Nevada – has been the underlying philosophy with which governmental bodies have regulated Nevada's casinos. Nevada has incorporated few moral positions about casino gaming into its regulatory framework, especially in comparison with other American jurisdictions with casinos. Few of the social concerns related to widely available casino gaming have affected Nevada's public policy towards gambling or its regulation of the casino industry. As far as the state is concerned, regulation should not adversely affect the economic performance of the casino industry unless an absence of regulatory action threatens the long run integrity, image or economic health of the industry itself. Such feelings are based in the formative period of Nevada's regulation; in the 1950s and 1960s, the real risk to the state's casino industry was the threat of federal intervention because of historic associations with organized crime and a federal view that gambling was morally wrong (Skolnick 1978; Cabot and Schuetz 1991).

The regulatory process in Atlantic City, by contrast, is far more cumbersome for casinos in terms of restrictions, requirements and costs of regulatory compliance. This is at least partially due to the position that New Jersey regulatory bodies have been reluctant to give up control of a variety of areas of decision making that in Nevada are left to the discretion of casino management.

In spite of its recent successes, there are questions about the Las Vegas casino economy that pose concerns over the next few years. There is an ongoing issue about if and when Las Vegas will become overbuilt. And if that does occur, there might be severe attrition among the older, smaller casino properties, which may not be able to compete effectively against the newest and largest 'must see' mega-casino destination resorts that have been built in that city. Most fundamental is the question of whether tourists will continue to visit Las Vegas, and spend as much time and money there, when they can find casino-style gaming facilities in a variety of other states and jurisdictions throughout the country.

THE INTERACTION OF ECONOMIC FORCES AND POLICY OBJECTIVES

As more forms of commercial gaming compete for what eventually will be a saturated commercial gaming market in the United States, some policy objectives will come into conflict with the economic viability and survivability of competing forms of gaming. As new gambling activities become available to the general public, they will displace other less convenient, less exciting, less cost effective or less accessible forms of gambling. For example, racing and *pari mutuel* wagering in the United States will likely continue to go through major contraction and down-sizing because of the proliferation of other competing forms of gambling, and racing's inability to effectively compete against them.

One of the effects of economic hardship on a socially regulated gaming industry is the pressure that arises at a political level to bring about a relaxation of the constraints under which the industry must operate. Initially, a casino industry may have been legalized because policy makers felt it could be controlled – symbolically or in reality – and made acceptable through constraints on location, operations or wagering conditions. Pragmatically, such rules may initially have been the only way to make enabling legislation politically palatable to opponents. However, once a gaming industry is established in a region, it begins the process of becoming legitimate – as a taxpayer, an employer and a member of the local or regional community. If its continued existence is threatened by competitive forces, it becomes far more difficult to argue to preserve the social constraints, especially if they have not been very effective in accomplishing their initial purposes.

This pattern has already emerged among some of America's new gaming industries. Iowa provides an excellent example. Though its riverboat casinos only began operations in 1991, by 1993 there had already been substantial attrition in the state's riverboat gaming industry. Three of the original five riverboat casinos closed after the first two seasons, and moved to more favourable gaming markets and regulatory environments in other states. A good part of Iowa riverboat gaming's problem was related to location, being some distance from the metropolitan Chicago area. However, some of the economic difficulties can be linked to the 'socially responsible' legislation they initially passed for their riverboat casinos. The $5 maximum wager and $200 maximum loss per excursion limitations were intended to protect customers from problems related to overindulging in gambling, but riverboat casinos in operation in the adjacent state of Illinois were not subject to such limitations and therefore were more appealing to customers who did not want to gamble under such constraints. The same can be said about Iowa's prohibition against casino credit in contrast to Illinois' allowance of credit.

Remote locations for gaming operations – which were initially tolerated because they were distant from population centres – may become the unwitting victims of the changing legal norms governing access to gambling. For example, Deadwood, South Dakota, may eventually find its casino industry contracting because of competition from more recently authorized gaming venues which are closer to their customer markets. In general, customers will choose the convenience of gaming venues close to where they live if they are able. In the same vein, Nevada's gaming industry is vulnerable to legal changes regarding gambling in California, where many of Nevada's casino customers live. It is clear that if California legalizes either casinos or non-casino gaming devices such as video lottery terminals, or ends up with substantial Indian casino gaming, there could be major negative impacts on Nevada's casino gaming industry. Furthermore, if California is forced to open the door to Indian casino gaming, it is likely that would be followed by a proliferation of non-Indian gaming as well. Any of these events could adversely affect Nevada's gaming primarily because Nevada would be at a distinct locational disadvantage.

Atlantic City is perhaps the most vulnerable of all the major tourism destinations in America to the proliferation of gambling, because it has a casino industry whose major advantage has been that it is the closest locale with casino gaming to the population centres of New York, Philadelphia, and Washington, DC. Atlantic City has not had much to offer its visitors beyond the gaming that can take place in its casinos. As a result, if new locations develop with casinos that are more convenient to its primary markets, Atlantic City will lose customers to those new venues. It has relatively little it can draw on to develop or retain the loyalty of its customer base in a more competitive gaming environment. The best Atlantic City's casino industry can hope for is to ask legislators and regulators to relax many of the expensive regulations so that they will be better able to compete with new jurisdictions. However, even that may not be enough.

CONCLUSIONS

The trend in recent years to exploit the opportunities associated with the changing social acceptance of gaming has led to a variety of experiments with legalization and regulation of casino gaming. Many of the constraints that were initially placed upon new casino industries to protect the 'public interest' will likely be relaxed in response to changes in public and legislative attitudes towards gambling. These may arise as a result of greater understanding of social costs and benefits associated with gambling, but also because of increased competition among commercial gaming industries and concerns over continued economic viability of established gaming industries.

In effect, society's acceptance of gambling as a mainstream recreational activity is becoming increasingly established. However, there is still going to be considerable political infighting over the question of who will be allowed to benefit from offering gambling services to the general public. Potential beneficiaries include governments through lottery commissions and as tax recipients, not-for-profit organizations through charitable gambling or as sponsors of other gambling activities, cities or communities hoping to be designated exclusive franchise locations for casinos in their market areas, Indian tribes or other groups who can achieve a special legal status for the offering of gaming services, and private sector interests such as casino operators, vendors of gaming equipment and purveyors of other gaming services.

One other point should be noted. The political process described in this analysis is driven largely by the opportunistic benefits linked to legalizing gambling. Such policies may be misdirected in the long term because the foundations for justification are planted in economic benefits that quite possibly will only be temporary. Job creation, tax revenue generation, investment stimulation and other related benefits which are by-products of tourist spending will become diluted as casino gaming proliferates into more and more jurisdictions. Such benefits to a region may only be sustainable if that jurisdiction can hold its monopoly on gaming for some period of time. In light of the cross-border competition that has spread across North America with the proliferation of casinos in the 1990s, such exclusivity is certainly at risk. Furthermore, many jurisdictions have not realistically weighed the economic benefits against the real social costs that are likely to result from commercial gaming in their communities. Therefore, many places that are legalizing casinos run the risk of being bitterly disappointed.

The unstable legal status of casino gaming in competing jurisdictions is usually taken into account by private investors, who evaluate the financial risks that are present in any project due to the possibility of changing legal status of gaming in neighbouring jurisdictions. However, the public sector also has to 'buy in' whenever gaming is authorized, either through infrastructure requirements, creation of regulatory bureaucracies or job creating or budgetary expectations. Governments quite often are not as conscientious in evaluating their commitments as are private sector investors because it is not their own money which they are committing. Furthermore, they may be more prone to err on the side of optimism in making projections on the job-creating or revenue-generating capabilities of new gaming industries. Not every jurisdiction can be as successful as the first one to legalize; economic benefits, especially those that depend upon capturing customers from other jurisdictions, must eventually be dissipated by continued proliferation.

Finally, with regard to the potentially damaging social effects, there is a strong asymmetric nature to regulatory and statutory commitments regarding the operation of authorized casino gaming. This is because it is difficult to increase the constraints on a legally created casino industry once it has been established, especially when it is already under increasing competitive pressures from other gaming jurisdictions.

Thus it would seem that the reasons why casinos are proliferating, in the United States and Canada at least, in the 1990s suggest the potential for considerable long-term costs. This trend creates risks and uncertainties not only for private investors, but for the general public as well – through the dimensions of social costs that might come along with the increased presence of casino gaming, as well as public sector financial considerations. Perhaps more important, however, is the fact that policy is being driven by the wrong motives. More and more frequently, autonomous jurisdictions – state and local governments, and Indian tribes – may decide they should move immediately on legalization because other competing jurisdictions have already done so or will soon do so; and that they *must* move immediately because, if they do not, other competing jurisdictions will beat them to the opportunity. The era of careful debate on the pros and cons of legalizing casinos in North America has given way to frenetic rhetoric suggesting a rush to legalize what gaming one can as quickly as one can. Yet, if too many casinos are legalized – if the trends of the early 1990s continue much longer – the only real benefits that will not be dissipated are those which will accrue to the consumers of gaming services. If these are positive enough to justify a substantial shift in society's legal tolerance of gambling, then that outcome would be fine. However, given the current level of public debate on gambling, such a justification is still far from the main considerations of policy makers.

REFERENCES

Cabot, A. and Schuetz, R. (1991) 'An economic view of the Nevada licensing process', in W.R. Eadington and J.A. Cornelius (eds) *Gambling and Public Policy: International Perspectives*, Reno: University of Nevada, 123–154.

Christiansen, E. and McQueen, P. (1993) 'Gaming's gross annual handle' and 'Gaming's gross annual revenues', in *Gaming and Wagering Business Magazine*, July/August and August/September, 1 ff.

Dombrink, J. and Thompson, W.N. (1989) *The Last Resort: Campaigns for Casinos in America*, Reno: University of Nevada.

Eadington, W.R. (ed.) (1990) *Indian Gaming and the Law*, Reno: University of Nevada.

Eadington, W.R. and Cornelius, J.A. (eds) (1993) *Gambling Behavior and Problem Gambling*, Reno: University of Nevada.

Mossenson, D. (1991) 'The Australian casino model', in W.R. Eadington and J.A. Cornelius (eds) *Gambling and Public Policy: International Perspectives*, Reno: University of Nevada, 303–362.

Neilson, A. (1991) 'Government regulation of casino gaming in Australia: The political and bureaucratic components and some of the myths', in W. R. Eadington and J.A. Cornelius (eds) *Gambling and Public Policy: International Perspectives*, Reno: University of Nevada, 363–394.

Reid, E. and Demaris, O. (1964) *The Green Felt Jungle*, New York: Pocket Books.

Rose, I.N. (1988) 'Gambling: From sin to vice to disease', *Journal of Gambling Behavior* 4, 4: 240–260.

Shaffer, H., Stein, S., Gambino, B. and Cummings, T. (eds) (1989) *Compulsive Gambling: Theory, Research and Practice*, Lexington, Mass.: Lexington Books.

Skolnick, J. (1978) *House of Cards: Regulation of Casino Gambling in Nevada*, Boston: Little, Brown & Co.

Sternleib, G. and Hughes, R. (1983) *The Atlantic City Gamble*, Cambridge: Harvard University Press.

Syme, D. (1992) 'The dilemma facing New Zealand's racing industry', in W.R. Eadington and J.A. Cornelius (eds) *Gambling and Commercial Gaming: Essays in Business, Economics, Philosophy and Science*, Reno: University of Nevada, 315–332.

Thalheimer, R. (1992) 'The impact of intrastate intertrack wagering, casinos, and a state lottery on the demand for parimutuel horseracing: New Jersey, a case study', in W.R. Eadington and J.A. Cornelius (eds) *Gambling and Commercial Gaming: Essays in Business, Economics, Philosophy and Science*, Reno: University of Nevada, 285–294.

Turner, W. (1964) *Gambler's Money*, New York: Signet Books.

Volberg, R. (1989) 'The prevalence of gambling in various states', in H. Shaffer *et al.* (eds) *Compulsive Gambling: Theory, Research and Practice*, Lexington, Mass.: Lexington Books.

Chapter 10

The economic evaluation of publicly assisted tourism projects

Stephen Wanhill

Around the globe governments have intervened to assist and regulate the private sector in the development of tourism. This is because the complex nature of the tourist product makes it unlikely that private markets will satisfy a country's tourism policy objectives to produce a balance of facilities that meet the needs of the visitor, benefit the host community and are compatible with the wishes of that same community. Incentives are policy instruments that can be used to correct for market failure and ensure a development partnership between the public and private sectors. The extent of public involvement depends on the economic philosophy of the government. The trend towards pure-market-led economics in recent years has led to a clawback of state involvement and the questioning of incentives as mechanisms more likely to lead to market distortions. When this reasoning is combined with increasing demands on government budgets worldwide and the larger public sector deficits that have been accumulating during the early 1990s, it is evident that governments are becoming much more cautious with regard to public spending and require more justification for supporting projects of all types, including tourism related ones.

This chapter reviews, in broad terms, the nature of investment incentives and examines the European Community (EC) and British approach to assisting tourism projects. The focus is on the evolving methodology which the author has identified in undertaking project appraisals to evaluate the worth of public sector support, and which is used to assist ministries of finance or government treasuries in deciding whether they are receiving value for money. The trend throughout the 1990s is likely to be one where government departments and agencies of all kinds will be under increasing pressure to provide performance measures for all their activities.

INVESTMENT INCENTIVES

Governments around the world offer a wide range of incentives to developers. They broadly fall into three categories (Bodlender 1982; Jenkins 1982; Wanhill 1986):

1 Reduction of capital costs: these include capital grants or loans at preferential rates, interest rate relief, a moratorium on loan repayments for a period of X years, provision of infrastructure, provision of land on concessional terms, tariff exemption on construction materials and equity participation;
2 Reduction of operating costs: to improve operating viability governments may grant tax 'holidays' (5–10 years), give a labour or training subsidy, offer tariff exemption on imported materials and supplies, provide special depreciation allowances and ensure that there is double taxation or unilateral relief. The latter are government to government agreements to ensure that no firm pays tax twice on the same profits;
3 Investment security: the object here is to win investors' confidence in an industry which is very sensitive to the political environment. Action here would include guarantees against nationalization, free availability of foreign exchange, repatriation of invested capital, profits, dividends and interest, loan guarantees, provision of work permits for 'key' personnel and the availability of technical advice.

It is from the above categories that governments will put together their package of incentives to attract investors, notably those from overseas.

EUROPEAN DIMENSION

European regional policy within the EC is about economic convergence and cohesion to ensure that all regions can compete effectively within the Single European Market. The programmes proposed within the locale of a Community Support Framework (CSF) in the main go forward for support by the European Regional Development Fund (ERDF). Pearce (1992) surveys the first fourteen years of the ERDF. As far as tourism is concerned, no special funds are set aside for tourism projects; they must take their place in the queue alongside all other industries. There are many ways of presenting projects, but tapping into ERDF grants requires that investment schemes are appraised from the standpoint of the regional economy as opposed to straightforward financial profitability.

The guidelines governing ERDF rest on the fact that a project cannot stand alone: its wider relevance and impact within a CSF must be demonstrated, as well as ensuring that it meets one or more of the overall regional objectives laid down by the Community. As a rule, tourism projects in this category tend to be public sector led and the principal aspects that should be addressed are:

1 Use of the project should be 50 per cent non-local;
2 The project should result in an increase in overnight stays;
3 The project should result in an increase in employment opportunities;
4 The economic position of the project within the local area should be examined;
5 The project should form part of a tourism strategy for the local area;
6 Tourist authority support will give weight to the application.

The overall regional Community objectives are quite broad; to be accepted a project must be concerned with the economic development of regions that are lagging behind, or the restructuring of regions seriously affected by industrial decline, or severely depressed rural areas.

IN BRITAIN

All assistance schemes administered by the tourist boards are discretionary and come within the terms of the 1969 Development of Tourism Act (House of Commons 1969) which states in Section 4 that:

4.– (1) A Tourist Board shall have power –
   (a) in accordance with arrangements approved by the relevant Minister and the Treasury, to give financial assistance for the carrying out of any project which in the opinion of the Board will provide or improve

> tourist amenities and facilities in the country for which the Board is responsible:
>
> (b) with the approval of the relevant Minister and the Treasury, to carry out any such project as aforesaid.
>
> (2) Financial assistance under subsection (1)(a) of this section may be given by way of grant or loan or, if the project is being or is to be carried out by a company incorporated in Great Britain, by subscribing for or otherwise acquiring shares or stock in the company, or by any combination of those methods.
>
> (3) In making a grant or loan in accordance with arrangements approved. Under subsection (1)(a) of this section a Tourist Board may, subject to the arrangements, impose such terms and conditions as it thinks fit, including conditions for the repayment of a grant in specified circumstances; and Schedule 2 to this Act shall have effect for securing compliance with conditions subject to which any such grant is made.
>
> (4) A Tourist Board shall not dispose of any shares or stock acquired by it by virtue of this section except –
>
> (a) after consultation with the company in which the shares or stock are held; and
>
> (b) with the approval of the relevant Minister and the Treasury.

It may be seen from the above that the terms of the Act are fairly general, and so it was left to the individual tourist boards to issue appropriate guidelines. These they agreed with the government body which acted as their reporting authority. Under the terms of the 1969 Act, incentives offered in Britain principally take the form of discretionary grants. These incentives are now only offered by the Wales Tourist Board; they were suspended in England in the latter part of 1988 and in Scotland in mid-1993. Both of these happenings were the result of government reviews of the tourist industry and the role of tourist boards in particular. The argument that has been given most weight in justifying the suspension of Section 4 assistance is the converse of the traditional infant industry case for protection. The infant has now grown up and, having reached maturity, no longer requires government assistance. However, this is not the same as the market failure argument, as, for example, put forward in the concept of sustainable development which challenges the ability of private markets to improve the distribution of income and protect the environment.

The appropriate guidelines which have been applied to Section 4 are best summed up in the words of the Wales Tourist Board (1992):

> The schemes administered by the Board are all discretionary and in general terms consideration can only be given to viable projects which involve capital expenditure and for which a need for Board assistance can be demonstrated. All projects must, in addition, be available to the general public when completed and be likely to attract visitors to Wales.
>
> Each application for assistance is assessed on its merits, the Board's decision being final. The Board seeks to maximise the benefits accruing to Wales with the limited resources available under these schemes and takes careful account of a number of factors in assessing applications. Priority is given to projects which:
>
> – Provide full-time employment opportunities;
> – Help extend the effective length of the season;
> – Enhance the range and quality of the facilities and amenities provided by the industry;
> – Have potential for attracting both domestic and overseas visitors;
> – Provide significant benefit to the community in terms of:
>   – income and employment creation
>   – improving local infrastructure
>   – preserving local landscape;
> – Are of good standard of design;
> – Exhibit sound marketing potential;
> – Are potential viable projects in their own right.

Being discretionary, Section 4 funding gives the Board a considerable degree of flexibility:

> – The option of switching sector priorities with the object of encouraging new developments, modernisation and achieving a balanced development of tourist facilities in specific locations;
> – Supporting projects which have high employment creating potential;
> – Selecting those projects which have the most chance of success;

    – Adjusting the amount of grant to oblige the applicant to meet the Board's project specifications in respect of type, quantity and quality.

Each project is considered on its own merits against the various criteria and a balanced view formed. Given that the number of applications for project support normally exceed the number that could be offered assistance by a factor of around 2.5:1, there is inevitably a rationing process, which, other things being equal, will usually favour employment creation. This is because the latter underpins the evaluation methodology and is a priority for public sector funding, as will be shown below.

BASIC METHODOLOGY

It is well known that tourism is an industry whose influence pervades many different sectors of the economy. There is no single industrial classification called tourism and so the usual starting point for evaluating tourism projects is to measure the economic impact of tourist spending and derive appropriate multipliers, in particular, income and employment multipliers.

    To derive the appropriate methodology, suppose that there exists a tourist destination with an attraction, a hotel and a beach. Visitors are surveyed at both paying sites and on the beach to ascertain what motivated them to come to the destination. Total spending at the destination (T) amounts to expenditure at the attraction (A) plus expenditure at the hotel (H) plus all remaining expenditure (R). The pull factor (reason for visit) for the attraction is x and the hotel is y, leaving 1–x–y as the significance of the beach. It follows therefore that attributable tourist expenditure by drawing power is:

$$
\begin{aligned}
\text{Attraction} &= xA + xH + xR \\
\text{Hotel} &= ya + yH + yR \\
\text{Seaside} &= (1 - x - y)(A + H + R) \\
T &= A + H + R
\end{aligned}
$$

In this example the local tourist board has put public money into the attraction and so wishes to evaluate its worth in terms of its contribution to tourist spending and employment in the area. The benefits (B) of the attraction are the difference between the situation with and without the project. The without situation is:

Attraction = 0
Hotel   = yH + yR
Seaside   = (1 − x − y) (H + R)
T_w = (1 − x) (H + R)

Hence

B   = T − T_w
           = A + x (H + R)   (1)

If visitors to the attraction would have come to the area anyway then the benefits would simply be A.

Ascertaining the fraction x is commonly achieved by visitor surveys, as for example in early work carried out in Wales by Archer and Shea (1980). Johnson and Thomas (1992) found in their study of Beamish Museum the pull or attribution factors for different types of visitors to be:

- Local home-based day trippers: 0.68;
- Non-local home-based day trippers: 1.00;
- Other day trippers: 0.98;
- Staying visitors: 0.05.

An alternative approach is to look at visitor behaviour patterns in relation to length of stay and *pro rata* their expenditure over the number of activities that they undertake, with appropriate adjustments for *a priori* information obtained from known visitor surveys and informed discussions with industry operators.

Employment effects

The benefits shown in equation (1) are in two parts. The first term on the right hand side is on-site expenditure and the second, off-site expenditure. The amount of off-site expenditure attributable to the attraction depends on its ability to generate additional visitors. Hence, this may be termed the visitor additionality factor. The application of employment multipliers per unit of tourist spending to equation (1), either on a full-time equivalent (FTE) or employment headcount basis, will give the gross employment (E) generated by the project. These multipliers are calculated so as to measure the direct employment effects of the project, the indirect effects arising out of intermediate purchases made by the project and the induced effects on the local economy as a result of the respending of local incomes derived from the project, and similarly for off-site expenditure. Thus:

$$E = Ae_a + xOe_o \tag{2}$$

where e_a is the employment multiplier appropriate to the attraction, O is the sum of off-site expenditure $(H + R)$ and e_o the required employment multiplier. However, equation (2) ignores any demand diversion from elsewhere in the area: this is termed displacement and in this respect it is important to define the boundary of the project. As observed by Johnson and Thomas (1990):

> In the case of the economy as a whole it is sometimes argued that all expenditure, and consequently employment, is diverted and there is in effect a zero-sum game. This point is of some importance from the point of view of public bodies providing funds. Local authorities and the Treasury for example might have very different views on what is the net impact because they are concerned with different reference areas.

At a national level this argument assumes that market forces are moving the economy towards full employment equilibrium so that public investment expenditure is simply displacing private funds in the capital market. Similarly, the operation of the project is displacing demand in the same or related product markets and likewise in the labour and property markets. In reality, economies do get stuck at a level of Keynesian unemployment disequilibrium, and one of the major objectives of regional policy is to 'kick-start' a demand-deficient economy so as to raise the level of output through the multiplier process. This discussion does not imply that displacement should be neglected so that policy decisions are made in terms of the gross effect only, but merely raises the issue that the logic of the crowding out effect ends up with a 'do nothing' policy.

As far as EC funding is concerned, displacement is a relevant factor to take into account, so that appraisals for ERDF support look at net employment effects (N). If d is the proportion of locally diverted demand (or demand diverted from another assisted area) in equation (1), then, from equation (2), net employment within the CSF boundary is:

$$\begin{aligned} N &= E{-}dE \\ &= (1{-}d)\,(Ae_a{+}xOe_o) \end{aligned} \tag{3}$$

CASE STUDY

Tourist project evaluation for ERDF funding essentially follows the methodology outlined in the previous section. This is best illustrated by considering an example of a successful submission undertaken for Cardiff City Council (1988) by this writer. This was the New Theatre which is now fully refurbished and considered to be a premier cultural attraction, and has gained much from the world standing of the Welsh National Opera. Cities offer important cultural venues for tourism purposes and are thus able to fit quite easily into the Community's tourism programmes, provided they are situated in a region designated for assistance. As the capital of Wales, but located in an area that had experienced industrial decline, Cardiff met all these conditions.

The New Theatre was opened in 1906: it is listed for its architectural value and is one of a family of twelve late Victorian/early Edwardian constructions designed by the theatre architects Runtz and Ford, of which the most famous are the Adelphi and Garrick in London. The project was chiefly one of refurbishing the theatre: the New Theatre is one of Cardiff's most significant venues for the performing arts, but prior to ERDF and local authority support it had suffered from cramped public areas and a steady deterioration in its structures both inside and out, to the point where standards of comfort and facilities were no longer acceptable in the market for a major theatre. The confidential business plan for the theatre was reviewed so as to position the project within the overall tourism strategy for Cardiff.

The key to theatre planning is the box office, since this is the major revenue-earning activity. By appropriate pricing and setting a range of performances from amateur through to opera, pantomime and children's theatre, the modernized New Theatre expected to attract audiences, not only from Cardiff City and South Wales, but also from beyond the CSF boundary (in this instance, defined as Industrial South Wales) in a radius of one and a half hours driving time. It would also draw tourists coming to the city, whether on holiday or on business.

Given that the theatre was intended to be an ongoing project, its impact was evaluated at the target operating capacity of 85 per cent. The latter was based on known operating statistics that were judged against what should be achievable in the light of the location of the theatre and its markets. A breakdown of annual audience figures at this level of usage is shown in Table 10.1.

Table 10.1 New Theatre visitor attendances at target capacity

Market segment	Numbers
Staying visitors:	
Overseas	8 150
Domestic	65 700
Day visitors:	
Industrial South Wales region	91 250
Outside region	115 650
Total	280 750

Source: New Theatre market analysis

The market analysis indicated that some 67 per cent of theatre attendances would come from outside the South Wales region which would satisfy the ERDF guideline that at least 50 per cent should be non-local. The latter is the displacement rule. Table 10.2 indicates the revenues that were likely to be generated by the audience numbers shown in Table 10.1.

The unit of account is European Currency Units (ECUs): at the time of writing (late 1993) one ECU is approximately £0.70 or $1.20. A summary of the economic impact of the trading operations of the theatre is shown in Table 10.3. The original money values used in the study represent 1988 figures adjusted to 1993 values by an index of the general rate of inflation.

Table 10.2 New Theatre revenue categories (1993 adjusted prices)

| Category | 85% capacity | |
	ECU (000s)	(%)
Activities		
Production:		
Box Office	4,387	90.0
Sales	94	1.7
Theatre lettings:	270	5.0
Fees and charges	97	1.8
Other(1)	37	0.7
Bars and catering	407	7.5
Management and buildings (1)	127	2.3
Total	5,419	100.0

Source: Estimates based on New Theatre Accounts
Note: (1) Main items are grants and contributions.

Table 10.3 Economic impact of trading operations

Trading operating capacity	Direct, indirect and induced effects	
	Cardiff	*Industrial South Wales*
Household income (ECU thousands, 1993 adjusted prices)	1,960	2,240
Employment		
Full-time job equivalents	124	139
Employment headcount	168	188

It is important, as Sinclair and Sutcliffe (1992) point out, to consider first round effects carefully as these have the most significant impact on what is to follow. The direct effects in terms of income and employment generation were taken from the theatre's operating budget so that multiplier values were only applied to intermediate purchases and other expenses incurred by the theatre, as well as expenditure out of trading surpluses. Income was measured in gross terms so that employment could be estimated by dividing through by average labour costs to give FTEs. The latter were then scaled up to allow for part-time work and thus give an employment headcount.

The values shown in Table 10.3 do include revenues generated from audiences coming from within the Industrial South Wales Region. Technically these revenues are displacement rather than additional and therefore outside the ERDF guidelines. However, the argument for including them rested on the view that without the modernization programme there was little future for the theatre and in all probability the custom would go outside the region. Thus the continued operation of the theatre was safeguarding jobs and the project was creating further jobs. At the operating capacity of 85 per cent, which was used to calculate the figures in Table 10.3, the theatre management indicated that they would be employing eighty-six persons (thirty six full-time and fifty part-time). The additional employment created indirectly and through the induced effects of the theatre's trading operations is eighty-two jobs in the Cardiff area and a further twenty jobs in the South Wales area, to give a regional total of 102 jobs in addition to those directly employed by the theatre.

The expenditure, income and employment effects presented so far do not constitute the total economic impact of the theatre

Table 10.4 Additional off-site expenditure by theatregoers (ECU thousands, 1993 adjusted prices)

Market segment	Total spent	Expenditure attributable to the New Theatre
Staying visitors		
Overseas	2,460	295
Domestic	5,437	534
Day visitors		
Industrial South		[1]
Wales region	895	[1]
Outside region	1,399	1,399
Total	10,191	2,228

Note: [1]Displacement expenditure within the region.

project. The refurbished theatre, as a prime cultural venue, contributes to raising tourism awareness and provides a reason for visiting Cardiff. Therefore, allowance had to be made for how much of tourists' total expenditure (on accommodation, meals, shopping, transport, etc.) could be reasonably attributed to the New Theatre. From survey information (Cardiff City Council 1988) it was estimated that for staying visitors just over 10 per cent of their off-site expenditure could be allocated to the New Theatre, as can be seen in Table 10.4.

Off-site expenditure generated by audiences from within South Wales were not included as they were likely to have incurred a similar level of expenditure elsewhere in the region, which implies that such expenditures are merely displacement within the regional economy. For day trip theatregoers coming from outside the region, the main purpose of their trip would be to visit the New Theatre, thus all of their additional expenditure was attributed to the project. The economic impact of the total allocated off-site expenditure shown in Table 10.4 can be found in Table 10.5.

The summation of Tables 10.3 and 10.5 gives the overall impact of the theatre project on incomes and jobs, as shown in Table 10.6. Apart from the qualitative arguments for ensuring the future of an important cultural attraction within the city of Cardiff, the New Theatre project would generate annually ECU 3.0 million of household income in the region, of which ECU 2.5 million would be in Cardiff.

Similarly a total of 241 jobs would be created in the region, with

Table 10.5 Economic impact of additional expenditure

| | Direct, indirect and induced effects | |
	Cardiff	Industrial South Wales
Household income (ECU thousands, 1993 adjusted prices)	511	727
Employment		
Full-time job equivalents	29	41
Employment headcount	37	53

Cardiff taking 205 of them. Of the latter total, eighty-six would be direct jobs in the theatre. The overall cost of the theatre's refurbishment (including compensation payments) was estimated at ECU 9.4 million in 1993 prices. This gave a capital cost per regional FTE of about ECU 52,000. The importance of this project to the city was acknowledged by the European Commission and ERDF support was forthcoming for up to one-half of the assessed cost of restoring the theatre, as is consistent with the matching grant nature of ERDF monies.

ADDITIONALITY AND DISPLACEMENT

The Section 4 legislation used in Britain is hedged about with the concept of 'additionality'. This lays down the criterion that a grant (or loan) would only be forthcoming if the project would not proceed without it. Assessment of this position by project officers involves considerable subjective judgment about the likely future behaviour of the investor and in practice requires the investor to sign a document to the effect that Section 4 funds are a necessary

Table 10.6 Overall economic impact of the New Theatre

| | Direct, indirect and induced effects | |
	Cardiff	Industrial South Wales
Household income (ECU thousands, 1993 adjusted prices)	2,471	2,967
Employment		
Full-time job equivalents	153	180
Employment headcount	205	241

condition for the project to go ahead. The reality of the addition-ality constraint was to make the Boards lenders of the last resort and mitigated against a proactive stance. It was for this reason that the Committee on Welsh Affairs (1987) recommended that the additionality criterion should be withdrawn. Operationally, project additionality is difficult to assess, but approaches to the problem include:

1 Discussions with investors on the key factors determining the decisions to implement the project;
2 Analysis of the financial performance of the project, on the basis that highly viable schemes would have gone ahead with-out grant aid;
3 Identification of analogous unaided investments;
4 Evaluation of market conditions;
5 Consideration of whether the project would have gone ahead but in some reduced form;
6 Assessment of projects that have been refused grant aid.

In this manner projects may be 'scored' on a scale ranging from complete additionality to zero additionality, as can be found in a study of inner city tourism completed by the UK Department of the Environment (1990). This study showed that most of the cases considered had a high incidence of project additionality. Critical to this was the fact that many of the schemes were very new to their locality and were therefore breaking new ground. Current practice, as used in further research involving this writer (Segal Quince Wicksteed 1993) is to define degrees of project additional-ity on the basis of whether the project would not have gone ahead without the grant (full additionality), or on a smaller scale or at a lower quality.

An important additional feature of Section 4 funding is its abil-ity to act as a catalyst in bringing forth other monies for the pro-ject once it had been given the 'seal of approval' by the Boards.

Also to be considered is visitor additionality which has been mentioned earlier in terms of attributable tourist spending. This is the measurement of the extent to which visitor flows generated by the project bring new money into the area. If visitor surveys on-site are to be the method of making such a judgment, then they require a particular line of questioning which involves:

1 Assessing visitors' prior knowledge of the project;

2 Discovering the significance of the project in influencing the trip decision;
3 Finding out whether the visitors would have been in the local area anyway;
4 Discriminating between stay visitors, day visitors and local residents.

Experience has shown that day visitors' additionality is more likely to be higher than that for stay visitors, because the latter often have many more reasons for coming to the area than the project in question. Some stay visitors may come for the specific purpose of visiting the project, in which case all their off-site expenditure is additional, while others may simply lengthen their stay because of the existence of the project, in which case only a proportion of their off-site spending is additional (Johnson and Thomas 1992).

Displacement may take two forms: business displacement and visitor displacement. Business displacement may arise in several ways:

1 The funded project crowds out a competing investment opportunity;
2 The project replaces an existing business on the same site;
3 The project may result in a property move to a new site leaving the old site vacant.

Replacement of an existing business may have a beneficial effect if there is a quality and cost improvement that raises long run viability. Many assisted tourist projects have been built on derelict sites and have therefore resulted in a net improvement.

Visitor displacement is simply demand that has been diverted from existing facilities in the locality as noted earlier. The commonest method of accounting for this tends to be the discounting of local resident usage as in ERDF procedures. The argument here is that residents have many other opportunities to spend in the local area, whereas, for visitors from outside, the whole purpose of the project is to augment the tourist product to encourage greater expenditure and a longer length of stay. An alternative approach to this issue is to estimate the diversion effect through discussions with operators. Under the assumption of separability of leisure consumption in the consumer's budget, which implies that if money allocated to leisure is not spent locally then it is spent outside the reference area, then if all competitive enterprises lie beyond local boundaries, visitor displacement effects can be ignored.

To conclude this section, and noting that equation (3) already includes a factor for displacement, then after allowing for a project additionality factor ($p < 1$), net employment becomes:

$$N = (1 - d) \, p \, (Ae_a + xOe_o) \tag{4}$$

But equation (4) does not allow for business displacement: if K is the project capital cost and S the level of grant/subsidy, then a polar case may arise where $(K - S)/K$ of investment is simply displaced project capital. If k is the proportion of additional capital funds that may be attributed to the project and $s = S/K$, then:

$$N = [s + k \, (1 - s)] \, (1 - d) \, p \, (Ae_a + xOe_o) \tag{5}$$

Putting $k = 1$ gives equation (4).

UNEMPLOYMENT

At a national level, unemployment benefits are income transfer payments which represent no real resource flows. At a local level, unemployment benefits represent a positive addition to income. They impact on the economy via the induced (Keynesian) effect of the respending of incomes earned by local residents, and serve to reduce income and employment multipliers to the extent of the impact of the project on the unemployed and the benefit payments to unemployed people. Designating e^* as the restricted employment multiplier, then

$$N = [s + k \, (1 - s)] \, (1 - d) \, p \, (Ae^*_a + xOe^*_o) \tag{6}$$

The ideal situation is where the impact of equation (6) falls on the local unemployment register, and this will be true even if there is job switching. However, e^* may need some fine tuning to allow for some employees commuting into the area and therefore spending their incomes outside the reference boundaries, and also part-time/seasonal workers on the project who previously would not have been in receipt of unemployment benefits.

TIME DIMENSIONS

So far the analysis has been carried out in terms of jobs created at working capacity of the project in steady-state, which implies that the time-slice under consideration is representative of the majority of the project's life. Introducing time into the analysis requires N to be specified in employee years and a planning horizon to be laid down, which may just be an estimate of the life of the project. The benefit of making this transition is that temporal patterns of employment may be accounted for, particularly construction work, although the UK Department of Trade and Industry uses a standard measure for a full-time job as one lasting ten years (Segal Quince Wicksteed 1993). Thus any construction job may be turned into FTEs by multiplying the number of employees, after adjustments for seasonal and casual workers, by the ratio of the construction period to the ten year standard. Once this step is taken equation (6) needs to be specified in income terms, discounted over the planning horizon and divided by the average cost per job year to make project comparisons. Thus:

$$N^* = \frac{Y}{w} = \frac{1}{w} [s + k(1-s)](1-d) p \left[\sum_{t=1}^{f} \frac{A_t m^*_a + xO_t m^*_o}{(1+r)^t} + K m^*_k \right]$$

$$(7)$$

Where

    N^* = accumulated present worth of job years;
    Y = present worth of the local income stream;
    w = average cost per job per year (including self-employed);
    m^* = appropriately adjusted local income multipliers;
    r = social discount rate;
    f = future time horizon;
    K = construction costs.

The time horizon f may be gauged from discussions with operators on the life of the project or to the point where the project requires significant reinvestment. The ratio N^*/f is the number of FTE jobs created by the project. This will differ from N in equation (6) even after the latter has been augmented by construction FTEs, because of the discounting process. The need for the latter hinges on whether there are marked differences in temporal employment patterns over the spectrum of tourism schemes being evaluated. Where this is not the case, then equation (6) will be adequate for the task, with an allowance for FTE employment generated in the construction phase.

PERFORMANCE MEASURES

The obvious performance measures relate to factors such as the number of FTEs created, job patterns in terms of educational attainment and skill levels, male/female ratios, the amount of part-time and seasonal work in relation to year-round full-time employment. In addition a number of financial indicators have been used in respect of the capital investment (K). The most common is the capital cost per job (K/N) but others include the grant/subsidy cost per job (S/N), the private capital cost per job ((K-S)/N) and the grant leverage effect ((K-S)/S).

PROJECT EXTERNALITIES

One of the main planks of UK tourism policy is to develop a balanced growth of facilities at tourist destinations to meet the many and changing needs of visitors. The expected outcome, as in the case of growth poles, is to produce agglomeration benefits, by virtue of the synergy of one project with another and its linkages with the rest of the economy, which makes the sum of the whole much greater than the individual parts that would apply if the resources were devoted to an equivalent number of dispersed projects. The generation of agglomeration externalities underpins the Local Enterprise and Development initiative in Wales (Wales Tourist Board 1992) and Tourism Development Action Plans (TDAPs) in England (English Tourist Board 1987). There are clearly a number of recognized successes, for example the repositioning of Portsmouth (Crouch 1992) as a city tourism destination under the banner of being the 'Flagship of Maritime England', away from the traditional seaside resort image of Southsea which occupies the southern part of Portsea Island. However, measuring agglomeration effects takes time and must depend on evidence of market expansion, particularly in relation to such items as repeat visits, increased investment activity, changing leverage ratios and improved asset prices.

Linkages are an important aspect of tourism projects which are accounted for in income and employment terms by the multiplier methodology. But the underlying assumption in what has gone before is that there is sufficient surplus capacity in the local economy to meet the production demands imposed by the tourist development. If this is not the case, then the project will either import from outside the locality or stimulate complementary bunches of investment in local suppliers. Increased local incomes and inward migration of employees generated by the project may also raise the demand for more public investment in housing, education, health, transport and other infrastructure developments.

Finally, the question of manpower must not be overlooked. Many large projects have important training elements which result in raising skills and productivity in the local workforce. Apart from improving incomes, this also feeds back into the agglomeration externalities by furthering the attractiveness of the location to outside investors.

CONCLUSIONS

During the 1980s a tide of economic liberalism saw questions being raised about the amount of state intervention and ownership in the economies of the world, and the implications this had for economic performance and public sector budget deficits. This heralded in programmes whereby many advanced economies divested themselves of state-owned assets to the private sector in order to reduce the size of the public sector and provide budgetary relief. The arguments advanced for privatization were for purposes of increasing efficiency and enhancing competitiveness by making greater use of markets for resource allocation. However, in the case of tourism, the complex nature of the product mitigates against the likelihood that private markets will account sufficiently for public sector interests and the needs of the host community in developing the tourist industry. The consensus view looks at tourism development as a partnership between government and the private sector, not least because many of the elements of the product sought by tourists lie within the public domain. Nevertheless, expanding budget deficits during the recession that began in the early 1990s made government treasuries far more conscious of deriving performance measures and criteria to justify state intervention.

The analytical methodology for publicly supported tourist projects discussed in this chapter has progressed from the rather broad approach, as exemplified by equations (2) and (3), through increasing levels of sophistication. One of the significant consequences of this is that as the analysis becomes more complicated so data requirements tend to spiral upwards. Given that data sources are imperfect and there is always pressure on time, the practical effect of this is to increase the level of economic assumptions in the model. The reality is therefore a trade-off of complexity against the more robust procedures illustrated by the ERDF model.

It is to be noted that the direct and spillover benefits of a tourist project are currently measured against the investment cost of the scheme alone. From a government finance standpoint this is perfectly acceptable, but from the position of the economy at large it is suboptimal. The multiplier impact of tourist spending may generate complementary bunches of investment to support such expenditure and so, at a further stage, the social benefits of tourism development, expressed here in terms of job creation, should be compared to any indirect or induced investment effects as well as the individual project capital cost.

REFERENCES

Archer, B. and Shea, S. (1980) *Grant Assisted Tourism Projects in Wales: An Evaluation*, Cardiff: Wales Tourist Board.
Bodlender, J.A. (1982) 'The financing of tourism projects', *Tourism Management* 3, 4: 277–284.
Cardiff City Council (1988) *Cardiff Tourism Study*, Cardiff: City Hall.
Committee on Welsh Affairs (1987) *Tourism in Wales*, London: HMSO.
Crouch, S. (1992) 'The way forward – Building public/private sector partnership', *Bulletin of the Tourism Society* 76, 6: 6–7.
Department of the Environment (1990) *Tourism and the Inner City*, London: HMSO.
English Tourist Board (1987) *Annual Report*, London.
House of Commons (1969) *Development of Tourism Act 1969*, London: HMSO.
Jenkins, C.L. (1982) 'The use of investment incentives for tourism projects in developing countries', *Tourism Management* 3, 2: 91–97.
Johnson, P. and Thomas, B. (1990) 'The economic impact of museums: A study of the North of England Open Air Museum at Beamish', Paper presented at a conference on Tourism Research into the 1990s, Durham: University of Durham.
—— (1992) *Tourism, Museums and the Local Economy*, Aldershot: Edward Elgar.
Pearce, D.G. (1992) 'Tourism and the European Regional Development Fund: The first fourteen years', *Journal of Travel Research* 30, 3: 44–51.
Segal Quince Wicksteed (1993) *Evaluation of Section 4 Assistance*, Cardiff: Wales Tourist Board.
Sinclair, T. and Sutcliffe, C. (1992) 'Keynesian income multipliers with first

and second round effects, an application to tourist expenditure', *Oxford Bulletin of Economics and Statistics* 44: 321–338.

Wales Tourist Board (1992) *Schemes of Financial Assistance*, Cardiff: Wales Tourist Board.

Wanhill, S.R.C. (1986) 'Which investment incentives for tourism?', *Tourism Management* 7, 1: 2–7.

Chapter 11

Resource constraints on tourism
Water resources and sustainability

John J. Pigram

A theme common to much tourism research in the 1990s is an emphasis on sustainability. Ecologically sustainable tourism calls for the endorsement of forms and scales of development which do not carry the risk of irreversible outcomes, or which impose unacceptable costs on future generations. Sustainability implies ongoing concern for the maintenance of those environmental qualities which attract and give satisfaction to visitors.

Tourism is, to a large degree, a resource-based activity, interacting with natural systems and with a capacity to initiate far-reaching changes on the environment. Many forms of tourism are seen as contributing to environmental degradation and tending to be self-destructive (Cohen Chapter Two). Erosion of the resource base, impairment of the built environment and disruption of the social fabric of host communities are common indicators of the negative impacts which can ensue from the predatory effects of a mass influx of tourists (Pearce Chapter Twelve).

An indication of the range of possible environmental impacts arising from tourism activity can be gained from the work of Buckley and Pannell (1990). Major impacts on the biophysical environment were categorized and linked to travel, accommodation and recreational activities associated with tourism. Significant environmental problems identified included trampling of vegetation, introduction of exotic species, pollution of air and water, disturbance to wildlife and visual impacts.

Whereas that study focused on effects on national parks and reserves, tourism has the potential to generate negative impacts in other bioregions such as the coastal zone, alpine areas and arid lands (Commonwealth of Australia 1991). Primary changes can include damage to vegetation and soil and degradation of the hydrological condition of waterbodies. These primary changes are often cumulative in effect and secondary impacts can arise altering the balances and relationships within habitats and ecosystems.

At a recent conference on the relationship between tourism and the environment, the potential for degradation of marine eco-systems in the Mediterranean was recognized (Stachowitsch 1992). The most serious threat to the ocean was seen as coming from increased input of organic material and nutrients from tourism developments along coastlines. Other negative effects identified include:

(a) destruction of coastal ecosystems to provide tourism infra-structure,
(b) damage to coral reefs and seagrass beds from anchoring of pleasure boats,
(c) disturbance of wildlife habitats and refuges,
(d) littering of beaches,
(e) depletion of fish stocks by recreational anglers, and
(f) collection of marine organisms as souvenirs

(Stachowitsch 1992: 30)

The author makes the point that not only does tourism contribute to these problems, it is also among the first industries to suffer from ecosystem deterioration. In some situations the problems stem from the pressure of numbers beyond a critical threshold or saturation point. In others it is not so much numbers as the char-acteristics of visitors and their activities which lead to deleterious consequences for the destination area.

Similar problems arising from tourism activity in the marine environment have been documented off the Queensland coast of Australia. Woodley (1989) identifies a number of interconnected issues with the potential to degrade the natural qualities of the Great Barrier Reef Marine National Park, the focus of tourism in the region. These include:

(a) discharge of sewage from vessels, floating structures, island-based resorts and the mainland,
(b) nutrients and toxic contaminants,
(c) oil spills,
(d) littering, and
(e) sedimentation

The major challenge seen as threatening the Great Barrier Reef is the maintenance of water quality (Craik 1992). Once again, the interrelationship with tourism is clear. Tourism activities account for part of the threat to water quality and to the sustainability of the Great Barrier Reef environment, on which, in turn, tourism depends. The link between water quality and the ecology and economy of the region has prompted the Marine Park Authority to implement measures to protect the Great Barrier Reef, both as a great natural asset and an important attraction for tourists.

These examples indicate the vulnerability of a particular environment – marine ecosystems – to disturbance, and the potential consequences for tourism-related activity in that environment. More generally, it is the inadequacy of environmental planning and landscape design which have failed to anticipate and keep pace with the incremental pressures which the growth of tourism brings. Numerous examples exist where developers and public authorities have failed to recognize the need for expanded services and facilities.

The emergence of tourism pressures on some of the villages and towns of rural England is symptomatic of the problem (Butler and Clark 1992). Ancient street layouts and outmoded traffic systems are simply incompatible with modern tourism. Thomas (1992) describes the difficulties which the historic city of Oxford experiences in trying to cope with traffic congestion and parking problems for an influx of tourist coaches and vehicles. The chaotic traffic and pollution problems evident in major urban centres in Asia, Bangkok, Hong Kong and Seoul, for example, are further illustrations of infrastructure being unable to handle the extra pressure imposed, at least in part, by tourist activity.

Planners and designers have been slow to put forward innovative systems of resource use, or creative approaches to environmentally compatible forms of tourism development to deal with such problems.

> It is the absence or weakness of planning which allows the development of types of tourism incompatible with natural systems and permits the expansion of tourism into areas at a rate inconsistent with the capacity of the infrastructure and society to cope with the extra pressure.
>
> (Pigram 1989: 217)

The challenge is to promote modes of tourism which upgrade the environment and serve as a positive influence in social and cultural dynamics; which 'can protect resources while improving quality and enhancing visitor satisfaction' (Gunn 1988: vi).

Typically, areas or sites targeted for tourism development differ in terms of their natural characteristics, their durability or fragility, and their significance. Sustainable tourism development implies the delineation of sensitive zones and selection of areas for more, or less, intensive use in keeping with the maintenance of environmental quality. Appropriate reference also needs to be made to human concerns and economic circumstances, as well as biophysical attributes. Water is a case in point, and the availability of water resources to sustain tourism can be a key constraint in the planning process.

WATER AND TOURISM

Water, with the right characteristics, should be a fundamental consideration in the location and siting of tourist developments. Adequate estimates of water availability require knowledge of surface waterbodies, groundwater, and climate and weather patterns over an extended period. The sources and suitability of water supplies for tourism purposes need to be determined, along with the costs of pumping, treatment, storage and disposal of water containing wastes. The form and quality of water for different forms of tourism and resort development are also important considerations. Wave, wind and flow conditions are obvious examples, as are shoreline and subsurface characteristics, and the quantity, permanency and seasonality of water bodies. The clarity, purity and temperature of water, including the presence of pollutants, are also critical to the success of water-related tourism. Too often, these aspects are ignored in project planning.

Water figures prominently in at least three aspects of tourism development:

1 The quantity and quality of available water can be major constraints on the location, siting, design and operation of tourism facilities. As pressure grows on increasingly scarce water resources, the potential of areas, otherwise suitable for tourism development, may be compromised by inadequate water supplies.
2 The presence of water serves as an additional dimension to a tourism facility, enhancing the scenic quality and appeal of the

setting, and contributing to the attraction and intrinsic satisfaction derived from the tourism experience. An environment rich in water often forms an aesthetically pleasing setting for tourism.

3   Water is essential for the operation of the tourism industry – for drinking purposes, sanitation and waste disposal, for cooling purposes, for irrigation and landscaping, and for the functioning of particular forms of water-related activities, for example, swimming and boating. Water for the making of artificial snow is also an issue in some tourist zones.

Ecologically sustainable tourism begins with site selection, planning and design. Proper attention to factors such as water availability can avoid subsequent managerial problems and help sustain worthwhile environmental values. Alternatively, poorly chosen sites with inadequate water supplies can conceal shortcomings and become problem areas calling for costly compensatory and mitigatory measures to remain functional.

The popular tourist destination of Portugal's Algarve region demonstrates how a precarious water supply and fierce competition from competing uses for the resource can threaten the viability of the tourism industry (Martin et al. 1985). In the Algarve, water supplies have not kept pace with burgeoning demands from intensification of agriculture and rapid urbanization. The tourist industry accounts for up to 40,000 users with peak demand coinciding with the period when water supplies are at their lowest. Groundwater is the primary source of supply and the major problem is the proximity of demand to the coast and the risk of saline intrusion as water levels in wells are depleted. Firm planning control and management of the groundwater resource and alternative sources of supply will be necessary to avoid contraction of tourist activity and possible abandonment of irrigation agriculture in the region.

The incidence of such problems is unlikely to recede as increasing population pressure and growing sophistication in water demand generate conflict between users and uses. The availability of water, in sufficient quantity and quality to satisfy such uses, has emerged as an important concern in many parts of the world in recent decades. As competition for water increases into the next century, tourism will be forced to justify its claims on the resource against a range of more conventional uses and priorities. The problem can be clearly illustrated with reference to the water situation in Australia, North America and Britain.

Water and Australian tourism

In water-deficient areas like much of inland Australia, water availability is a very real constraint on all forms of resource use. Yet, despite its intrinsic importance, water often appears to be viewed as a non-critical factor in the location of tourism developments. This leads to conflict when new claims are made on scarce resources, especially for uses which are seen as non-essential. On the one hand, allocation of water for tourism and recreation is resisted by current water users. On the other, increasing pressure is being experienced on water resources at those sites which *are* available to meet a growing demand from domestic and foreign tourists.

Already environmental problems, both biophysical and social, are becoming apparent and parts of inland Australia may soon face a situation similar to that described in North America:

> In a number of locations in the Western United States, *legal appropriations for water currently exceed available water resources*. Developers are faced with rising costs as well as growing environmental and regulatory constraints. In some regions in the nation, developers now have to prove a 200- to 300-year supply of water in order to receive approval to go forward in the development process. In other areas, ski area expansion or development is being held up pending assessment of adequate water resources. In some cities, developers of golf courses are unable to utilize municipal supplies and have to purchase water from other sources. As water supplies become more scarce, the development and approval process may more frequently include the cumbersome, and time-consuming process of acquiring water rights. This adds additional associated costs and inherent risks. Finally, there is the growing possibility which developers fear most – that development or expansion plans may be put on hold, or be prohibited entirely, as environmental pressures and conflicts grow.
>
> (Arnold 1990: 9)

In many areas, the problems are made worse because of conflict with other water uses. Water serves a range of important functions –

domestic water supply, irrigation, hydropower and industry – in addition to its role in tourism. Some of these lend themselves to multipurpose use in tandem with tourism and recreation; others are incompatible or involve use of the water resource in such a way as to detract from its suitability to support tourism. Conflict can occur over use of the water surface as well as over accessibility to the water resource. In some cases, access is denied to tourists seeking use of water bodies; in other cases, especially along shorelines, access problems are created by tourist development intruding into public space. Confrontation between tourist developers and other resource users, and the communities affected, could be reduced if conditions of water availability and access were established at the outset.

As with the example from the Mediterranean coast noted earlier, externalities generated by so-called 'productive' forms of water resource use can erode amenity values and be detrimental to tourism projects (Martin *et al.* 1985). Eutrophication and resulting algal blooms, for example, can have serious implications for tourism along inland rivers and water bodies. Paterson (1989) reports the problems caused by an algal bloom on the Gippsland Lakes of southeast Australia, coincident with the peak summer tourist season, as having a lasting effect on the A$180 million tourist industry based on the lakes. Paterson likens the impact of such an event in economic terms to a season of poor snowfall in an alpine resort.

Further difficulties arise because of the prevailing attitudes of water management authorities to instream uses of the resource. Many authorities in Australia continue to regard the provision of water for uses such as tourism as merely ancillary to other accepted functions of the resource, for example domestic water supply, commercial and industrial use, irrigation, hydropower, navigation, flood mitigation and waste disposal. This approach has eliminated or excluded many options for use of waterbodies for recreation and made conditions for others less than satisfactory. Examples of poor planning and mismanagement include:

(a) discharge of pollutants into streams serving recreation sites,
(b) release of water from storages without regard for the effect of stream flows, velocity and temperature on recreation pursuits downstream,
(c) operation of storages without regard for the effect of draw-down on recreation opportunities,

(d) construction of storages without provision for future recreational use of the waterbody and shoreline, and

(e) prohibition on the recreational use of domestic water supply storages and catchments.

(Pigram 1993)

Water resources management for tourism

Managerial initiatives for the tourism industry can also be inhibited by fragmentation and overlap between decision-making bodies, and confusion regarding the responsibility of respective government sectors and agencies. Referring to the analogous area of outdoor recreation planning in Australia, Pitts argues:

> The management of outdoor recreation resources and facilities in Australia is characterized by a myriad of government departments, authorities and agencies operating in apparent isolation of each other. Outdoor recreation has rarely been allowed to develop as a secondary function associated with more traditional government activities such as forestry, conservation, water supply and town planning. This approach has inevitably led to problems of coordination, conflicts in connection with overlapping responsibilities and doubts about the effectiveness of the whole delivery system in meeting community needs.
>
> (1983: 7)

With tourism specifically, there is little coordination between the various public agencies, private groups and voluntary organizations interested in attracting the tourist dollar to Australia. Moreover it is only in the most recent times that water supply projects in Australia have been planned with future tourism and recreation potential in mind. Lake Wivenhoe, built to augment water supplies for the city of Brisbane, Queensland, and Split Rock Dam in northern New South Wales, are two of a very few examples where a framework of recreation opportunities has been incorporated into the storages during construction.

More typical is Lake Hume on the Murray River, which forms the state border between New South Wales and Victoria. The lake, which was built primarily as an irrigation storage some seventy years ago, was of decidedly marginal importance. Any amenity values created were incidental to the benefits perceived for river regulation and irrigation downstream which were the primary purposes of the storage. This situation becomes readily apparent when summer discharges draw down the storage level coincident with peak recreational demand. The exposed shoreline is aesthetically undesirable and difficult for boat launching, and recreational use becomes hazardous as dead trees and other obstacles, not removed prior to inundation, appear at the water surface. Interestingly, a recent study found that retaining more water for longer periods in the lake during the summer to serve recreation needs was not economically justified compared with returns from the released water for irrigation and other purposes (Pak-Poy and Kneebone 1990). Therefore, resolution of the conflict will not be easy to accomplish.

Fragmentation of administrative responsibility for Lake Hume also represents a significant obstacle to management of the storage as a resource for tourism and recreation. The lake is owned by the Murray-Darling Basin Commission, but day-to-day operation of the storage is the joint responsibility of the New South Wales Department of Water Resources and the Rural Water Corporation of Victoria, which also shared in construction of the lake. Protection and maintenance of the catchment are also divided between resource management agencies in the two states. On the Victorian side, for example, part of the foreshore is in private hands and can legally be fenced to exclude people. To complicate the management picture further, five local government bodies control different parts of the shoreline, sections of which have been leased to private organizations. Finally, control of recreation activity on the water surface is the responsibility of the New South Wales Maritime Services Board.

Fragmentation at this scale is common on inland waterbodies in Australia, even away from state borders. At Lake Hume, efforts are being made to overcome the problem with the creation of a Recreation Coordinating Committee embracing representatives of bodies with managerial input into the storage. However, until the committee is given statutory power to coordinate overall recreation planning and management, its role in developing a more effective spectrum of opportunities for water-related recreation and tourism at the lake will be frustrated (Lamb 1988).

Further downstream on the Murray River, more evidence can be found of the magnitude of the task in achieving consensus between a number of interests and planning bodies. A Strategic Tourism Plan drawn up by the Murray River Region reflects the gap between public regulatory authorities, the community and the private sector (Atkinson and Bochner 1988). The challenge in finding common ground among such diverse interests was noted previously (Pigram 1993). Added to the complexity of the operational environment is the perception in many quarters that tourism represents a new and non-essential (Nash Chapter Three) claim on an already stressed water resource; a claim that water users believe can only be met at the expense of existing entitlements to water held by established interests.

Clearly then, there is ample scope for conflict over allocation and use of water for tourism in Australia, and competition is likely to be even more intense in regions away from the coast where water resources for any purpose are in short supply. As might be expected, the more demanding the environment, in terms of pressure on water resources, the more critical the issue of water adequacy becomes. This is not a problem confined to Australia. The quantity and quality of available water resources are key concerns in the development of tourist opportunities in parts of North America, Britain and elsewhere.

Water for tourism in North America and Britain

The low priority given to instream uses of water for tourism and recreation is also apparent in North America. In the USA, recreation resource allocation, especially in rural areas, has tended to be *ad hoc* and provision of opportunities for tourism is often the byproduct of other major resource developments. The result is resistance encountered to tourism initiatives seen to threaten established claims on the resource base. The negative reaction in Hawaii to proposals to develop or expand golf resorts, for example, is probably partly a reflection of anti-Japanese sentiment. It is also based on the consequences for agriculture from increased pressure on limited water resources on some of the islands.

More recently, a number of initiatives have been taken in the USA in an attempt to revitalize tourism as a tool for rural economic development (Economics Research Associates 1989; Eadington Chapter Nine). In particular, the potential of community-driven, tourism-specific rural enterprise zones as the platform for tourism development is receiving serious consideration (Messerli 1990). Of course, tourism enterprise zones require the existence of resources with tourism potential, and accessible and attractive waterbodies may well serve as the focus for designation of such zones.

In Canada the value of rural water for tourism and recreation is explicitly recognized in the resource appraisal procedures of the Canada Land Inventory. However, public sector initiatives to develop this potential have been intermittent and generally reactive to perceived exploitation of the natural environment by private interests (Butler and Clark 1992). Again in park development, the emphasis has been mainly on environmental protection and attempts to implement an integrated approach to the provision of opportunities for water-related tourism have received less attention.

In Britain, people have long enjoyed comparative ease of access to rural land and waterbodies for tourism and recreation. The coastline is generally within easy reach and increments to the stock of recreation water space continue to occur from the construction of new reservoirs, restoration of canals and the flooding of disused gravel pits and mineral workings. Since 1974 regional water bodies have had a statutory obligation to provide for recreation in all new water projects. Yet, few authorities have the personnel or skills necessary to plan and manage facilities to satisfy an increasing demand for water-related recreation and tourism (Blenkhorn 1979). Some concern has also been expressed regarding recreation opportunities for both domestic tourists and foreign visitors to Britain at water supply projects following privatization. Although legislation provides for public access to water authority land, the requirements are vague and open to differing interpretations.

More generally, the value of water for leisure and tourism in rural Britain has been recognized by the Countryside Commission (1988) and the English Tourist Board (1991). In its guide to sustainable tourism, the English Tourist Board acknowledges the role of clean waterbodies as an attraction for visitors, as well as the need for adequate water, in quantity and quality, for human and operational needs at tourist destinations. Clearly, the emphasis is on management of water to cater for the many ways in which it can function as a resource for tourism.

The managerial response

The question of how to deal with emerging claims on water resources for tourism is an important and legitimate focus of concern for water managers. Demands for water to support tourism can become particularly contentious in situations where competition for limited supplies is great and pressure to use the resources in a sustainable manner is high.

A simple, but unimaginative response by resource management agencies might be to refuse approval altogether for tourism development in areas where the adequacy of water (or other attribute of the resource base) was in question. This was the situation in Wilpena Round in the arid zone of South Australia where a proposal for a resort development was challenged because of the limited groundwater resources in the area (Department of Environment and Planning 1989). However, care is needed with such responses, and any decision to exclude tourism on the basis of some apparent or perceived inadequacy in the resource endowment should always be qualified. Improved information and technology, coupled with enlightened planning and management, may permit innovative measures to be implemented and make the initial cautionary reaction irrelevant and redundant.

A range of measures is possible in response to questions over the adequacy of water supplies to support instream uses such as tourism. The most constructive approach is to work towards better use and management of what water is available. More efficient irrigation, for example – 'doing better with less' – may allow the same agricultural production, but with some water to spare for other uses including tourism (Pigram 1993). A further refinement would be to link water allocations to the adoption of 'best management practice' in water use. Adjustments to the price of water may also be necessary to stimulate efforts to economize in use, and to recycle and reuse water. A system of transferable water entitlements is another mechanism which would permit tourist developers to enter a water market and bid for a share of available water (Pigram et al. 1992).

In some situations, it may be possible to generate new opportunities for water-related tourism development by encouraging multiple use of waterbodies or the creation of additional water resources by the construction of artificial lakes. This has been the strategy adopted in arid inland areas of the Northern Territory, Australia. Lakes intended solely for recreational and tourist use are planned for sites in parts of the Territory with few permanent waterbodies. Even in the wetter northern zone near Darwin, such lakes would provide an important resource for water-related tourism. Domestic water supply reservoirs in this area are not open for recreational use and the ocean and estuaries are hazardous because of crocodiles and venomous sea creatures (Lawrence 1987).

WATER FOR TOURISM IN ARID ENVIRONMENTS

It is clear that considerable scope exists for mitigation of water supply problems through management of water demand and supply, and through conservation measures. In these circumstances, insistence on unrealistically high levels of resource security before approval of new tourism proposals could effectively confine tourism to inherently well-endowed environments, perhaps already facing visitor pressure (Cohen Chapter Two). Such a policy would preclude the provision of exciting tourism settings in regions regarded as inherently inhospitable. Desert oases, for example, and sites with tourist potential in arid zones would be excluded from consideration. Moreover, resource managers would be denied the opportunity to overcome basic resource deficiencies and establish viable forms of tourism in harmony with the limitations of a harsh and demanding environment.

As available water supplies dwindle and competition for water increases, activities seen as less essential, such as tourism, must justify claims on a scarce resource, and demonstrate the capacity to achieved sustainable use. The Palm Springs resort area in the California desert is a good example of the way in which the application of sound water planning principles and management practices can contribute to ecologically sustainable tourism in an arid environment.

Tourism in the California desert

Palm Springs is only one of a collection of urbanized areas located in the Coachella Valley of southern California 100 miles (160 kilometres) southeast of Los Angeles and north of the Salton Sea (Figure 11.1). The region is true desert with annual rainfall averaging less than three inches (approximately 76mm) and only 15–20 days of rainfall each year. Summer temperatures are extreme; the July mean maximum is 108°F (42°C) and humidity is very low. The valley is surrounded by mountains up to 10,000 feet (approximately 3,050 metres) high, which are snowcapped in

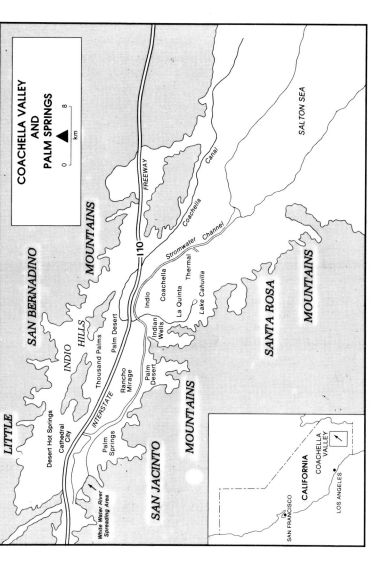

Figure 11.1 Coachella Valley and Palm Springs (location)

winter and which, at times, funnel winds of great force through the valley.

The area was originally settled by the Agua Caliente Indians who were attracted by the healing powers of the mineral waters. European and Hispanic settlers later used the springs to raise date palms and citrus crops. Today, over 60,000 acres (approximately 24,000 hectares) of irrigated farmland use some 300,000 acre feet (approximately 369,000 megalitres) of water annually to produce a wide range of fruit, vegetable and field crops with a total gross value of US $347 million in 1990 (Coachella Valley Water District 1991).

Of even greater significance to the regional economy is tourism. By the mid-1980s, one in four Coachella Valley jobs was attributed to tourism which had become a US$1.3 billion industry and was still expanding. The area was first made popular for vacations by Hollywood film stars, such as Bob Hope and Frank Sinatra, who have homes there. At present the warm dry climate attracts more than two million visitors annually to the valley's 200 hotels and resorts, which offer 12,000 rooms. There are 7,500 swimming pools and over eighty golf courses in an area approximately 35 miles by 15 miles (55 kilometres by 25 kilometres). Visitors and resident golfers spend nearly US $300 million annually and generate 7,000 jobs. It is little wonder the valley has become known as 'the golf capital of the world' (Figure 11.2).

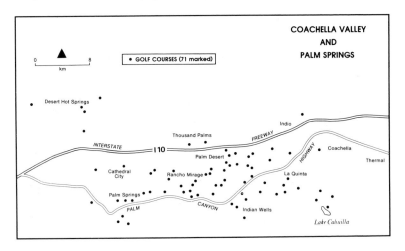

Figure 11.2 Coachella Valley and Palm Springs (golf courses)

The ready availability of water made possible by sound management practices has led to the transformation of the desert into a series of oasis-like settlements supporting a thriving economy based on irrigated agriculture and tourism. Moreover, careful management of the resource appears to have ensured the sustainability of these human activities in the face of increasing demand.

Early settlers in the Coachella Valley quickly realized the value of water. Initially, irrigation supplies were drawn from the extensive aquifer underlying the basin. However, with limited natural recharge and increasing use, groundwater levels began to drop. Agitation for access to Colorado River water grew, and in 1948 the Coachella Branch of the All-American Canal was completed. The availability of this water not only boosted irrigation acreage fourfold, but brought with it additional water conservation measures. These include an underground piped distribution system and drainage system, sophisticated metred control of water deliveries and the lining of a large section of the Branch Canal to contain seepage losses (Coachella Valley County Water District 1978).

The reduced agricultural demands on groundwater, as a result, eventually made possible the emergence of the western portion of the valley into the world famous tourism resort area it has become. In turn, tourism development in Palm Springs benefited from the application of computerized technologies for water control, and the array of other innovative water saving practices already in use in agriculture. Moreover, the measures in place to intercept surface flows and encourage the percolation and replenishment of groundwater storage for agricultural users became an essential part of a water management strategy to sustain tourism in this arid region.

This is all the more remarkable in view of the extensive use of water typical of all phases of the Palm Springs tourism industry. Beyond the city limits the open sandy landscape is broken only by stunted vegetation, twisted by the relentless desert winds. Within the urbanized area, water and the evidence of water use are everywhere. Lush turf and flowerbeds line the streets and the golfing fairways. Lakes, fountains and waterfalls feature prominently on the country club estates. In one leading hotel, diners are taken to the restaurant by barge along an artificial stream misted with a fine rainforest spray (see Cohen Chapter Two). In the more luxurious estates, multimillion dollar residences feature up to five bathrooms, plus a powder room, pool and spa. Casual visitors, ignorant of the background of conservation, tend to view the scene as prof-ligate waste of water. In fact, sound planning and management of the water resource help integrate the city and its tourism industry into its hostile desert surroundings.

Water resources management in the desert

As noted earlier, measures already in place to cope with agricul-tural water demands were equally relevant to the emerging water needs of tourism in the Coachella Valley. The keys to success are an impressive artificial recharge programme to replenish the aquifer and an extensive range of water conservation techniques to eliminate waste.

Some thirty years ago, with groundwater levels in the Palm Springs area dropping an average of 1.4 feet (approximately 43cm) per year, the Coachella Valley Water District and the adjoining Desert Water Agency opted to join the California State Water Project. This scheme comprises a system of storages and aqueducts designed to import water from northern California. However, no facilities exist to get state project water to the desert. Instead, the valley water agencies entered into exchange agreements with the Metropolitan Water District in southern California to trade Coachella Valley's project water for an equal amount of Colorado River water. Under the agreement, water is diverted from the Metropolitan Water District's Colorado River Aqueduct for groundwater recharge in wet years, in exchange for the local agencies' contracted state project water in dry years. The diverted water is trapped in a series of earthen intake basins north of Palm Springs from where it percolates into underground storage.

Between the wet years of 1985 and 1987, for example, some 600,000 acre feet (approximately 738,000 megalitres) of river water, which otherwise would have flowed into the Gulf of California, was captured and 'banked' in Coachella Valley's groundwater basin, providing a ten-year supply for desert water users. This had the added advantage of allowing groundwater withdrawals from higher water tables with less pumping, while giving the benefit of addi-tional water supplies to southern California during drought.

An indication of the success of the system can be gauged from groundwater elevations in wells monitored throughout the valley. During the past twenty years, water levels rose an average of 9 inches (approximately 23cm) per year. In one well which was dropping 2.4 feet (approximately 75cm) per year twenty years ago, the average annual decline over the whole of that period was reduced to 10 inches (approximately 25cm). During the last five years, as the plume of recharged water moved down valley from the spreading area, the water level actually increased 1 foot (approximately 30cm) per year (Coachella Valley Water District 1991).

Despite the success of the groundwater recharge scheme in stabilizing the aquifer, the Coachella Valley Water District is also engaged in a wideranging programme of management of water supply and demand. Among the measures being implemented are:

(a) improvement of water extraction techniques to maximize the supply potential of the aquifer,
(b) improved application systems, including drip irrigation, and the use of electronic timers, with moisture probes and wind sensors,
(c) monitoring of water use to reduce waste, and
(d) adoption of increased water charges to reduce demand.

With continued urbanization of the valley, the need for water reuse has been recognized. An ambitious programme is in place for reclamation of water containing wastes. All the tertiary treated water currently produced (3 million gallons/11.36 megalitres per day) is pumped, through a separate reticulation system, to golf courses and parks which welcome the reclaimed water as a cheaper alternative to the domestic water supply.

A further initiative in water conservation is the strong emphasis on water-efficient design and landscaping. Developers are required to submit landscape plans for approval prior to construction, and low interest loans are provided to encourage the installation of facilities to improve water efficiency. New golf courses are being designed with less turf, using about half the water of older courses. Many golf clubs water only the greens and essential parts of fairways, and are turning to water-efficient vegetation and natural landscaping on other parts of their courses.

Xeriscape, or the practice of low water use landscaping, is also being promoted for residences, streetscapes, public buildings, hotels and resorts. The Coachella Valley Water District employs specialist water management staff to advise on appropriate landscaping, irrigation techniques and use of desert native plants and materials. A school and community education programme is part of this initiative and a guide to water-efficient landscaping and desert gardening has been published (Johnson and Harbison 1988). Despite reluctance by some interests to adopt the desert-style landscaping, the city has reduced outdoor water use by 10 per cent in five years, while at the same time increasing the overall area of urban parkland.

Palm Springs is a success story of sustainable tourism in a desert setting. The unique combination of a large reservoir or ground-water used conjunctively and opportunistically with surface water supplies, and a comprehensive programme for managed use and reuse of the resource, has averted the prospect of water problems for the foreseeable future. Questions remain regarding the long-term viability of tourism and other development in the Coachella Valley, among them, air pollution, seismic activity and the eco-nomic implications of seasonality of patronage. However, from the perspective of water adequacy, Palm Springs remains an exciting tourist oasis in stark contrast to its arid surroundings.

CONCLUSION

In a now more environmentally conscious world, the tourism industry faces increasingly stringent conditions on development proposals. Many of these conditions reflect a concern for sustain-ability; for the long-term health of the resource base on which tourism depends. A key constraint in the establishment, operation and expansion of tourist developments is the availability of water. Water is a desirable attribute of tourist resorts and facilities and the provision of water-related activities for visitors is a common feature of tourism developments. Yet, natural attractions of climate and scenic splendour sometimes are the prime determinants of the location of tourist activity. In the absence of a secure water supply, the sustainability of these ventures calls for effective management of the resource in the face of competing demands.

It takes only a drought of the dimensions of the recent disaster in California, for example, to underscore the fragility of many tourism developments in water-deficient regions. In these circum-stances, tourism is seen as a dispensable, low priority activity and the scarce water resources which are available are allocated to needs perceived as more basic and urgent. The challenge for the tourism industry is to demonstrate its capacity to adopt sustainable management of the water resources at its disposal. In adopting this response, tourism not only justifies its claims on the resource, but becomes a model for alternative users of water to pursue more sustainable modes of use.

As global pressures on space and resources grow with increased population, technological change and greater mobility and awareness, the tendency may be to push tourism activity into areas marginal in terms of a secure resource base. This trend will make even more urgent the development of sustainable forms of tourism consistent with the prevailing constraints on resource use, yet responsive to the potential of human ingenuity and managerial skill in working within those constraints.

REFERENCES

Arnold, M. (1990) 'Water resources. A critical constraint to development', Unpublished Master's thesis, Cornell University.

Atkinson, W. and Bochner, S. (1988) 'Planning for tourism at the regional and local levels', *Planner* 3, 5: 45–9.

Blenkhorn, A. (1979) 'The attraction of water', *Parks and Recreation* 44, 2: 17–23.

Buckley, R. and Pannell, J. (1990) 'Environmental impacts of tourism and recreation in national parks and conservation reserves', *Journal of Tourism Studies* 1, 1: 24–32.

Butler, R.W. and Clark, G. (1992) 'Tourism in rural areas: Canada and the United Kingdom', in I.R. Bowler, C.R. Bryant and M.D. Nellis (eds) *Contemporary Rural Systems in Transition*, vol. 2: *Economy and Society*, Wallingford: CAB International, 166–186.

Coachella Valley County Water District (1978) *Coachella Valley's Golden Years*, Coachella: Coachella Valley County Water District.

Coachella Valley Water District (1991) *Annual Review 1990–91*, Coachella.

Commonwealth of Australia (1991) *Ecologically Sustainable Development – Tourism*, Canberra: Australian Government Publishing Service.

Countryside Commission (1988) *The Water Industry in the Countryside*, Manchester: Countryside Commission.

Craik, W. (1992) 'Water quality: Promoting tourism and recreation', Paper presented to Australian Water Resources Commission National Conference on Water Quality Management and Ecologically Sustainable Development, Adelaide, December.

Department of Environment and Planning, South Australia (1989) *Proposed Wilpena Station Resort, Flinders Ranges National Park*, Adelaide: South Australia Government Printer.

Economics Research Associates (1989) *The National Policy Study on Rural Tourism and Small Businesses*, Virginia.

English Tourist Board (1991) *The Green Light. A Guide to Sustainable Tourism*, Manchester: Countryside Commission.

Gunn, C. (1988) *Vacationscape*, New York: Van Nostrand Reinhold.

Johnson, E. and Harbison, D. (1988) *Lush and Efficient. A Guide to Coachella Valley Landscaping*, Coachella: Valley Publishing.

Lamb, A. (1988) 'Applying the ROS to water storages – The case of recreational fishing at Lake Hume', Unpublished BA Hons thesis, University of New England, Armidale, NSW.

Lawrence, J. (1987) 'Water-based recreational issues in the Northern Territory', Paper presented to Engineering Conference, Darwin, May.

Martin, L., Bennett, R. and Gregory, D. (1985) 'The thirsty Algarve', *Geographical Magazine* 57: 321–324.

Messerli, H. (1990) 'Enterprise zones and rural tourism development', Unpublished MA thesis, George Washington University, Virginia.

Pak-Poy and Kneebone Pty Ltd (1990) *Hume and Dartmouth Reservoirs. An Economic Study of Changed Operating Strategies*, Canberra: Murray-Darling Basin Commission.

Paterson, J. (1989) 'Water management and recreational values', in B. Rigden and L. Henry (eds) *Water Quality and Management for Recreation and Tourism*, Proceedings of the IAWPRC Conference, Brisbane, July 1988.

Pigram, J. (1989) *Outdoor Recreation and Resource Management*, London: Croom Helm.

—— (1992) 'Planning for tourism in rural areas: Bridging the policy implementation gap', in D. Pearce and R. Butler (eds) *Tourism Research: Critiques and Challenges*, London: Routledge, 156–174.

—— (1993) *Issues in the Management of Australia's Water Resources*, Melbourne: Longman.

Pigram, J., Delforce, R., Coelli, M., Norris, V., Antony, G., Anderson, R. and Musgrave, W. (1992) *Transferable Water Entitlements in Australia*, Armidale, NSW: Centre for Water Policy Research, University of New England.

Pitts, D. (1983) 'Opportunity shift. Development and application of recreation opportunity spectrum concepts in park management', Unpublished PhD thesis, Griffith University.

Stachowitsch, M. (1992) 'Tourism and the sea: The world's largest ecosystem in danger', in *Proceedings* of International Society for Environmental Protection Conference on Strategies for Reducing the Environmental Impact of Tourism, Vienna, November, 30–36.

Thomas, J. (1992) 'The built heritage: Tourist attraction or financial liability? A case study of Oxford, United Kingdom', in *Proceedings* of International Society for Environmental Protection Conference on Strategies for Reducing the Environmental Impact of Tourism, Vienna, November, 494–507.

Woodley, S. (1989) 'Management of water quality in the Great Barrier Marine Park', in B. Rigden and L. Henry (eds) *Water Quality and Management for Recreation and Tourism*, Proceedings of the IAWPRC Conference, Brisbane, July 1988, 31–8.

Chapter 12

Planning for tourism in the 1990s
An integrated, dynamic, multiscale approach

Douglas Pearce

The identification of trends in tourism and a concern with factors shaping future events and developments can themselves perhaps be heralded as two of the significant trends to have emerged in tourism in recent years. An established interest in technical studies for modelling and forecasting demand in tourism (e.g. Archer 1980; World Tourism Organization (WTO) 1981; Edwards 1985; van Doorn 1986) has recently been complemented by more wide-ranging, often qualitative, assessments of how tourism is going to develop throughout the world to the end of the present century and beyond (e.g. Tourism Management 1987; Edgell 1990; WTO 1991; Buchanan 1992; Hawkins 1993). This growing interest reflects not only the increasing social and economic significance of tourism but also appears to have been prompted by the ever-nearing approach of the mystical Year 2000 and realization of the far-reaching effects of recent events in Europe – particularly the collapse of communism in 1989 and moves towards completion of the Single Market in the European Community in 1992 (Butler Chapter One) – and other parts of the world, notably the fast emerging economic role of the Asia-Pacific region.

All these latter studies indicate that the 1990s will be a decade of growth, with the WTO (1991) projecting an average annual growth rate of 4.2 per cent and an estimate of 637 million international arrivals in the Year 2000. Moreover, this growth will be accompanied by significant changes in the structure of tourism, including a fragmentation of demand, diversification of supply, intensification of competition, further concentration within the industry and changes in regional market share. Other changes have been heralded by earlier chapters of this book. Butler and Mao, for example, highlight some of the consequences of far-reaching political events (Chapter Six); Cohen, Nash, Graburn and Richter underline the significance of broader societal changes (Chapters Two to Five) while Pigram draws attention to the growing need to respond to resource constraints (Chapter Eleven). The message is clear: tourism will continue to evolve and in the future will exhibit different characteristics than it does at present.

Envisioning the future, as a number of writers remind us, is an essential step in planning for tourism. Mill and Morrison (1985: 15), for example, note 'All planning involves an analysis of the future' while Gunn (1988: 15) observes: 'Planning is predicting. Predicting requires some estimated perception of the future. Absence of planning or short-range planning that does not anticipate a future can result in serious malfunctions and inefficiencies.'

While the global assessments of tourism futures by the WTO, Hawkins and the other writers mentioned above provide valuable insights into world or regional trends in the 1990s, most planning will continue to be concerned with more specific trends and future perceptions of particular places, be they countries, regions or individual resorts, for it is at these levels that plans are usually prepared and implemented. The purpose of this chapter is to present and discuss an innovative approach to planning for tourism, using as an example the conceptual framework underlying the recent preparation of a state tourism plan for Sarawak, a small but developing destination in South East Asia, part of the world's fastest tourism growth region in the 1980s and 1990s (Figure 12.1). Although the framework was developed specifically for Sarawak it has the potential for wider application as the issues raised are much more general in nature and are particularly relevant to addressing the changing conditions of the 1990s.

CONCEPTUAL FRAMEWORK

Three fundamental principles were recognized as being important in developing a conceptual framework for a comprehensive long-term masterplan:

1 Tourism is a multi-faceted phenomenon involving the provision of a range of interrelated goods and services by the public and private sectors. Identifying and understanding the interplay and interrelationships between these different elements and sectors is essential for successful tourism planning.

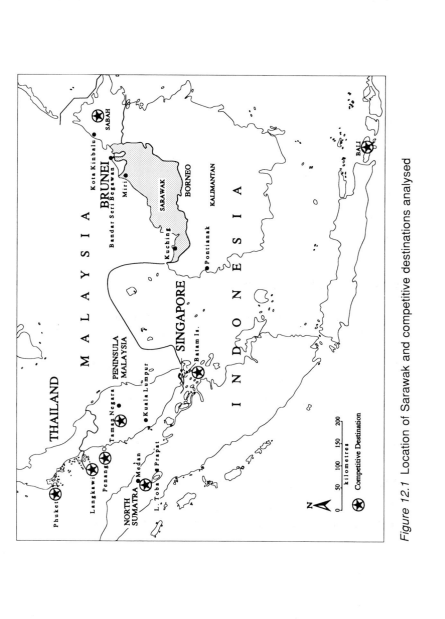

Figure 12.1 Location of Sarawak and competitive destinations analysed

2 Preparation of a long-term development plan must take account
   of the dynamic nature of tourism and the factors which influence its development.
3 Preparation of a state masterplan involves planning at an intermediate scale, setting the state in the broader national and
   regional context while at the same time coordinating and integrating activities at the local level.

In short, the need to draw together a large number of elements
over time and space called for an 'integrated, dynamic, multiscale'
approach to planning for tourism in Sarawak. This approach is
depicted graphically in Figure 12.2, which shows that for each scale
of analysis, a number of interrelated elements are examined over
time and the resultant implications of the trends identified are
brought together in a series of recommended actions that constitute the basis of the implementation component of the plan.

The planning process depicted in Figure 12.2 draws on established tourism planning practices but also incorporates several
distinctive and interrelated features, notably:

(a) the comprehensiveness of the elements included and inte-
     grated,
(b) the determination of trends for each of these, that is analyses
     and evaluations undertaken are dynamic, not static, and
(c) the explicit multiscale approach adopted – although a state
     plan, the state is not the sole focus and explicit linkages with
     phenomena at other scales are examined.

These features are relevant to planning for tourism in general, not
only in Sarawak, for they might be applied to other destinations at
other scales and would seem particularly appropriate for meeting
some of the challenges which the 1990s are bringing. To this end,
the remainder of this chapter elaborates on the underlying ration-
ale involved and outlines some of the methodological issues which
arise.

ELEMENTS TO BE INTEGRATED

Many different levels and types of tourism plans have been
prepared (WTO 1980; Gunn 1988; Pearce 1989; Inskeep 1991).
The elements included in any particular one may vary widely.
Two major components common to many plans are an analysis of

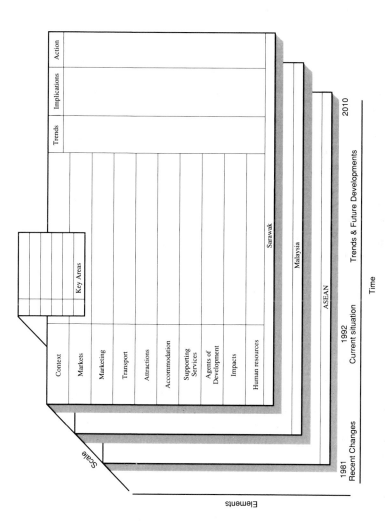

Figure 12.2 A conceptual framework for the preparation of the Second Sarawak Tourism Masterplan

existing and potential markets and an evaluation of the destination's resources (attractions, accommodation, transport, infrastructure, etc.). To this end, visitor statistics are analysed, satisfaction surveys undertaken, inventories of accommodation compiled, resources mapped and evaluated. Bringing these two components together – that is matching demand and supply – to meet specified goals (e.g. increasing foreign exchange earnings, generating employment, minimizing environmental impacts) constitutes the basic approach of many tourism plans. Plans may also give greater or lesser emphasis to other matters including the impacts tourism creates, labour demands and future training requirements.

Traditionally the emphasis has been on questions of what; that is, what markets are to be tapped, what resources are to be developed? Usually, little explicit consideration has been given to the who and the how elements, that is, who is marketing, who is developing the resources evaluated and how? Failure to examine these elements in association with the markets and resources may result in a less than complete understanding of a destination's strengths and weaknesses and seriously reduce the likelihood of the plan being implemented successfully.

Such considerations become particularly significant in medium- and long-term planning when extended time horizons make accurate demand projections increasingly difficult (Mazanec Chapter Eight). An effective strategy in such circumstances is to ensure that good systems are in place to monitor and respond to the changes in the markets which will inevitably occur and to meet the opportunities and threats which will develop. This requires a systematic examination of the structure and functions of a wide range of agents of development and of the institutional framework supporting tourism. Moreover, the type of tourist development which occurs in any area is as much a reflection of the ways in which these different functions are exercised and by whom, as by what is actually being developed. The framework depicted in Figure 12.2 makes explicit this concern with who is doing what by matching the market analysis with an evaluation of marketing activities and incorporating a section on agents of development after the evaluation of resources.

Thus in addition to analysing existing and potential markets through compiling visitor statistics, commissioning an exit survey, discussions with outbound operators and an analysis of competitive destinations, a comprehensive review was undertaken of the ways in which tourism in Sarawak was being marketed and by whom. The market analysis requirements, for example, drew attention to what market research was being done and what databases underpinned current marketing efforts. In particular, the review focused on the resources, priorities and programmes of the state and federal bodies charged with tourism marketing. What was being done, how and with what results were key issues examined. Likewise, the marketing activities of the hotels, tour operators and carriers were reviewed. Some assessment of these activities was also derived from the exit survey which included questions relating to visitors' use of different sources of information and their responses to the statement that Sarawak 'is well publicised abroad'.

The review of agents of development was undertaken in two parts. Attention was directed first at the different organizations, predominantly public sector, which have become involved in various aspects of tourism in Sarawak. Consideration was then given to the structure and operations of the tourist industry in the state.

The organizational framework for tourism in Sarawak was examined by means of inter-organizational analysis (Pearce 1992). Figure 12.3 was used as a framework for wide-ranging consultations, assessment of current practices and evaluation of available documentation. This involved systematically identifying key functions undertaken by different organizations, assessing the resources (funding and personnel) available to each and examining the nature of the relationships and linkages among them. Particular attention was paid to issues of coordination and to the identification of gaps or deficiencies in the present system. Were, for instance, those involved in development drawing on available market intelligence in the location, design and construction of accommodation and tourist facilities? What research support was available to planners, policy makers and marketers? How did major agencies with other more dominant responsibilities, such as forestry, see their tourism functions? Were any key functions not being carried out or insufficiently resourced? Figure 12.3 also served as a means of summarizing the major findings and displaying clearly and succinctly gaps and overlaps when the cells were filled out or left blank. This basic function/organization matrix can be applied in any situation and readily incorporated in the planning process.

The inter-organizational analysis was complemented by the review of different sectors of the industry, notably accommodation,

Functions Agency	Marketing	Visitor Servicing	Development	Operations	Planning and Policy	Research	Regulation	Training
State tourism agency								
National tourist organization								
Private sector organization								
Development corporations								
Other government agencies								

Figure 12.3 A framework for interorganizational analysis

tour operators and attractions. The size, structure and ownership patterns of the different sectors, together with details on levels of profitability and employment, were obtained from census statistics while operational information was sought through in-depth interviews with selected businesses. Industry attitudes towards issues such as promotion, access and labour were elicited through small group discussions. Interviews with offshore operators and carriers provided some evaluation of the state's tourist industry, as did the satisfaction section of the exit survey. When combined, the information from these different sources enabled a good overall assessment of the strengths and weaknesses of Sarawak's tourist industry to be made. This, in association with the inter-organizational analysis, contributed to the development of coherent strategies for both the public and private sectors.

TRENDS

Recognition of the dynamic nature of tourism, particularly in a fast growth region such as South East Asia, led to a second emphasis in the preparation of the masterplan, the identification of recent and future trends and the implications of these. The analysis of market trends is a common practice in tourism planning (Mazanec Chapter Eight), time series of visitor arrivals being a frequently used means of projecting growth in the tourist traffic from different markets. Other elements, however, are often dealt with in a more static fashion. Inventories of attractions, for example, usually just depict the current situation with little or no temporal dimension being included. The approach adopted with the preparation of the Sarawak masterplan was to examine the changes which had occurred with each of the elements over the previous decade as a means of better understanding past obstacles to growth and likely future developments and opportunities. The approach is not dissimilar to the more general identification of world-wide trends noted earlier except that the process is more specific and directed. It is also consistent with Haywood's (1986) call to take account of the evolution of tourist areas and with the first stages in Acerenza's (1985) planning process in which he advocates beginning with an analysis of previous tourist development and an evaluation of the economic and political significance of tourism.

In terms of the analysis of visitor trends and accommodation developments, conventional quantitative approaches were used.

The integration of the results of these different trends proved particularly useful. Analysis of visitor arrivals throughout the Association of South East Asian Nations (ASEAN) region in the 1980s, together with recent regional growth projections (Edwards 1990; Buchanan 1992), highlighted the increase in demand that had been experienced and was expected to occur, suggesting region-wide opportunities to develop tourism would continue through the 1990s. However, a review of projected hotel room construction indicated that many areas in the ASEAN region were seeking to exploit this demand and that competition would correspondingly be keen.

Varying degrees of quantification were possible in other areas. No systematic database on domestic tourism demand from Sarawakians themselves, for example, currently exists. However, examination of a range of social indicators (e.g. population growth, per capita GDP, degree of urbanization), access factors (e.g. vehicle ownership, road construction) and available recreation figures (notably national park visits) provided insights into local recreational and tourist demand. More detailed examination of the evolution of the road network, the upgrading of airports and changes in air schedules, both internal and external, together with projected works in those areas, provided crucial measures of, and vital insights into, improvements in accessibility. Likewise, a systematic recording of the spatial and temporal development of national parks and other recreational amenities, in association with available visitation records derived primarily from entry permits or payments, enabled trends to be established in the attractions and activities sector. Particularly important here was the identification of changing locational patterns and potential new destinations which improved access and the opening up of new parks permitted. This potential could then be matched with visitor preferences as a critical step in defining the spatial dimensions of the plan. In other instances a much more qualitative approach to the analysis of trends was adopted. Much of the scene-setting undertaken in terms of the contextual element of Figure 12.2 involved a review of national and state five-year plans, particularly in regard to the tourism policies they contained. This review enabled some assessment of the state's role in the federal system and of changing attitudes towards tourism at both levels and permitted the identification of persistent key issues.

These and other trends identified do not enable one to spell out what tourism in any destination will be like at any given point in the future. Taken together, however, they do provide a reasonably clear indication of directions in which tourism might evolve in the short to medium term and steps which might be taken to direct future growth. In this respect the approach is not simply a reactive one, with planners and developers just responding to external forces. By taking an integrated approach and looking across a wide spectrum of trends, it is possible to identify at an early stage areas where different elements are getting out of balance and to take measures to rectify this and to coordinate activities so as to exploit better opportunities which arise. The continuing need to match supply and demand, whether in quantity or type, and to ensure physical development is adequately supported by management, marketing and maintenance, requires having good organizational systems in place. All external changes may not be accommodated in this way, particularly in turbulent times, but most developments directly affecting tourism will be incremental and subject to such monitoring rather than abrupt changes. If planning processes can encompass these incremental changes effectively by taking explicit account of the dynamic nature of tourism then they may also be better positioned to respond to the sudden and dramatic impacts which occur on a less regular basis and over which tourism planners have no control.

QUESTIONS OF SCALE

A third distinctive feature of Figure 12.2 is the weight given to the interrelationship of the elements at different scales. Tourism plans have commonly been prepared at a range of scales – national, regional and local (WTO 1980; Pearce 1989). There may even be some direct linkage between these, as when a national plan is accompanied by a corresponding set of regional plans, for example in the case of the 1976–80 Tourist Development Plan for Ireland (Pearce 1992). More often, however, plans prepared at one scale focus almost exclusively on that scale, disregarding developments at a higher, lower or equivalent scale elsewhere. The Dutch tourism and recreation development plans (TROPs) of the 1980s, for instance, were prepared on a province by province basis, each plan largely ignoring the effects of projects in neighbouring provinces with the consequence that total demand throughout The Nether-lands was severely overestimated (Boonman 1986; Pearce 1992).

If there has been a tendency in recent years, it is to become more inward looking in response to calls for more community involvement in the planning process (Murphy 1985, 1988; Haywood 1988; Simmons 1991). While such involvement adds an important perspective, external linkages should not be overlooked. During the 1990s it will become even more imperative to set the planning of any area in a wider context as trends towards the globalization of tourism intensify. As, for example, long-haul markets become increasingly important, destinations will find their spheres of competition are more complex and their links into these distant markets ever more crucial. Moreover, these two seemingly divergent tendencies – greater community involvement and growing external linkages – need to be brought together. This is particularly critical in regional tourism planning as the regional plan constitutes a vital intermediate stage between national and global issues and forces and local needs, impacts and product developments (Wanhill Chapter Ten).

The framework for the Sarawak masterplan makes this multiscale approach explicit, acknowledging that conceptually and functionally such a plan must:

(a) reach upwards and outwards, setting tourism in Sarawak within the context of tourism in Malaysia and the development of the national economy, while also taking account of developments elsewhere in the ASEAN region, and

(b) look downwards and inwards to provide direction for the development of tourism within Sarawak and to mobilize all resources efficiently and effectively at the state and local levels.

In practice the relative weight given to the upwards and downwards components varied from element to element. Issues of markets, marketing and transport were given the greatest external orientation, with factors being traced through to the local level. Conversely, the social impact assessment and the physical planning of product development were largely focused on the local level, in the case of the latter by a series of key area plans. But, given the integration between these different elements, the overall effect is essentially to channel external markets progressively into localized areas within Sarawak and to plan for the physical development and integration of these areas.

Hierarchies of international tourist flows, for example, were established by the analysis of ASEAN-wide visitor arrivals and then related to the more specific patterns determined for Malaysia and Sarawak. While published statistics were drawn upon here, the exit survey also contained explicit questions on international and internal travel patterns in addition to standard sections on visitor profiles, expenditure and the other factors mentioned previously. Trip Index values (Pearce and Elliott 1983) were used to assess the relative importance of a visit to Sarawak within respondents' over-all trips. Other information was collected to indicate the nature of the external and internal circuits favoured by different markets.

A feature of the market research was the competitive destination analysis undertaken. Systematic appraisal and comparison of key tourism elements among competitors can constitute a more objec-tive basis for evaluating the strengths and weaknesses of the focal destination, provide a better appreciation of its competitive advan-tage and contribute to the formulation of more effective develop-ment policies by broadening the context in which the focal destination is set. Relatively few studies of this sort have been undertaken so far (MacLaren Plansearch Corp et al. 1987; PATA 1988). The basic approach is to evaluate the focal destination systematically against a series of competing destinations in terms of a set of a destination attributes or elements, in this case markets, air access, attractions, accommodation, prices and development processes. The latter can provide particularly useful insights into the dynamic behind the growth of individual destinations, enabling some assessment of likely levels of future competition. Whether a desti-nation is growing spontaneously in response to market demand, for instance, or being developed by aggressive supply-led policies can provide some insights into what may happen in the future.

From the large number of possible competing destinations, eight were chosen for detailed comparison with Sarawak from Indonesia, Thailand and elsewhere in Malaysia (Figure 12.1) on the basis that they:

(a) offer similar products to Sarawak in the areas of beach, cul-tural and nature based tourism,
(b) were perceived by Sarawak operators to be major competitors,
(c) are located within one to two hours flying time from Singapore, the main regional hub,
(d) are intermediate scale destinations similar to Sarawak, that is they are destinations of a subnational scale but larger than a single resort.

The competitive destination analysis, which was undertaken by means of field visits and the analysis of available statistics and documentation, proved particularly useful in providing touchstones against which Sarawak's resources and policies could be measured and its competitors judged.

CONCLUSIONS

To meet the challenges of the 1990s tourism planning must become more comprehensive and responsive to changing conditions. The integrated, dynamic, multiscale approach depicted in Figure 12.2 and discussed in preceding sections is one attempt to meet these challenges. Figure 12.2 suggests that tourism planners must broaden their approach, by increasing both the range of elements taken into account and the scales at which these are considered. At the same time, these elements and scales must be brought together and the dynamic nature of the phenomena and their interrelationships recognized and provided for. The example here has also highlighted the importance of incorporating the agents of development and the institutional framework within which they act, for if plans are to be implemented successfully close attention must be paid to who is to do what and how. Broadening the approach to planning in this way may also mean adoption of a wider range of tools and techniques, for example the use of inter-organizational and competitive destination analysis. Resource requirements are also likely to be increased. Data needs and problems will be magnified as the scope of the exercise is extended in scale and over time, compounding definitional difficulties and issues of equivalence. However the greater utility and effectiveness of the resultant plan should more than compensate for this, especially over the medium and long term. While these factors have been examined here from the perspective of an intermediate level state or regional plan, the basic approach can be readily adapted to national or local level planning. With the former there is a need to reach further downwards than is usually found in most such plans, while many local plans would benefit from a more explicit linking to regional, national and indeed international structures and phenomena.

In summary, as tourism evolves towards the Year 2000, tourism planning must develop with it, becoming more flexible and capable of accommodating a wide array of potential changes. This will require new approaches, new techniques, perhaps even new ways of conceiving tourism. As the earlier chapters have shown, these considerations are not just limited to planning, for change in tourism is becoming increasingly pervasive. As a result, if we are to continue to understand this multifaceted phenomenon we must explore in greater depth the causes, processes and consequences of change. The contributors to this book have outlined a wide variety of ways in which these issues might be addressed and this challenge met, but considerable scope exists for extending these approaches to other problems and other topics.

ACKNOWLEDGEMENTS

This chapter draws on research undertaken by the writer as a member of the Tourism Resource Consultants–Lincoln International Consortium engaged in the preparation of the Second Sarawak Tourism Masterplan. The author wishes to acknowledge the assistance of other members of the project team but remains solely responsible for the views expressed.

REFERENCES

Acerenza, M.A. (1985) 'Planificación estratégica del turismo: esquema metodológico', *Estudios Turisticos* 85: 47–40.

Archer, B.H. (1980) 'Forecasting demand: Quantitative and intuitive techniques', *Tourism Management* 1, 1: 5–18.

Boonman, A. (1986) 'De TROPometer: Een TROP evaluatie', unpublished eindexamenscripte, Breda: Nederlands Wetenschappelijk Instituut voor Toerisme en Recreatie.

Buchanan, I. (1992) 'Intra-Asian travel and tourism: Identifying growth trends', in *Proceedings* 2nd Pacific Asia Travel Association Asia Business Forum on 'Intra-Asian Tourism: Harnessing Business Opportunities', Singapore: PATA.

Edgell, D.L. (1990) *International Tourism Policy*, New York: Van Nostrand Reinhold.

Edwards, A. (1985) 'International tourism forecasts to 1995', *International Tourism Quarterly* 2: 52–64.

——(1990) *Far East and Pacific Travel in the 1990s*, London: The Economist Intelligence Unit, Special Report no. 2939.

Gunn, C.A. (1988) *Tourism Planning*, 2nd edn, New York: Taylor & Francis.

Hawkins, D.E. (1993) 'Global assessment of tourism policy: A process model', in D.G. Pearce and R.W. Butler (eds) *Tourism Research: Critiques and Challenges*, London: Routledge, 175–200.

Haywood, K.M. (1986) 'Can the tourist-area life cycle be made operational?', *Tourism Management* 7, 3: 154–167.

—— (1988) 'Responsible and responsive tourism planning in the community', *Tourism Management* 9, 2: 105–118.

Inskeep, E. (1991) *Tourism Planning: An Integrated and Sustainable Development Approach*, New York: Van Nostrand Reinhold.

MacLaren Plansearch Corp., Tourism Research Corp., Addison Travel Marketing (1987) *Guest Ranches of British Columbia: Product and Market Analysis*, Vancouver: Ministry of Tourism, Recreation and Culture.

Mill, R.C. and Morrison, A.M. (1985) *The Tourism System: An Introductory Text*, Englewood Cliffs: Prentice-Hall.

Murphy, P.E. (1985) *Tourism: A Community Approach*, New York: Methuen.

—— (1988) 'Community driven tourism planning', *Tourism Management* 9, 2: 96–104.

PATA (1988) *Tourism Development of Bantanyan Island, Cebu*, San Francisco: Pacific Asia Travel Association.

Pearce, D.G. (1989) *Tourist Development*, 2nd edn, Harlow: Longman and New York: Wiley.

—— (1992) *Tourist Organizations*, Harlow: Longman and New York: Wiley.

Pearce, D.G. and Elliott, J.M.C. (1983) 'The trip index', *Journal of Travel Research* 22, 1: 6–9.

Simmons, D.G. (1991) 'Local input into destination area tourism planning', in *Leisure and Tourism – Social and Environmental Change*, Proceedings of World Leisure and Recreation Association World Congress, Sydney, 16–19 July.

Tourism Management (1987) 'Special issue, Proceedings of the International Conference on Tourism in the 1990s', 8.2.

van Doorn, J.W.M. (1986) 'Scenario writing: A method for long-term forecasting', *Tourism Management* 7, 1: 33–49.

World Tourism Organization (1980) *Physical Planning and Area Development for Tourism in the Six WTO Regions, 1980*, Madrid: WTO.

—— (1981) *Tourism Forecasting*, Madrid: WTO.

—— (1991) *Tourism to the Year 2000: Qualitative Aspects affecting Global Growth*, Madrid: WTO.

Index